PRAISE FOR

Through a Screen Darkly

Jeffrey Overstreet is a spiritual bloodhound, rabidly tracking the voice of God through his own experience of the history of cinema. In *Through a Screen Darkly,* he leads the way for all of us, demonstrating how we can look closer and experience the divine invasion of film for ourselves.

Scott Derrickson
Writer and Director, *The Exorcism of Emily Rose*

Jeffrey Overstreet has taught me a great deal not just about how to watch movies, but also how to glean truth, beauty and redemption from films of all types—even those that aren't necessarily comfortable to watch. I am learning the art of looking closer, and this book takes that art—and that education—to even deeper, and thus more rewarding, levels.

Mark Moring
Editor, ChristianityTodayMovies.com

Jeffrey Overstreet is a witness. While habituating the dark caves of movie theaters, he gives articulate witness to what I too often miss in those caves—the contours of God's creation and the language of Christ's salvation. In these theaters, assumed by many to be unholy temples in a wasteland of secularism, he writes what he sees and hears. I find him a delightful and most percipient companion—a faithful Christian witness.

Eugene H. Peterson
Professor Emeritus of Spiritual Theology, Regent College

God the Maker made us to be makers as well. That is why, as Chesterton said, "Art is the signature of man." Filmmaking is an art form that is the unique invention of the twentieth century. Nothing quite like it had ever existed before, and through it, millions have had powerful, even profoundly spiritual, experiences. Jeffrey Overstreet is a guide eminently qualified to show us how to see the way in which films both illumine the terrain of the human spirit and probe the eternal mysteries of God.

Mark Shea
Senior Content Editor, CatholicExchange.com

Jeffrey Overstreet understands the art of understanding art and believes it is too important a task to leave to the experts. *Through a Screen Darkly* is a trustworthy guide as you sort through the enriching, exhilarating, messy, dangerous and important business of loving God and film.

Dick Staub
Author, *Christian Wisdom of the Jedi Masters* and *The Culturally Savvy Christian*

Through a Screen Darkly constitutes a milestone in Christian reflection about contemporary film. This is not simply because it is full of insightful analysis and a generous, open spirit, but because its vision grows out of a passionate, personal journey. This is film criticism with a soul and a sense of urgency growing out of the conviction that faith and the imagination need one another—the better to open our eyes to the flickerings of God's grace.

Greg Wolfe
Publisher and Editor, *Image*
Author, *Intruding Upon the Timeless: Meditations on Art, Faith and Mystery*

JEFFREY OVERSTREET

Regal

From Gospel Light
Ventura, California, U.S.A.

PUBLISHED BY REGAL BOOKS
FROM GOSPEL LIGHT
VENTURA, CALIFORNIA, U.S.A.
PRINTED IN THE U.S.A.

Regal Books is a ministry of Gospel Light, a Christian publisher dedicated to serving the local church. We believe God's vision for Gospel Light is to provide church leaders with biblical, user-friendly materials that will help them evangelize, disciple and minister to children, youth and families.

It is our prayer that this Regal book will help you discover biblical truth for your own life and help you meet the needs of others. May God richly bless you.

For a free catalog of resources from Regal Books/Gospel Light, please call your Christian supplier or contact us at 1-800-4-GOSPEL or www.regalbooks.com.

Library of Congress Cataloging-in-Publication Data
Overstreet, Jeffrey.
  Through a screen darkly / Jeffrey Overstreet.
    p. cm.
  Includes bibliographical references (p.   ).
  ISBN 0-8307-4315-4 (trade paper)
  1. Motion pictures—Religious aspects—Christianity. 2. Motion pictures—Moral and religious aspects. I. Title.
  PN1995.5.O94 2008
  791.43'75—dc22   2006033137

1   2   3   4   5   6   7   8   9   10   /   10   09   08   07

Rights for publishing this book in other languages are contracted by Gospel Light Worldwide, the international nonprofit ministry of Gospel Light. Gospel Light Worldwide also provides publishing and technical assistance to international publishers dedicated to producing Sunday School and Vacation Bible School curricula and books in the languages of the world. For additional information, visit www.gospellightworldwide.org; write to Gospel Light Worldwide, P.O. Box 3875, Ventura, CA 93006; or send an e-mail to info@gospellightworldwide.org.

By means of all created things, without exception, the divine assails us, penetrates us and molds us. We imagined it as distant and inaccessible, whereas in fact we live steeped in its burning layers.

TEILHARD DE CHARDIN, *THE DIVINE MILIEU*

The world speaks of the holy in the only language it knows, which is a worldly language.

FREDERICK BUECHNER, *A ROOM TO REMEMBER*

Contents

Part Three: Fools and Jokers

Part Four: Art of Darkness

Part Five: Summoned by Music and Light

Acknowledgments

Many people have inspired me with their art and have contributed their time, wisdom and editing to make this book a reality. I owe them my gratitude. To name a few:

- My beloved Anne, for her patience during the madness and her sharp editor's eye;

- Don Pape and Lee Hough, my agents at Alive Communications, for their affirmation and amazing work;

- Marsha Marks, who literally dropped out of the sky to answer my prayers;

- Alex Field and everyone at Regal Books, for inviting me to share;

- Mike Demkowicz, Brian Friesen and Margaret Smith, who volunteered hours of reading, volumes of insight, long telephone discussions and meticulous corrections;

- Fritz Liedtke, Danny Walter and Wayne Proctor, who critiqued first drafts;

- Ted Olsen, Mark Moring and Steve Lansingh at *Christianity Today*;

- Greg Wolfe and *Image* journal;

- Scott Derrickson and Ralph Winter;

- Jonathan Bock and Ted Gartner at Grace Hill Media;

- My teachers, Luke Reinsma and Rose Reynoldson; my supervisor, Jennifer Gilnett; and my patient coworkers at Seattle Pacific University;

- Promontory Artists Association, for laying the foundation;

- Critics Steven Greydanus, Peter Chattaway, Doug Cummings, Alan Thomas and the artsandfaith.com gang;

- The Milton Center Workshop, for helping to keep my instruments in tune;

- Luci Shaw and John Hoyte, for their generous hospitality;

- Nathan and Sarah Partain, Will Uppinghouse, Henrik Lind, and Pastor Michael Kelly, for prayer and encouragement;

- And, finally, the artists whose work lit my way: Wim Wenders, Krzysztof Kieslowski, Terrence Malick, J.R.R. Tolkien, Madeleine L'Engle, C. S. Lewis, Sam Phillips, Over the Rhine, and U2, to name just a few.

Introduction

"You didn't like it? Why not? That movie changed my life!"

"How can you call *that* piece of trash your favorite movie of the year?"

Over the last decade of writing film reviews for magazines such as *Christianity Today* and websites such as LookingCloser.org, I've received all kinds of questions, some of them charged with emotion: "How can I know if a movie is safe for my children?" "Aren't you taking this too seriously? Isn't it just entertainment?" "*American Beauty* is the best movie *ever*—so how can you say that it's flawed?" "How could you recommend something that moves as slowly as *The New World*? It bored me to tears." Many of these questions require more than short answers, more than an argument.

Movies inspire passionate feelings. And those feelings, once expressed, can inspire strong bonds between us or cause us to clash. As I sort through my e-mail and talk with moviegoers at work, church or film festivals, I find that once we get past these initial emotional responses and begin to explore our shared experiences and differing interpretations, we can learn a great deal about each other and ourselves.

Because I am a Christian and a movie critic, I wrestle with certain questions that other film reviewers may never face. Religious readers are particularly interested in what filmmaking and faith have to do with each other. Viewers raise questions about "worldly" or violent movies, or films in which they perceive a political agenda. One asks, "Is it okay for Christians to watch R-rated movies?" Another writes, "You gave that Bruce Willis film a good review, but what about the foul language?"

Some are troubled by depictions of sex in *Cold Mountain* and *Little Children*, or unflattering portrayals of Christians in *The Da Vinci Code* and *Talladega Nights: The Legend of Ricky Bobby*. Some are worried about witchcraft in the world of Harry Potter, while others declare that Hollywood is preoccupied with attacking traditional values. "The Bible says we should have nothing to do with darkness," a reader reminded me. "So how can you justify spending so much time at the movies?"

I've wrestled with many of the same questions in past years. The answers did not come easily. While other Christian moviegoers were quick to instruct me on which movies were good or bad, backing up their arguments with Bible verses and statistics, my experience and understanding of Christian freedom and responsibility has led me to different conclusions—and to new questions, as well. And as readers continue to write in and condemn my perspectives as "too liberal" and "too conservative" (I'm regularly accused of both) or "subversive" and "elitist," I never cease to be amazed at their need to slap a convenient label on me, as if human beings can be divided into simple categories and thereby judged.

Thus, when I respond to readers, I find my answers require something more than a simple explanation. I end up sharing stories about my journey. I talk about my changing relationships with certain films, my conversations with moviegoers and filmmakers, and events that transformed me.

So I decided to write a book.

And the book became another chapter in that journey. I retraced my steps from Michael Haneke's *Code Unknown*, Krzysztof Kieslowski's *Three Colors* trilogy and Wim Wenders' *Wings of Desire*, all the way to the days when *Raiders of the Lost Ark* and *Star Wars* stimulated my young imagination. As I did, I began to see how the power of art has led me to growth and understanding. I realized that I was already responding to the light shining through art when I was nine years old, delighting as Kermit the Frog headed out of the swamp on a rickety bicycle to pursue his dreams in *The Muppet Movie*.

I was also startled to discover how profoundly time and experience have changed my perspective. As I reread my own review of Spike Jonze's film *Adaptation*, I was ashamed to find that I had reacted hastily to the film. The characters' reckless behavior had made me uncomfortable, so I judged the film prematurely without perceiving the film's meaningful observations on human depravity. Revisiting the film since then, I've been moved and inspired. Other films that at first ignited my enthusiasm may seem heavy-handed or derivative—even shallow—after a second or third viewing.

This is one of the things I've learned along the way: A first impression is rarely the final word on a movie. In fact, there is probably no final word at all. Art needs time to settle in our minds and hearts so that the process of contemplation, discussion and ongoing exploration can open up possibilities that never occurred to us in the theater.

Gene Siskel and Roger Ebert first modeled this process for me on television. Even as a 10-year-old, I wanted to understand how two experienced and respected moviegoers could disagree so passionately and glean such varying insights from the same movies. Their heated exchanges made art seem so much more mysterious, so full of possibilities. I began to understand that interpretation, conversation and revelation were what art was all about. Even though Siskel and Ebert concluded with "thumbs up" or "thumbs down," moviegoing was not really about casting judgments. No simple checklist of dos and don'ts and no quick scan for certain volatile ingredients could lead me to a fair assessment of a film. This was to be a journey.

I'm sure that many of my strongest friendships would never have grown without the art that provoked me to share feelings with others and learn from their perspectives. I'm also sure that I would have never met and fallen in love with my wife if I had not learned a few things from movies about love and looking closer.

Writing this book has shown me how movies have enhanced my life. It has reminded me of why I do this, why I see movies two or three times (or more), why I examine the truth that shines darkly through the veil of the movie screen, and why I go home to write about the experience. Just as Christ's listeners attended to His metaphors and parables and heard Him say, "Those who have ears to hear, let them hear" (Matt. 13:9), so too I have found that we can glimpse transforming truth through the beauty of art if we put aside fear and judgment and look with "eyes to see."

This book is not a catalogue prescribing which movies you should see and which you should avoid. It's not a technical manual on the finer points of filmmaking. It is, rather, an invitation to a journey. To those who wrote to me with challenging questions about moviegoing and never received a reply, I apologize for the delay, but I could not give you a satisfactory response without presenting the bigger picture—without taking you to the movies along with me.

I hope you'll come along and join the conversation.

Jeffrey Overstreet

PART ONE

How We Watch

How a Camel Made a Grown Man Cry

The show was delightful. No, no. It was brilliant. No, no, no, no.
There is no word to describe its perfection, so I am forced to make one
up. And I'm going to do so right now: Scrumtrilescent!

WILL FERRELL AS FILM EXPERT JAMES LIPTON
ON *SATURDAY NIGHT LIVE*

A Forgotten Language

A camel is standing alone in the middle of the Gobi Desert, wind whipping back her golden mane. And she is singing.

I'm not kidding. I'm looking at her.

The cinema is dark and I'm squinting at the pale pages of the notebook in my hand. Then I look up into the vibrant screen and stare at this beautiful redhead—this camel singing somewhere in Mongolia at dusk—and my vision blurs through tears.

No, this isn't a goggle-eyed, knobby-kneed Disney camel. This is a living, breathing camel standing in the lavender dusk of the shifting dunes, staring into the distance and singing.

The moviegoers in Seattle's Guild 45th cinema are breathless with what they're seeing. Some of us who have ventured into air-conditioned darkness—the local film press, the publicist, and the "line people" who picked up giveaway tickets and waited outside on the sidewalk for an hour—are experiencing what we always hope to find, never quite expect, and will remember for years to come.

That *thing*.

Evening is like recess in my high-tech, highly caffeinated hometown. Everyone runs out to play, chasing their own particular passions, escaping the daily demands and drudgery. Weary from our work, we scatter in search of conversation, concerts, poetry slams, karaoke, baseball, beer, exercise, night classes. Students hunker down at Zoka Coffee Roasters, studying textbooks and sucking caffeine, peering over their PowerBooks and scanning the faces of others while they ponder pick-up lines. Gamblers hurry northward into the neon of Aurora Avenue's casinos, where other stops promise cheap cigarettes and *girls! girls! girls!*

When the evening is over, they'll return to the confines of the next day, some poorer, some weaker, and some a little wider. A few will be richer, stronger, and maybe even wiser. So much depends on the nature of their escape.

Tonight, I'm pursuing my own after-hours discipline. I'm in a chair in a darkened theatre watching a documentary called *The Story of the Weeping Camel*, wincing every time the person in front of me rocks her chair back against my bruised knees. Sticky seat cushions, talkative teens, annoying big screen commercials—it's all worth enduring for those occasional moments of revelation. It's like waiting through a season of disappointing baseball just to be there at that magic moment when the angle of the pitch and the timing of the swing meet with a crack that will echo in your memory for days. And yet, unlike a home run, this occasion on the big screen doesn't merely change the score. It changes you.

*   *   *

It's 1987. I'm 17 years old and on my second date . . . sort of.

Her name is Melissa, and she's spirited, funny and pretty. I'm thrilled that she has agreed to go with me to a new film called *Dances with Wolves*, because I hear it's three hours long. That's three hours in a darkened theatre with Melissa. *Melissa*, who doesn't really seem drawn to me *in that way*, but who is a lot of fun and who's happy to flirt with me so long as I don't respond to her with any earnest romantic intentions.

Sweaty-palmed, hoping that the evening might mark a change, I settle in for the long three hours.

During the course of the movie, Melissa will take at least three breaks, probably because she's rather small and has consumed a jumbo Diet Coke. But while she's gone, I remain riveted, caught up, transported through time and space. I'm not thinking about my chances with Melissa anymore. I'm thinking about the chances of that poor soldier, John Dunbar, against those natives—the mean ones, not the good ones.

By this time in my early high school experience, my understanding of Native Americans had been shaped by Disney movies, cartoons and family-friendly television dramas. That is to say, I'd believed in a caricature of scalp-hunting savages in face paint and headdresses. To see John Dunbar discover companionship and care amongst softhearted, nature-loving Sioux challenges my perspective. This version of the Old West is more complicated and it makes me uncomfortable. I thrill to the chases and bask in the panoramic landscapes captured by Dean Semler's cinematography. I laugh at the budding friendship between man and wolf. But contrary to my usual moviegoing experience, I suddenly don't know what to expect or where the story will take me.

Then the moment comes—one I still don't completely understand. Dunbar sits in a tent with a Sioux chieftain. Between them sits an agitated woman. Her wardrobe is like the chief's, but her features are more like Dunbar's. This is Stands With a Fist. When she was still a child, her white parents were butchered by Pawnee attackers and she was taken into the care of the more compassionate Sioux. Uprooted from the language of her family, she grew up as a Sioux, adapting to their language and locking the horrible truth about her family into a vault deep in her memory.

Now, here in the tent, as she encounters a white man for the first time in ages, her brow furrows. Terror flashes in her eyes. Under orders to translate for Dunbar, she struggles to find the right words, turning them over as if they are strange keys. When they snap into place, she trembles and begins to speak. That box of nightmares opens.

I'm frightened. Paralyzed. I don't know what's happening to me. There's a lump rising in my throat, and I feel I might choke. So I sit there covering my mouth with my hand, hoping Melissa won't notice that tears are spilling down over my fingers.

It remains *the scene* that draws me back to Costner's overlong epic, even as an adult, after I've come to view *Dances with Wolves* as a rather sentimental work. It's a scene that no one else really cares much about, but it somehow tapped into the core of my emotions. It still devastates me.

I'm still not sure why that scene affects me so intensely. It is not the climax of the film. It's not even intended to be a tear-jerking scene.

Perhaps it has something to do with my personal interest in helping people understand each other through art. I started journaling about my love of cinema and music when I was 14, and I'm still striving to capture the mysteries of movies in words. Perhaps it's because Stands With a Fist is being set free from the identity she has assumed out of necessity. As she wraps her tongue around this forgotten language, she is pried kicking and screaming away from what she knows, dragged back through a river of pain, and at last returns to walk again in the world from which she came—a homeland she's only now remembering.

I've always had this sense that there is another language I once knew, a joy that was mine before I was born. When I get a glimpse of that glory through art, I can feel the memory of it pressing against the back of my mind, and the longing for that peace and resolution wells up inside me. I can't quite grasp it. I can't speak my native language. Not yet . . . but I'm learning.

If I do the difficult thing and pull myself away from art that is merely entertaining and start searching for those currents of truth that reside within beauty and mystery, I will be drawn off the path of familiarity and comfort. The reality of God is not bound to a particular earthly language, country or style. His spirit can speak through anything. But He is far more likely to be encountered in those things that are excellent rather than shoddy, particular rather than general, authentic rather than derivative. I will find myself investigating art and expression that never played for audiences in this country—art that waits overlooked on the shelves full of foreign and independent films at the video store. And I will be changed, concerned with cares and disciplines that make no sense to Hollywood movie publicists.

It could be a lonely road. But it's a road that leads farther up, farther in, to greater majesty and more transforming truth.

First Steps into a Larger World

Like a pillar of cloud or fire, sometimes a movie offers us mysteries that draw us out of the captivity of our own perspective.

Growing up in a Christian home in Portland, Oregon, I lived in fear of the world of *sinners* beyond the walls of my sanitized religious subculture. My family showed up at a Baptist church on Sunday morning and socialized in a Christian community. My younger brother and I attended Christian schools from kindergarten through college. Word around the Sunday School room convinced me that I lived in a place like Rivendell in J.R.R. Tolkien's *Lord of the Rings*, where all was beautiful and good, while everything "out there" was like Mordor. I came to believe that I was safe around believers but endangered by the worldly.

In our church community, the artwork of pop culture was treated with grave suspicion. Only rare exceptions such as cute and innocuous children's stories, *Sesame Street* and the Disney cartoons were beyond reproach. *Snow White and the Seven Dwarves* was the first movie I saw projected on a big screen, and it planted the seeds of curiosity about cinema in my mind. But commercial fiction, the Weekly Top 40 on Z100 FM in Portland, the block-buster movies of the week and all other secular stuff was considered dangerous because it showed all kinds of behavior that could lead people into temptation. After I accidentally stumbled into a friend's basement bedroom and glimpsed posters for the rock band KISS on the walls, I had nightmares and became convinced that boy was going to hell.

The homes my family visited were full of Christian books—usually the same volumes we had on our own shelves. So it was that I became fascinated with the larger world of literature through the neighborhood public library. The library contained books that didn't talk about Jesus but whispered about other perspectives, cultures and experiences. Most of the time, those stories were more interesting. They explored different subjects, and sometimes they didn't end the way I wanted or expected.

Advertisements in the newspaper for that forbidden world of movies—those "worldly" stories—intrigued me as well. I remember being troubled and fascinated by Marlon Brando's fearsome expression on the original newspaper advertisements for *Apocalypse Now*. And when something called *Star Wars* showed up on the page, my imagination grew extremely restless.

One afternoon in my grandparents' living room, Uncle Paul announced to the family that he was going to go see George Lucas's special-effects sensation. When he said that he wanted to take along his seven-year-old nephew, I braced myself to hear my parents refuse. They had heard rumors that the movie was scary and violent, and in retrospect, I completely understand their concerns. But then from his La-Z-Boy chair in the corner, my grandfather, who rarely spoke, stunned the whole family by announcing that he too wanted to see what all of the fuss was about. And he promised that he'd keep an eye on me. That tipped the scale in my favor.

At the Hollywood Theater in Portland, Oregon, in 1977, I took my first steps into a larger world. And I would never think of going back.

* * *

The next important step in my moviegoing journey took place a few years later when I watched Hugh Hudson's film *Chariots of Fire*.

Should the Olympic hopeful Eric Liddell compromise his Christian convictions and run a race on the Sabbath in order to pursue a gold medal? Would God be so unfair as to punish him for pursuing his dream?

I worried about these issues. Sunday School, Christian education and family devotion hour had taught me the inflexibility of the Ten Commandments. "Remember the Sabbath." The appeals of Liddell's missionary sister made sense in my practical, Protestant world. Why should he waste his time competing in worldly races when he could be on the mission field, saving souls by preaching the gospel? Despite the fact that most of the men in my church went home from Sunday services to watch the afternoon's NFL match-ups, no one had ever mentioned that you could serve God by running laps.

Then Eric's father looked him in the eye and spoke words that shattered so many of my assumptions about a good life: "You can glorify God by peeling a potato if you peel it to perfection."

Excellence. By doing something well, I could please the Lord. I remembered Mr. Liddell's words when I stepped out on to the basketball court in high school. I could glorify God if I followed Coach Remsburg's instructions for making a perfect free throw. And when I studied for Mr. Zimmerman's algebra tests, I could glorify God by learning to solve complex equations perfectly. In fact, I could glorify God when I was running, singing in Mr. Barber's championship concert choir, raking up the wet autumn leaves from the apple and cherry trees in the backyard, writing stories or making films. When we give others something excellent, we reflect the standards of heaven. We make others curious. When they get curious, they're open to discovering things they would not otherwise understand. Such discoveries provoke growth and a particular joy.

"When I run, I feel His pleasure," said Eric Liddell.

When the three o'clock buzzer droned in the school's hallway, I hurried home and shut myself in my room to write stories of my own, stories I'd considered only guilty pleasures until I saw the glory of God reflected in Eric Liddell's ecstatic smile as he ran pell-mell, head thrown back, wind buffeting his white shirt marked number 451 and broke the tape at the Olympics. He honored God's law. He refused to run on Sunday. But he did run, and those swift strides spoke of glory in a way that a Sunday School lesson could not.

* * *

A film called *Amadeus* took me a step further. The popcorn thrills of *Star Wars* and the gospel message of *Chariots of Fire* had won acceptance in my community. They were fun and portrayed good guys and bad guys in easy-to-recognize forms.

But director Milos Forman and screenwriter Peter Schaffer showed me that excellence—no matter where it comes from—can reveal a greater picture of the truth. I learned that God sometimes uses very naughty people to lift our spirits through art. Wolfgang Amadeus Mozart, that scoundrel of a composer, played with such memorable vigor by Tom Hulce, informed me that art by any artist, even the most reckless, could contain glimpses of the sublime.

I soon found that I could even learn something from the films of Woody Allen, Quentin Tarantino or that troublemaker Oliver Stone. I could gain insight by watching films from other countries, from pagan cultures where the characters didn't speak English.

Why did this surprise me? The psalms, the staple of my daily devotion time, had been composed by David, who as a king would murder, betray and fornicate, then write the psalms out of deep, heart-tugging confession. This deeply flawed individual was called a man after God's own heart.

Perhaps the wisdom of Sunday School and the wisdom of worldly art were not so separate after all.

Moved in Mysterious Ways

Maybe you're thinking back on very different films: *Citizen Kane. Schindler's List. Bruce Almighty. Amelie. It's a Wonderful Life. Manon of the Spring. Braveheart. The Passion of the Christ. March of the Penguins. Crash. Babel.* Transforming moments at the movies will differ substantially from person to person.

I once polled a group of 80 adult moviegoers about the films that had most inspired them and those that had most upset them. Several titles, including *Saving Private Ryan, The Silence of the Lambs* and *Apocalypse Now*, earned multiple mentions in *both* categories.

In a *Mars Hill Review* interview, the brilliant novelist Chaim Potok said that art is "a relational experience. Art happens somewhere along a relational arc, between what you are and the object of creation."[1] The things that move you will depend, in part, on your own experiences as well as the artist's own history and personality. Generations to come who watch *United 93* will feel very differently from those who lived in New York during the attacks that destroyed the World Trade Center. Most of us cannot imagine what *Saving Private Ryan* feels like to veterans of World War II, or what *The Queen* feels like to Londoners who took flowers to the gates of Kensington Palace after Princess Diana died. *The Passion of the Christ* was a different experience for Catholics than it was for Protestants and different for Christians than for Muslims. *Brokeback Mountain* and *The Da Vinci Code* have received almost every response imaginable, from the highest praise to the most mean-spirited condemnation.

As a Christian trying to find his footing in a complicated world, *Chariots of Fire* resonated with me. It probably said something different to agnostics or professional athletes. Even the artist cannot guess what his or her art might reveal.

After all, by arranging elements of plot and aesthetics, we create something dynamic. Madeleine L'Engle describes the creative process as collaborating with God. In reflecting the way life works, we present a complex experience from which different people can draw differing—but not necessarily contradictory—interpretations. In sharing our different views, we can test our interpretations for weaknesses and piece together fuller revelations.

Does this mean that there is no such thing as a good or bad movie and that everything is relative? Certainly not. A double cheeseburger could do some good for a starving man, so it's not worthless, but let's not confuse it with a healthy meal. It's difficult to train ourselves to consider a film's quality: how it makes us feel, its flavor and what it all means. Taste is important, but so are the ingredients, their proportions, their preparation, the arrangement and presentation of the plates, and whether or not the meal is nourishing. Excellence matters.

These days, as a film critic, I am learning that a film succeeds when it makes me forget that I have a pen in one hand and a legal pad in the other. I long for those moments when I'm swept up in revelation, oblivious to all else.

Back in 2004 in Beverly Hills, I joined a few journalists to talk with the accomplished actor Michael Caine. After Caine regaled us with amusing anecdotes about working with Robert Duvall on the set of *Secondhand Lions,* one of the reporters spoke up. He asked if there was something that the actor wished moviegoers and film critics would learn to understand about movies, something we just don't get. Caine thought for a moment, furrowed his brow, made a tent of his fingers, and then said with great confidence, "If you are sitting there watching the film and thinking to yourself, *That is Michael Caine giving a great performance*, then *I have failed*! My job as an actor is to make you forget you're watching Michael Caine. You should be absorbed in the character and the story."

That is a mark of filmmaking excellence. The work carries us up out of our critical faculties and sweeps us to a galaxy far, far away . . . or to a desert in Mongolia where a camel is singing at the sunset. It is something distinct to movies. We are presented with flickers of light preserved, one moment after another, motion and change reflected in a way that cannot happen in a painting, in writing, in music.

In that state of childlike attention, we are vulnerable to shocks both pleasant and discomforting, both instructive and damaging. We are open to revelations that change us. Receiving our attention, the artist bears some responsibility to behave with integrity, to serve the work and craft it with excellence, but even he may not anticipate what his arrangement of light and shadow will reveal. It's possible we will glimpse the glow of glory, truth that cannot be reduced to a simple paraphrase, glimmering through the screen darkly.

*   *   *

Moviegoers buy their tickets for all kinds of reasons. Some just want to turn off their brains and be entertained. Others pursue any new work by particular actors or directors—Julia Roberts, Juliette Binoche, Robin Williams, Robert De Niro, Steven Spielberg, Spike Lee. Some invest themselves in the study of film, discussing the differing effects of a Robert Altman tracking shot; the long, slow, meditative scenes of Yasujiro Ozu; or the way that the Dardenne brothers aggressively pursue their characters with handheld cameras. Some just want an excuse to sit and whisper quietly to their dates in the dark.

But most of us have some sort of expectation when we spend that money. We expect laughs, chills, jolts or tear-jerking drama. More often than not, we get just enough of what we anticipated to go home happy. A few days or weeks later, we move on to the next big blockbuster.

Occasionally, we get *more* than what we came for, and we're impressed. We might even talk about it for more than five minutes on the way home. In the morning, we tell our coworkers, "Don't miss that film! It was hilarious! We laughed until our faces hurt. Awesome!"

I often catch myself saying, "It really *moved* me."

Moved? As in from point A to point B? Do I mean that I'm in a different place now than I was before seeing the movie? Am I seeing the world from a new vantage point?

Normally, no, I don't mean that. Usually, I'm just saying that I *felt* something. I was drawn out of my routine and experienced a strong emotion, something out of the ordinary. There's that moment when the curtain pulls back, the music swells, the camera zooms in on the hero's eyes, and I share her epiphany. Even when those revelations are terrifying—"He's not just looking for ghosts! Oh man . . . he *is* a ghost! He's been a ghost all along!"—on some level, I know that I'm safe in my seat. And I thrill with the vicarious experience.

But sometimes, yes. Sometimes, I *am* moved from point A to point B. I *want* to be moved, to glean more from moviegoing. I don't want to waste time with disposable box office sensations. I want to be challenged and nourished. I try to listen to those who have a passion for movies from around the world. While I occasionally run into something unpleasant when I follow their recommendations, I'm bound to make discoveries that make me glad I listened. The more I explore, the more I learn about navigating the dangers of moviegoing.

It's been my preoccupation for decades to experience those moments when an artist, intentionally or unwittingly, pulls back the veil of the everyday and gives us a glimpse of a wilder world than we had previously known. It has led me to discover the rewards of Disney, *Die Hard*, David Lynch and the Dardenne brothers. I've gone sightseeing to exotic corners of international cinema under the guidance of Poland's Krzysztof Kieslowski, France's Robert Bresson, Austria's Michael Haneke, Russia's Andrei Tarkovsky and Andrei Zvyagintsev, China's Edward Yang and Zhang Yimou, America's David Gordon Green and Terrence Malick, and beyond.

I've found redemptive insights and moments of piercing brilliance in places that I'd been told were off-limits to conscientious moviegoers. Like Stands With a Fist, I have a strange compulsion to sit down between Christian culture and secular society, trying to help them understand each other—and, ultimately, God—better through a shared experience of art. The more I apply myself to this, the more I realize that this compulsion grows from having learned that my own assumptions were wrong and my view too narrow. Now I want to understand more and apprehend beauty wherever I can find it.

And I can tell you, beauty will mess with you if you let it.

*   *   *

As my friend Jason Bortz watched a film about Africa, a little African girl came into the scene and happened to glance into the camera. Jason suddenly felt as if he'd been struck by lightning, because the girl's big brown eyes, radiant with joy, blazed out from her desperate circumstances, and he *recognized* them. *Those are my daughter's eyes,* he said to himself. *That may as well be my daughter.*

What Jason meant was that a connection had been made—across continents—to tell him that he could no longer sit still knowing about his "daughter's" need. He was compelled to leave his family for a few weeks to go, to serve, to learn more and to face the enormity of the need.

When some people encounter glory, they do the strangest things. They build an ark. They write stacks of psalms in gratitude. They go up against Pharaoh and all of his minions. Jason Bortz never recovered. He soon touched the same ground he had seen in the film and made a documentary about the contagious joy of Africans who live in nightmarish circumstances and the ways in which we can help them. Intent on blessing them, Jason finds himself awakening to new joys. The world is incrementally changed.

If you thought it might happen to you, would you hand over 10 bucks for the possibility?

Revelation Where You Least Expect It

The search for those deeply transformative moments at the movies is a costly discipline. It requires investments of time, money and ego.

If you take up this pursuit, you'll find yourself less and less satisfied with most of the titles listed in the box office top 10. Frequently, popular movies have been assembled from standard parts by a committee, designed to appease what are often rather base appetites, and packaged to meet audience expectations. In search of authentic expressions and compelling visions devoid of advertising and calculated entertainment, you'll find yourself more likely to venture off to those out-of-the-way theaters to see films most of the viewing public hasn't even heard about. While they rush out to see *The Wedding Crashers* or its inevitable sequel, you might find yourself riding on a train through Tokyo with a lonely, troubled young woman in a film called *Café Lumiére*. You may even end up seeing it alone.

Am I asking you to become a snob? Great *Naked Gun* . . . no! I'll fess up: I *enjoyed* Michael Bay's *Armageddon* (that confession alone could lose me my film critic's license). When I watched Will Ferrell hurl crass insults at his coworkers in *Anchorman: The Legend of Ron Burgundy*, I laughed until I was sore. I'm much more likely to pop Tom Hanks' forgotten comedy *The 'Burbs* into the DVD player than I am to watch him in *Saving Private Ryan, Philadelphia, Cast Away* or (heaven forbid) *The Terminal*. Given a choice between *Pirates of the Caribbean: The Curse of the Black Pearl* and *The Sea Inside*, I'm as likely to join Johnny Depp as I am Javier Bardem.

I love movies—all kinds of movies. I love them the way others love baseball, classical music, wine or great literature. I want to understand the subtleties of Claire Denis' French imports like *L'Intrus*, but I don't want to miss *Ocean's Thirteen*. I try to resist the pull that turns so many cinephiles into snobs. I want to watch movies with my nephews and nieces and be pleasant company. If a professional baseball fan cannot attend a community softball game without scoffing at the amateurs on the field, he has a problem. The symphony maestro shouldn't blush at singing along with Alanis Morissette on his car stereo.

C. S. Lewis once said, "When I became a man, I put away childish things, including the fear of being childish, and the desire to be very grown up." Madeleine L'Engle insists that her age is not an isolated chronological statistic, but only the most recent addition of a year to her life: "I am also four, and twelve, and fifteen, and twenty-three, and thirty-one, and forty-five and . . . and . . . and . . ." There is genuine joy to be shared in simpler, or more popular, experiences. And revelation happens there too, on occasion.

I once read an e-mail from a moviegoer who claimed he dedicated his life to God because of something he saw in *Herbie the Love Bug*. Another arrived from a woman who experienced a transforming realization during the Julia Roberts and Richard Gere throwaway called *Runaway Bride*. My friend Dick Staub has written a whole book on insights to be found in the *Star Wars* series. Staub, who teaches a class called "The Culturally Savvy Christian" at Seattle Pacific University, invited students to share the movies that shook them up, and he was moved by the testimony of a woman whose life was changed by watching the forgotten Val Kilmer action film called *The Saint*. I rest my case.

That doesn't mean these films were examples of superlative filmmaking. Not even close. So what does it mean when predictable mediocre work changes lives? Does it mean that excellence doesn't matter? No, it simply means that art reflects life, and when we meditate on life, we might see something in a new way—and that might awaken us to possibilities, problems, hope, doubt, salvation or sin. As a wise arts patron once said, "The play's the thing wherein I'll catch the conscience of the King."

* * *

For example, I was relatively unmoved by Zach Braff's debut feature *Garden State*, yet the film is a favorite for a whole generation of moviegoers who relate to the plight of the protagonist. It's a well-crafted film—Braff drew winning performances from his cast and performed some creative camerawork. However, it's the problem facing the young seeker that resonates most with young audiences.

Here's the premise: Andrew has been dosed with prescription drugs well into adulthood to numb the pain of his childhood. Through the influence of a nosy, courageous girlfriend, he learns that a life of buffering pain through medication has hindered his growth. In fact, it has paralyzed him. Andrew realizes that he will grow up only if he chooses to move through the pain instead of around it. In the culminating scenes, he has a face-off with his father that is all about his demand for pain and his rejection of a life lived in denial.

Those who have grown up wrestling with these issues may find themselves powerfully moved by the truth of Braff's film. I can see the merit in the story, but my experiences do not make that subject particularly compelling to me. When I watched *Garden State*, I became more concerned with some of its structural faults and the fact that the final confrontation occurs abruptly, taking place between Andrew and a character that has not been developed very well over the course of the film. It didn't resonate with me.

On the other hand, director Michel Gondry's visionary film *Eternal Sunshine of the Spotless Mind,* which explored similar issues, has become one of my favorites. Charlie Kaufman's screenplay gave us a sci-fi parable about two lonely souls, Joel and Clementine, who had memories deleted from their brains to excise the wounds of their breakup. As a result, they became developmentally disabled—by eliminating the scars of their rocky relationship, they ensured that they would never again enjoy lasting romance or a healthy marriage. The film offers powerful insights about the challenge of true love by showing us two individuals who cannot meet that challenge.

This is a story that speaks powerfully to me. I have watched so many friends' marriages collapse due to the loss of the initial thrill and the reality of dealing with one another's differences on a daily basis. When I asked Kaufman about what led him to make such an unusually honest film about the difficulties of love, he said, "It's important to me, when I'm doing this stuff, to be truthful. Truthful, in a sense that it's truthful to me . . . because that's all I can do. If I feel like I'm doing something honest, then I feel like I'm not putting garbage into the world. It's my experience, and therefore it has some veracity. This is a true moment as I've understood it . . . and then I try to translate it into a scene."

Eternal Sunshine of the Spotless Mind troubles many viewers, and it should. Joel and Clementine treat each other with deplorable,

R-rated selfishness and cruelty. But the critics writing for *Christianity Today* voted Kaufman and Gondry's work the best film of 2004 for its creativity, intensity and meaningful exploration of romantic love. It is, after all, one of the few recent love stories to affirm that true love is sustained beyond the first flush of infatuation by a spirit of trust, longsuffering and forgiveness.

That is one of the ways in which art enlightens us. It reflects our mistakes, our flaws and our pain back to us so that we must acknowledge them and find hope to move beyond them. Poetry, wrote Robert Frost, "is a way of remembering what it would impoverish us to forget." At its best, cinema becomes that kind of poetry. We hear the language we have forgotten luring us back to wisdom. In Ecclesiastes 3, we read that eternity is written in our hearts. Art helps us learn to read.

Visions That Hurt, Visions That Heal

As Stands With a Fist discovered in *Dances with Wolves*, being truly *moved* can be a painful thing. When we realize or remember something that tells us our view has been too narrow, we suddenly prefer to stay put. Who wants to be reminded that he is incomplete, misguided, weak or in need of help and healing? Just as we may feel pain when looking at a troubling X-ray, we can find some of the big screen's diagnoses discomforting.

In Mike Leigh's *Secrets and Lies*, Brenda Blethyn plays a worrywart named Cynthia who is invited to a café to meet a stranger. She has no idea what this invitation is about, but when the stranger explains, we watch as Cynthia slowly, reluctantly, realizes that this unfamiliar face is the face of the daughter she abandoned years earlier. It's as if Cynthia has deleted some files from her own memories and this stranger has come along to restore them. Cynthia almost disintegrates in front of our eyes. Her sins have found her out.

It is here that Leigh's mastery as a filmmaker makes a difference. Some directors would zoom in on Cynthia's tears to exaggerate her emotions and force us to feel something. Leigh's camera does not flinch. It stays put, letting us observe as if we are sitting across the table from Cynthia. He does not make any cuts. He just lets the film roll. This increases the realism and authenticity, sharpening the pain of the moment. It feels less *manufactured,* more *natural.* Many of us cry with her. We know how hard it is to face the consequences of our own foolishness. Even the most painful situations can, in the hands of an artist, reveal a sort of magnificence. We cry not just for Cynthia's grief but also because of the excellence with which it is portrayed.

Watching *Secrets and Lies,* I did not for a moment think, *Amazing. This scene is filmed uncut. There isn't any music. There are no special effects!* No, those thoughts came later as I sought to understand *how* it was that Leigh's work affected me so intensely. I'm accustomed to directors who can't communicate effectively and try to enhance their shoddy workmanship with overbearing effects: a bombastic soundtrack or camera tricks. They deliver their points with blunt instruments, hammering the audience in order to get a reaction.

Not Leigh. He captures life in a way that is distinct to the art of filmmaking: He delivers us into a particular passage of time—full of movement, shifting light, pauses and dialogue.

That particularity is not meant to merely suggest life but to represent it in all of its temporal complexity. We can revisit those moments again and again, searching for significance in what seems incidental. Some filmmakers do this and reveal very little. The ferocity of Leigh's gaze can take us into the heart of the matter. By paying attention to every detail and allowing his actors some measure of spontaneity, he creates a lifelike scene. Through this verisimilitude, he gives us an opportunity to discover meaning in a reality very like our own.

We sit there and suffer, unable to find the will to put more popcorn into our mouths. We want this rift between two people to be healed so that we too can be at peace.

* * *

Speaking of suffering in front of a movie screen, I can't remember many scenes that made me more uncomfortable than watching that poor Mongolian camel give birth.

She, too, wept. Just as Cynthia of *Secrets and Lies* did not want to accept that she owed a great debt to the stranger next to her, that four-legged female in *The Story of the Weeping Camel* did not want to accept the responsibility of mothering that shaky-legged, bawling baby that had caused her so much pain during pregnancy.

The Story of the Weeping Camel documents for us, in graphic footage, the rather messy birth of this baby camel. The mother walks around in agony, her offspring only half-sprung from her bleeding hindquarters. No wonder the mother wants nothing to do with the baby once he's born! He's left to cry and stagger after her, even though she kicks him and leaves him to starve in the sand.

But then, something remarkable happens. The worried Mongolian nomads, distressed that they cannot convince these two hairy beasts to reconcile, send their oldest son (his name, believe it or not, is Dude) into town to summon an unlikely source of help—a music teacher from the local school. The dutiful musician travels back to this remote, old world settlement and unsheathes an instrument that looks something like a cello.

The animals' caretakers strap the instrument up against the mother camel's neck, and the wind moves across the strings so that they hum quietly. The camel's ears swivel back. The ethereal tones have her attention. She listens.

Then the musician takes back his instrument and draws his bow across the strings. It's a slow and haunting tune. The grandparents, the parents, the children—three generations—gather in reverence to observe.

The mother camel stands in rapt attention, concentrating. And then it happens . . . a marvelous and mysterious event. She begins to weep. Her baby approaches her. Instead of lashing out with her hooves, as she has done so many times before, she stands still and the baby begins to suckle. The suspense seems to dissolve into the desert air, carried away on the strains of the song. When the performance is over, the rift between mother and child has been healed. In the next scene, the mother stands there staring into the sun, vocalizing in a way that sounds as though she's continuing the song. The baby bleats along with her. It's an astonishing sight.

In Scripture, when a man encounters the glory of God—whether it's in a blinding light, a burning bush, a pillar of cloud, a dream, or a talking donkey—that man is changed. Sometimes he goes back to his friends with his face shining.

Like the weeping camel, I felt my own weary, distracted, broken soul touched, encouraged and transformed by observing those windswept dunes and that multi-generational family, dusty animal and concert in the Gobi Desert. Just as exposure to the mystery of the musician's song somehow healed what was broken in the camel's heart, so this mysterious story penetrated my own heart and restored my spirit. I walked out of that theater with my heart humming.

I can describe it best by borrowing some words from an artist and music-lover named Jessica Poundstone, who came back from a Bill Frisell concert recently and wrote, "Sometimes music is like one of those programs you run on your computer to optimize your hard drive: it heals a million little broken things you didn't even know needed attention."

God repairs us through creation and through art. This has something to do with why the camel sings.

Note
1. Michael J. Cusick, "Giving Shape to Turmoil: A Conversation with Chaim Potok," *Mars Hill Review*, Winter/Spring 1997. http://www.lasierra.edu/~ballen/potok/Potok.interviews.MHR.html (accessed November 2006).

Viewer Discretion Advised

*The eye is the lamp of the body. If your eyes are good,
your whole body will be full of light. But if your eyes are bad,
your whole body will be full of darkness.*

MATTHEW 6:22-23

*Do not participate in the unfruitful deeds of darkness,
but instead even expose them.*

EPHESIANS 5:11

Beside Quiet Waters

Low tide at Richmond Beach can be generous, and as I walk on the slippery wet rocks this evening, they glitter like pirate's treasure in a children's book. The setting sun rolls a gold carpet across quiet Puget Sound water toward me, a shimmering path like a dream of heaven's own avenues.

A few teenagers skip stones, ducks paddle near the shore, and farther out a loon (a bird I don't see very often, but its speckled wings are unmistakable) mopes along. The wind drags a dark curtain of rain across Bainbridge Island.

I can't tell you why, exactly, but the place calms me down. I come here when I'm wounded. Like this afternoon, for instance.

Somewhere in my chest, I feel a bruise. It's the ache of helplessness and outrage I feel when a good friend has unfairly suffered some insult. Someone took a sledgehammer to an admirable work of art, and there was nothing I could do to stop it.

In that agitated state, I couldn't finish my film-review assignment for *Christianity Today*. So I've come down to let the whispering tide, the gulls and the sunset do their work on me. It's what I love best about my neighborhood—the seven-minute drive to this panoramic glory. The psalmist knew what he was talking about when he implied that walking beside quiet waters would restore his soul (see Ps. 23:2). He also wrote that every day pours forth speech (see Ps. 19:2). This scenery is murmuring through stone and tree and tide. I'm not sure what it's saying, but something inside me responds.

* * *

Yesterday I saw a film called *Don't Come Knocking*, and it's been on my mind ever since. Sam Shepard played Howard Spence, a foolish film star famous for playing Old West gunslingers. Spence comes to the conclusion that his life is rather empty, so he sets out to find his way back to opportunities that he missed in hopes of salvaging some of the relationships he let dwindle.

In the dark I scribbled down "the prodigal father." As I did, I laughed, knowing I would find those same words in the reviews composed by other Christian film critics.

As part of my responsibilities for ChristianityTodayMovies.com, each week I read and excerpt a wide variety of religious press film reviews. I then line up those excerpts in a sort of round table format so that it sounds as if these writers have gathered after the movie to share their observations and argue. I'm quite accustomed to juxtaposing reviews in which one Christian heralds a new release as a powerful story with a redeeming message while another feels it exhibits shoddy craftsmanship and a formulaic narrative.

When I opened up my notes and compared them with the other Christian press reviews of *Don't Come Knocking*, I expected to find similar views. But I was disappointed to find that very few critics had been able to see the film as of yet. Then I ran into one of *those* reviews—the sort of "Christian movie review" that I grew up reading. The writer condemned the film *and* the filmmakers, slapping a long list of derogatory labels on their work. It was like watching a guest at a generous feast stand up, spit on what is served to him and storm out.

Appalled at this display of contempt and skewed judgment, I was tempted to post a sharp retort online. But the words of a friend who once sent me a stinging e-mail came back to me: "Jeffrey, you might become a decent film critic someday if you learn to get over your outrage." So I'm trying.

I think back to the beginning of *Don't Come Knocking*. I try to watch the story again through different lenses. Was I fooled? Is this actually a dangerous and deceptive movie? Have I been corrupted by Hollywood poison?

A Tale with a Timeless Theme

Howard Spence is sitting on an old couch in the middle of the street in Butte, Montana. He has run away from the set of his latest film, a Western being shot against the desolate backdrop of Moab, Utah. Something has drawn him to Butte, where he once fell in love with a waitress.

As he sits there, troubled and alone, enjoying a moment of stillness, there's a sense that he's opening his eyes for the first time. He seems bewildered, as if he's never stopped to notice time passing before.

Through the lens of director Wim Wenders, Butte has the spacious silence of a ghost town, haunted with echoes of the past. In the stillness, Spence begins to ponder all that he's missed during his pursuit of pleasure and fame. His success, his self-indulgence (which has landed him some impressive tabloid headlines) and his compulsion to escape into the ego-boosting fantasy of the American Western—all of these things have proven powerfully distracting.

Maybe here, at "the scene of the crime," Spence will wake up and start living for the first time, drawn by the possibility of love and a family. It won't be easy for Howard to re-enter relationships he left in shambles. That journey must begin with repentance and forgiveness. Is he up to it?

*   *   *

This story of the wandering father does not have the same glorious climax as Jesus' parable of the prodigal son. Howard's fractured family does not fall into each others' arms and live happily ever after. But we can still catch glimpses of grace and redemption along the way.

The film's power grows from the authentic performances of seasoned actors. It resonates in the wry humor of the soft-spoken script. Above all, vivid imagery (stunning scenery, time-weathered faces and the disintegrating architecture of Butte) communicates volumes about this desolate spiritual territory.

It was bound to be an unusual outing—a German filmmaker telling the story of an American road trip. He had done it before in the masterful, Cannes-award-winning *Paris, Texas,* his only other collaboration with Sam Shepard. That was 20 years ago. *Don't Come Knocking* is a lighter, funnier fiction, and some of its scenes feel more haphazard than meaningful. But once again Wenders and Shepard have crafted an evocative, contemplative journey full of characters who are longing for wholeness. And this time, Shepard takes the starring role of the wayward Hollywood icon, bringing rough authenticity both to the minimalist script and his performance.

Wenders has made his cowboy movie, and it is the antithesis of the classic Western. We're quite accustomed to seeing the all-American hero win the heart of the girl, outwit and outgun the bad guys and then, when the woman begs him to stay home on the ranch, ride off with a tip of his hat to wander and seek adventure. In Wenders' perspective, however, this is a distinctly American dream—self-reliance and independence that lead ultimately to regret and emptiness.

Wenders starts at the other end of the story, when the wanderer decides to turn back and reconsider the choices he's left behind.

*   *   *

The story of Howard Spence is a prevalent tale in movies today, as generations growing up fatherless seek to fill a void and as men who have run from family and responsibility begin to yearn for what they might have chosen.

It's an ache that we can feel in a wave of recent films: Wes Anderson's *The Royal Tenenbaums* and *The Life Aquatic with Steve Zissou*, Hirozaki Koreeda's *Nobody Knows*, Tim Burton's *Big Fish*, Andrei Zvyagintsev's *The Return*, Noah Baumbach's *The Squid and the Whale*, and Jim Jarmusch's *Broken Flowers*. We can trace it back to *The Empire Strikes Back*, when Luke Skywalker finally learned about the betrayals of his own particularly irresponsible papa.

Yet *Don't Come Knocking* is charged with personal passion. Sam Shepard admitted that this story reflects his troubled relationship with his own father. And Wenders heard echoes of *his* past as well. "[My father] was a great father," he told me. "I loved him very much. He was always there for me. And then . . . we sort of had a falling out when I was 16, 17 and 18 years old. We actually didn't speak for a number of years. And then we slowly talked to each other again and became very good friends . . . I spent his last six months with him on a day-to-day basis."

The reconciliation clearly meant a great deal to Wenders, especially in view of the lack he has seen in others' lives. "When I grew up, I only had one friend who didn't have a father, and that was always horrifying to me. I had so much pity for the guy . . . [The] fact that he didn't even know his father was inconceivable to me. And then, eventually, it was as if this friend multiplied. I knew more and more people who grew up without a father. The absent father became a regular cultural and social phenomenon. . . . It almost seemed during the '90s that there were more people *without* a father than people *with* a father."

As Wenders realized the "incredible lack" he would have felt without his father, he became interested in "telling the story of that absence." But, in his characteristic style, Wenders told that story in *Don't Come Knocking* from different perspectives in order to understand it as fully as possible. "From the beginning, I wanted to tell the story from both sides: the guy who missed being with his kids . . . and receiving their love and giving his love, and . . . from the perspective of these young adults who have this guy waltz in and say, 'Hi, I'm your father,' and how they feel about it."

He was surprised at how closely *Don't Come Knocking* paralleled another movie, Jim Jarmusch's *Broken Flowers,* which was finished around the same time. "I think it's in the air. . . . Jim Jarmusch is one of my best friends. We are not in any way competitive. And the fact that Jim, unbeknownst to me, made a film about the same subject made it clear for both of us that we had hit on something that is of grave contemporary concern."

* * *

That ability to tap into timeless themes through the particularity of his work is what has earned Wenders a reputation as a poet amongst other filmmakers, even if his movies aren't flashy enough to grab the attention of mainstream moviegoers.

Scott Derrickson, the director of the thought-provoking thriller *The Exorcism of Emily Rose* and one of Wenders' good friends and collaborators, talked to me about how to appreciate Wenders' work. "Unlike Hollywood films, Wenders' films assume that you will bring your own thoughts and feelings to the moviegoing experience. He won't tell you what to feel, so when you watch his films, you have to think about what *you* are seeing, what *you* are hearing and what *you* are feeling—in short, you have to interact with the film. Hollywood movies manipulate your emotions, but his films give you freedom to respond without coaxing.

"Pay attention to Wenders' great muse, which is 'a sense of place.' He understands that human longing drives us to travel— to move beyond our houses into our own cities and often across our countries and out into the world. He is more sensitive to 'place' than any filmmaker I know, and you must always pay attention to his locations and landscapes; try to see how his visual space ties in to his characters and stories."

In that sense, *Don't Come Knocking* is a fine summation of Wenders' strengths. The silences are as important as the conversations. The landscapes are as important as the characters in the foreground. They all contribute to questions that the viewer is encouraged to consider.

*   *   *

Watch the sky. Pay attention to weather, light and shadow. Watch the streets. Search the lines in each character's face. Attend to the words they choose to use.

That's one of the disciplines that those who get the most out of going to movies learn to develop. I'm still a beginner. I've got to watch everything and relentlessly ask, "Is this significant? What does it mean? Why is it there?"

If the filmmaker lacks talent, I probably won't find many answers to those questions. But if he or she is a true artist, I'm often surprised by the relationships I find between different elements of the film. And I continue to discover surprising possibilities when I watch it again. When I'm scribbling in my film notebook, it's just like combing the stones of Richmond Beach to find souvenirs. Any of these elements could turn out to be treasure, reflecting light, revealing insight. Hold some of them to your ear—you'll hear the voice of an ocean.

Consider the following: An antique harmonium. A sugar cube held an inch above the swirling surface of coffee in a cup. A beam of blue light. A whiskey bottle. A tablet dissolving in water. A trapeze.

In the pages to come, I'll show how each one of these has been revelatory for me. If I hadn't been paying attention, I would have missed them. This tells me that I've missed thousands of other meaningful moments along the way. So I go back, again and again. I pursue conversations with other moviegoers to learn what they saw so that I can fill in more of the picture. I want to learn how to train my attention and judge what is meaningful and what isn't. In a word, I want to learn discretion.

"Discretion" is a word much abused. We've come to relate it to the warning "Viewer discretion advised," meaning, "Watch out! Potentially offensive and lurid material ahead! Turn back!" But any good dictionary will tell you that discretion is about having good judgment.

"Details are confusing," said Georgia O'Keeffe. "It is only by selection, by elimination, by emphasis, that we get at the real meaning of things." I want to learn the science of sifting art for meaning. It might be the pin holding a woman's braids in place. It might be a small bird carved from a piece of wood.

It might even be a red wheelbarrow, sitting beside a puddle of rainwater and some chickens.

So Much Depends Upon . . .

Oh, that confounding red wheelbarrow.

"What is this poem about?" Mr. Demkowicz, my red-bearded high school English teacher, leaned patiently against the front of his desk and scanned the half circle of students, watching our pained expressions.

It was 1988. We were seniors at last. Surely we could understand this four-line poem by William Carlos Williams called "The Red Wheelbarrow":

so much depends
upon

a red wheel
barrow

glazed with rain
water

beside the white
chickens.

"Is it about life on the farm?" a student ventured.

"No, don't ask *me* what it's about," said Mr. Demkowicz patiently. "What do *you* think it is about?"

A student sitting next to me shifted uncomfortably. I could see that she wanted to say something, but everything about this class made her—and most of the students—a bit jumpy.

First of all, "Mr. D" was a formidable, broad-shouldered fellow. His behavior in the classroom was startling and unexpected. He had introduced himself by rising and walking around to the front of the desk, removing that barrier between us. Then he had told us about the general outline of the coming quarter and how he was going to offer us an opportunity for a different kind of classroom experience.

"You're seniors now," he said. "Theoretically, that means you're young adults. This would suggest that I don't have to treat you like children anymore. And I want to think that's true. Perhaps we can lift some of those rules and formalities that you've become accustomed to, some of the restrictions that are intended for . . . for younger people. Restrictions that have come to seem stifling to you."

Normally, a class would begin with a list of the familiar rules of engagement. This had to be a trick.

"Let's try, for example, pulling these desks out of the rows they're in and placing them in a half-circle around the room."

This was a change of pace.

"You don't have to raise your hands when you want to say something. You don't need permission. Let's be grownups. We're here to learn about literature and art, and that happens through reflection and conversation. Show respect to each other by listening, and then offer your observations."

College students grow accustomed to this dynamic. But for high school classmates who had grown up together in rows and with hand-raising to get the teacher to call on us, this was an emancipation proclamation. If there is anything that seniors in high school despise, it's the idea of being treated like children. So we accepted the challenge.

Fortunately for the rest of us, one young woman found the courage to venture into uncharted territory and venture a guess about the poem. "Isn't the poem about the simple things?"

"What is the poem saying about the simple things?" Mr. D responded.

"Well, everything in it is very simple. The wheelbarrow. The chickens."

"Go on. What else?"

"Well, I'm not sure about the first line. But it seems like it's stressing that these things are very important."

"'*So much depends upon* . . .' Yes. That's rather loaded, isn't it?"

The student went on, fumbling around in new territory. Then others stepped in with their own thoughts. Before long, 20 seniors were taking turns, offering thoughts. Slowly, the quality of their contributions shifted from *guessing at the answer* to something altogether different: *offering their impressions*.

"Don't worry," Mr. D assured us, holding up a printed copy of the poem. "This is not a case of guessing the meaning *behind* the poem." He flipped the paper over, and we laughed—it was blank on the other side. "The meaning is *in* the poem in many ways. It is not a puzzle to be solved. This isn't a math problem. Your interpretation of the meaning will depend somewhat on your own experiences."

We would, indeed, see different things in Williams' poem. And likewise, today, Wim Wenders' *Don't Come Knocking* might fail to resonate with some viewers, even as it seizes and shakes a viewer who grew up fatherless or strikes a spark of conscience in a man who senses that he has selfishly wasted his life. Wenders told me that he has seen tears in the eyes of fathers and sons as they emerge from the dark theater where his film was playing. Others have called it a somewhat amusing but forgettable film. Does this suggest that a poem, a movie, or a work of art can mean whatever we want it to mean? Mr. D resolutely denied this. "No, there are two erroneous extremes that we could reach: first, that there is one *and only one* proper interpretation, and second, that the meaning is arbitrary. Neither is true."

He went on: "There is truth in a good work of art, but it is a fluid and complex mystery. We will all see different pieces of it because we are all looking at it from different points of view and bring different things to it from our experiences. Insightful observations will hold up under scrutiny and correspond with other interpretations. Misguided interpretations will collapse when we look closer at the work. Interpretation is the search for the truth through a process of trial and error. The 'trial' happens when we 'try' our impressions against the work; the 'error' happens when we see that our impressions come more from ourselves than from the work."

Some interpretations of "The Red Wheelbarrow" resonated with many, and others seemed far-fetched. But my classmates and I were excited that so much could be drawn from one sentence. It felt like staring at one of those Magic Eye paintings, when a square full of small multicolored spots suddenly reveals a three-dimensional image to the patient observer.

Williams' poem is just four short broken lines, yet each line is broken in such a way as to lend special importance to simple things such as rain and chickens. There is a sort of music to it, a rhythm made of long, lilting vowel sounds, which we discovered after reading it a few times. The words are specific, bold and colorful, giving a vivid picture of a particular wheelbarrow, a particular place, a particular moment.

Eventually, someone noticed that the way the lines themselves were divided took a curious shape. In each line, a longer descriptive line rests upon a short word. In this way, four sections become four little wheelbarrows, each one carrying meaningful cargo.

There was a sense of exhilaration in realizing that we would not be penalized or belittled for a "wrong" answer. What mattered wasn't getting it right so much as playing a part in this communal journey forward. And yes, that's what it was—"play." By participating and playing with the words and considering their relationships, we began to do our part to fill in the picture.

It would have been easy for someone to respond by saying, "This is boring. There's nothing here. You're all just making it up." But if the rest of us were reaping rewards, that rash judgment would have been exposed as a sign of ignorance or, worse, arrogance.

That's not to say that every attempt at art is meaningful. Some contain clumsy contradictions. Some make a lot of noise, puffed up with their own importance, and then proceed to point out the obvious. There are works that strive to make us feel good about ourselves by telling us what we want to hear. And there are others that exhibit just how little thought the artist has committed to his work. The more we discover excellence in art, the more we can discern rich pickings from landfills. Discretion.

So, to remind us of this lesson, Mr. D wrote a few words on the chalkboard. Those words remained there all year long and became a sort of mantra for many of us. We even had it printed on T-shirts: "*Things mean things . . .*"

Signposts in a Strange Land

When we approach art with humility rather than a readiness to judge, we open ourselves to discovering that any particular detail might be a signpost that will point us in the direction of the truth.

Julie, the central character in Krzysztof Kieslowski's *Three Colors: Blue*, keeps a mobile made of blue glass fragments. What does it represent? In *Au Hazard Balthazar*, a donkey moves from abandonment to humiliation to abuse. As we follow him, we learn a great deal about human nature from the treatment he receives from various characters. What does Balthazar represent?

If we sum up a work by reacting to the first things that jump out at us—if we condemn *Blue* because Julie chooses to sleep with an admirer or *Balthazar* because a cruel man ties a flaming newspaper to the donkey's tail—we may miss what these events show us about human nature, or about grace, and remain unchanged. It can seem impractical. A useless preoccupation. But the more we enter into the artistic imagination, the more we might begin to suspect that the world itself could be the design of a Supreme Artist and that creation is full of meaning . . . pouring forth speech.

God's truth is not available *solely* in Scripture or in the mouths of preachers—it can also be discerned in the way a tree grows or the way a sugar cube absorbs coffee. God may be revealing Himself not just through the charity of a compassionate saint (*Dead Man Walking*) but also through the shocking evil of a desperate preacher (*The Apostle*). In Romans 1:20, Paul tells us that what can be known about God is plain for all to see: "For since the creation of the world God's invisible attributes—his eternal power and divine nature—have been clearly seen, being understood from what has been made, so that men are without excuse."

This unsettles Christians who have come to believe that the only source of God's revelation is the Bible. I get letters from them; they warn me that I'm playing with fire if I look anywhere else. But the Scriptures relentlessly point us outward, teaching us how to hear God's voice in the natural world, in human events and in history. "The heavens declare the glory of God" (Ps. 19:1). "I lift up my eyes to the hills—where does my help come from?" (Ps. 121:1). "Go to the ant, you sluggard; consider its ways and be wise!" (Prov. 6:6).

Christ gave us metaphors He found in nature and in the folly of human behavior to show us the truth about holiness. As the writer of Colossians assures us, "For by him *all things* were created: things in heaven and on earth, visible and invisible, whether thrones or powers or rulers or authorities; *all things* were created by him and for him. He is before *all things*, and in him *all things* hold together" (1:16-17, emphasis added).

If the kingdom of God is like a mustard seed, for all we know it might also be like a red wheelbarrow. Or the black and white keys in Jane Campion's *The Piano*. Or the old turntable playing music for the inmates of *The Shawshank Redemption*. Or even the quiet streets of Butte, Montana, in *Don't Come Knocking*.

Christ's incarnation teaches us that spiritual things and fleshly things are not separate. The sacred is waiting to be recognized in secular things. Even those artists who don't believe in God might accidentally reflect back to us realities in which we can see God working.

"If thine heart were right," wrote Thomas à Kempis, "then should every creature be a mirror of life and a book of holy doctrine. There is no creature so small and vile but that it showeth us the goodness of God." In the same vein, George MacDonald wrote, "When we understand the outside of things, we think we have them: the Lord puts his things in subdefined, suggestive shapes, yielding no satisfactory meaning to the mere intellect, but unfolding themselves to the conscience and heart."

Mathematics, science, art—these are languages through which God is speaking. *All truth* is God's truth. We mustn't be afraid of science, numbers or surrealist paintings. If God is sovereign in the world, as we assert that He is, these explorations affirm and increase the faith of those who look closely.

But isn't this a dangerous endeavor? You bet your life. (And isn't that what we all bet?) There are dangers: pieces of broken glass, glimpses of death, and obscenities spray-painted everywhere. We've done a bang-up job of polluting God's world and making paths to glory fraught with peril.

But those who let the dangers discourage them from engaging the world are not really saving themselves. They're cutting themselves off from sources of God's revelation. If we think that by withdrawing we can get away from sin's influence in the world, we have forgotten that sin is active within our own walls and within our own heart. When characters in horror movies run from the monster and lock themselves inside the house, we all know where the monster is going to show up next.

* * *

I'm learning to write in the dark. Important images and lines jump out of the film, and I want to remember them. My notebooks would be as illegible to you as some doctors' prescription slips. But they're useful to me when I think back through how the filmmaker employed different elements to convey meaning or explore a theme.

While watching *Don't Come Knocking*, it occurred to me that very few filmmakers make Westerns anymore, and when they do, the movies don't look like old-fashioned John Wayne Westerns. And yet here was Howard Spence, starring in an old-style Western in 2006 on a movie set in Moab, Utah. Odd, to say the least.

Was Wenders misguided? Ignorant about contemporary Hollywood productions? Or did he include this anachronistic production on purpose to represent something? Could it be that the characters in the film hadn't noticed that time has passed and that the age of the cocky American gunslinger is over? Could it be that their nostalgia for the individualistic hero has blinded them to the consequences of such individualism?

I was also intrigued by the character Sutter, an investigator sent from the Utah movie set to find Howard in Montana and bring him back to fulfill his contract. Sutter, played by Tim Roth, is a well-groomed man who dresses in a suit and small, mirrored glasses that seem to emphasize his blindness. His attention is entirely focused on finding the lawbreaker and bringing him to justice. He seems just as lost in the vast silence of the desert as he is when a gracious old woman welcomes him in and offers him chocolate chip cookies.

Sutter, too, has seized on a limiting view of life. His narrow, legalistic mind has cut him off from true humanity, just as the runaway actor's self-indulgence and recklessness have cut him off from the same. They're on two different extremes of delusion. Wisdom lies elsewhere.

Don't Come Knocking affirms that there are many different ways we can approach our lives. We can give in to the whispers of ego, temptation or distraction. We can put on the mirrored glasses of piety and condemn what we see, making ourselves feel superior in the process. Or we can walk this corrupt ground with humility, discernment and grace.

If we watch *Don't Come Knocking*, we can see characters who take that third path and learn how their behavior stands in sharp contrast to those they encounter along the way.

"Abhorrent!"

So there I was, considering the rewards of Wim Wenders' *Don't Come Knocking*, pondering what it meant, when I finally found a review written by a prominent and popular Christian film critic.

Had he discovered any of the same things that I had? Had he found deeper meaning in Wenders' parable? No. This Christian reviewer condemned not only the movie but Mr. Wenders as well, declaring that "discerning moral viewers should all together avoid this piece of trash."

The reviewer went on to present a checklist of potentially offensive items he witnessed in the film. He catalogued "strong instances of foul language and miscellaneous immorality such as gambling, drinking and drugs." He warned his readers about a scene involving "naturalistic upper male nudity." (In other words, we see a grown man take off his shirt.) "This is a movie that is just not good," he concluded.

Because the movie contained these elements, he branded the movie with a red bar and the rating he reserved for the worst of all movies: "Abhorrent."

*　*　*

Are the reviewer's claims about the content of Wenders' movie true?

There *are* scenes in *Don't Come Knocking* that include foul language, gambling, drinking and drugs, just as Christ's tale of the prodigal son involves a man who wishes his father was dead, sinks into debauchery, and ends up eating pig slop.

Wenders includes these elements so that we can see the power of the traps that have been set for Howard Spence. I wouldn't bring small children to the film. They wouldn't understand Howard's dilemmas, and they might be frightened by the rough behavior the lost cowboy encounters.

But none of this misbehavior is presented as rewarding activity. In fact, just as the traveler in *Pilgrim's Progress* struggles through Vanity Fair, so Howard Spence falls victim to old addictions when he visits a casino. These elements are clearly included to show his weaknesses and why he needs to be saved.

We don't see any Christian characters, like those in Wenders' collaboration with Derrickson in 2005's *Land of Plenty*. Nor are there any angels commenting on the work of the Holy Spirit, as in 1987's *Wings of Desire*. But there are other factors to consider: the characters' choices and consequences, the way that stillness prompts them to reflection, and the cinematographer's interest in the scenery and run-down buildings, which serve in the film as suggestions about the passage of time and the failure of an old world. (Others may catch visual allusions to Edward Hopper's body of work.)

If we were to approach the Bible the way that this dismissive reviewer approached Wenders' story, what would we do with the story of Lot's sexually misguided daughters, those last dark days in Sodom and Gomorrah, Ehud's evisceration of a king, or Solomon's love poetry . . . for starters? How would we deal with those bloody, bawdy Shakespeare stage plays? Imagine editing "strong instances" of violence and suffering from Dante's *Inferno*.

I once received a letter from a furious reader who did not like my recommendation of a movie about gangsters. The foul language of these characters, I had written, was troubling, but I felt it was an accurate reflection of this corner of society. The reader wrote:

> You say that this honestly depicts our society. Well, no, it does not depict mine. I don't work with people who speak that way and I'm not around them away from work. If someone attempts to use this kind of language around me, I will quickly point out that I don't like it and then remove myself from the situation.

The reader is telling the truth. I don't doubt it. But is this the response that Christ would have us cultivate toward our fellow sinners?

If a depiction of evil causes us to sin, by all means, we must respond to our conscience and withdraw until we have become stronger. How many of us are humble enough to admit when we are what Scripture calls "the weaker brother"? But if we can look at evidence of sin, consider its consequences and resist the temptation to imitate it, this can lead to wisdom and resilience.

Christ did not turn and walk away from sinful people because of their imperfect behavior. His enemies, the Pharisees, were the folks who were appalled to find Him spending time in the homes of sinners and sin.

In an article titled "Should Christians Read Dirty Books?" Barbara Pell asks if the sensitivity of many American Christians toward foul language in art might have more to do with being middle-class than with being conscientious.

> I was once told that some naturalistic scenes in a contemporary novel that particularly offended me were moderate compared to the scenes of human squalor and hopelessness witnessed by my friend, who was a public health nurse in a city slum. She implied that if I could get out of my ivory tower and my middle-class suburban community and experience the degradation and suffering of the majority of the world's people, if only through the realism of a modern novel, maybe I could begin to understand what the nurses and social workers and street missions were trying to do in a society where one couldn't run away from the consequences of human sin and need simply by closing the covers of a book.[1]

If we are shocked by something as common as a spoken obscenity, it may reveal more about our distance from people in need than it does about the person who blurted out such coarse language. As children of God, we have not been instructed to create an insulated commune in order to wall ourselves off from the corrupting influences of the world.

In John 17, Jesus said that He was sending His disciples *into* the world, even though they were not *of* the world. They were to engage their corrupt culture armed with a spirit of courage and character. In Acts 17, Paul was able to walk among the Athenians' altars to false gods and then point people toward the inscription to the "unknown god" on one of those altars.

For us, art serves by showing not only what is happening in the world around us but also the perspectives with which others are viewing and interpreting those events. It is bound to be fraught with deception, distortion and damage. Should we shield our eyes and run away?

In his book *Whistling in the Dark*, Frederick Buechner has a strong answer: "If we are to love our neighbors, before doing anything else we must see our neighbors. With our imagination as well as our eyes, that is to say like artists, we must see not just their faces but the life behind and within their faces. Here it is love that is the frame we see them in."[2]

Proceed with Caution

That spiteful review of *Don't Come Knocking* may have rankled my nerves, but it was nothing new. I've become well acquainted with this type of Christian movie review in many different

Christian publications. But seeing such brash ignorance and contempt for a fellow Christian's artistic exploration of spiritual themes . . . well, this time, it just kicked me in the gut. That's why I'm down here walking on the beach.

There's a grown man lying on a beach blanket just ahead of me, even though the air is cooling down. He's not wearing a shirt. Farther on, I happen upon some boys in their early teens who are wearing black jackets and splashing around in the water unsupervised. Three of them are cussing, throwing rocks at each other and bragging about sexual exploits that probably never took place.

I start making mental notes. I've already seen something that qualifies as "naturalistic upper male nudity," if I understand that category correctly. I've encountered "strong instances" of profanity. The occasional broken beer bottle. Hunks of eroding Styrofoam. A discarded condom in the sand. Pieces of a dead crab. Should we close off this beach and rate it as "abhorrent"?

Again, I'm wrestling with my inner cynic. If I can't get over my aggravation, I won't ever find the right kind of spirit for effective review writing. That critic's complaints came dangerously close to eclipsing the virtues of Wenders' movie in my mind. I do not want to dwell, as he does, on the evidence of sin, or I'll become the very thing that grieves me.

There's something about this vast grandeur—water, storm, mountains and sky—that helps me regain my perspective. Suddenly, an aggravating movie review doesn't seem like such a crisis. This shoreline is loaded with distracting memories, most of them pleasant, and they begin to glide into view like the sleepy gulls.

*   *   *

When my parents took my brother Jason and me on vacation, we always drove from Portland to the Oregon Coast. Mom and Dad would stroll arm in arm along the sand at Lincoln City while I ran ahead to explore every tide pool. When I stumbled onto a wonder—a small red crab, a sea anemone, a purple starfish—I'd scamper back to tell them what I'd seen.

As I carried my six-year-old curiosity onto that glittering span to greet the great, breathing sea, my parents would shout the same warnings every time: "Jeff, don't run barefoot! There might be broken glass!" "Don't pick up jellyfish. They can sting!" "That's not drinking water." "Those rocks are sharp and slippery." "Stay where we can see you."

All of this was good advice. Even so, I once cut my hand so badly that my parents told me to submerge it in a bucket of ice water to numb the pain while they looked up a local hospital in the phone book. You never know. There are all sorts of dangers in such a place.

I am grateful that my parents steered me clear of perils I was not yet smart enough to avoid. I'm glad they considered it important to risk those perils in order to expose Jason and me to the splendor of Lincoln City tide pools, the giant crashing waves of Gleneden Beach and the bluffs above the water at Rocky Creek State Park. I suspect that my own creative efforts in writing, and those of my brother in composing music and singing, grew from a desire to respond to those natural marvels.

I'm even more grateful that my parents taught me how to recognize the dangers of rock, tide and litter for myself so that I could eventually show some discipline on my own and avoid hurting myself. We all mature and outgrow the need for constant supervision. We find satisfaction in going it alone with discernment.

But there are those who think we should remain fearful children. They strive to convince us that exposure to corruption will contaminate us. They cultivate contempt for those who have the strength and maturity to move about in dangerous places. Before we go out on the beach, they burden us with reminders of all of the possible threats that might be waiting there. Educating ourselves to danger is an essential part of maturity, but if we *dwell* on such threats, we will complicate our enjoyment of freedom and blessing. If we proceed with caution, open to the possibility of revelation, we never know what treasure we'll discover.

Don't Come Knocking is a story about how a lifelong fool, Howard Spence, paid the price for living recklessly and tried to make up for his mistakes before it was too late. But by contrast, Wenders also shows us that one can become *too* concerned with law and order. He gives us the story of Sutter, who spends his day looking for fault in others and lives a lonely, stifled life that is closed off from pleasure and joy. As such, *Don't Come Knocking* is a story about wisdom for those with eyes to see and ears to hear.

* * *

On the morning of September 11, 2001, my wife, Anne, and I turned off our television shortly after the second World Trade Center tower collapsed. We'd seen enough. It was time to pray and to seek reminders of God's sovereignty. So we drove down to Richmond Beach and walked the short trail across the bridge over the railroad and out to the shimmering golden water.

At first, it seemed that we were the only Seattleites who had been able to break free from the gravity of the morning's televised destruction. But we eventually encountered some environmental scientists in wading pants, dragging nets through the water, pulling their catches free and placing them in different buckets. They showed us a variety of fish they were testing for various toxins, including a red lion's mane jellyfish, its translucent body crimson and cold. "It's dead," a woman explained to us. "Probably floated in from the ocean. Pollution."

We watched these gentle, patient scientists work for a while. The quiet was unsettling. Anne reminded me that all air traffic had been grounded due to the attacks.

These two events—the attacks on America and these wading scientists—seemed strangely connected. The spectacularly colorful images of a smoky maelstrom engulfing New York. The frantic attempts of the anchormen to discern what lay at the root of such devastating evil. The exotic, beautiful sea creatures. The quiet waters hiding poisonous secrets. The patient dedication of these scientists, with their nets and needles, studying their specimens in an attempt to understand what was poisoning them. They were laboring in faith that what is wrong with the world can be made better. That, I believe, is what we all must do.

It's a muddy and dangerous business: We must face the mess we've made of the world, brave the dangers of corruption, tend to what is broken, and do what we can to prevent evil from gaining further ground. To become doctors who treat the corruption in the world and in ourselves, we have to first understand the sickness and what causes it. The scientists wore gloves. When handling toxic material, we should take proper precautions to guard ourselves. With caution, we must proceed.

* * *

Today as I'm pondering the parallels between beachcombing and moviegoing, my review of *Don't Come Knocking* waiting unfinished back home on my desk, I'm suddenly distracted by one of those teenagers in the water. He's standing a short distance away from his posse, directly between me and that shining path of sunlight, and the blaze reduces him to a vague silhouette. His pant legs rolled up to his knees, he stands ankle-deep in rippling fire and concentrates fiercely on the deep blue cloudburst mushrooming over the islands. Perhaps there's something on his mind. Perhaps the immeasurable glory of this place has, for a moment, won out over juvenile banter, danger and trash.

That's when I notice the bold white print across the back of his T-shirt: "Viewer Discretion Advised."

Notes
  1. Barbara Pell, "Should Christians Read Dirty Books?" *Christian Educator's Journal*, February/March 1989, pp. 6-7.
  2. Frederick Buechner, *Whistling in the Dark: An ABC Theologized* (New York: Harper and Row, 1988), pp. 15-16.

CHAPTER
THREE

A Feast of Movies

To eat good food is to be close to God.

PRIMO IN *BIG NIGHT*

*There comes a time when our eyes are opened
and we come to realize that mercy is infinite.*

LORENZ LOWENHIELM IN *BABETTE'S FEAST*

A Scene from Babette's Feast

The letter was delivered with some gravity by a man in a red uniform on horseback. A villager carried it quickly to the designated house, where it was received with surprise and apprehension by Martina and Philippa, the two aging daughters of the Protestant minister who had fostered this close-knit community in the mid-1800s on the Jutland coast of Denmark.

The words "from France" worried them immediately. The letter was addressed to Babette, their faithful servant of 14 years. Babette had come to them for refuge during the 1871 revolution in France, finding purpose and solace in serving these saintly women while they continued their father's legacy of caring for the villagers. Would this letter summon her back home, leaving them to cook their simple meals of dried fish and bland bread soup for themselves?

During a pregnant pause, Martina and Philippa watch as Babette opens the letter. Babette's bewilderment deepens into incredulity. No, she has not been summoned home. She has won the lottery!

At first, it's thrilling. Out here on the edge of the world, among people of meager resources, they can barely comprehend such a fortune. But then the sisters' fears return. What will Babette do with this opportunity? Only a fool—or a saint—would remain here unnecessarily.

Babette, the letter heavy in her hand, walks out of the house and down the slight, stony slope to the edge of the sea. (How often the great heroes of the big screen must, in their moment of decision, stare out into open space!) There, she gazes into the expanse of the sky and its blurred reflection on the waves as if she is sending out a kind of silent signal and waiting for a response. She could do anything with this money. But what *should* she do?

Her decision is mysterious. She decides to bless her dear employers and their community with yet another meal. But the menu's going to blow their minds.

Their suppers have been simple and practical, the same thing every day. This feast will be extravagant, made with things they've never seen, much less tasted, before. Their meals have been easy to swallow. Babette will offer dishes that confound them, and they may or may not be comfortable with such exotic ingredients. They have abstained from alcohol. Assistants from the kitchen will fill their glasses with wine. Babette's feast will challenge more than their stomachs. It will awaken some of their deepest fears.

"The God Room"

When I watch *Babette's Feast*, I feel a deep gratitude to the director, Gabriel Axel, and the writer, Isak Dinesen. And I'm thankful too for Mr. Demkowicz, who showed it to our senior class back in 1988 as we began to learn about how "things mean things."

The film is filled with themes worth talking about, fodder for discussion of differing religious traditions, and characters who reveal tendencies in our prideful human nature. But what I saw reflected back to me was a picture of people gathering for a work of art—culinary art—and how their varying fears prevented them from understanding extraordinary and available blessings.

Ever since, lines and images from *Babette's Feast* have come to mind as I've talked with others about the art of film. I've heard myself speaking with the same prejudice and paranoia that afflicts Babette's guests. And I've seen others reject great cinematic feasts out of fear.

* * *

Film reviewing was, at first, a way for me to cultivate conversations such as those I had enjoyed in university literature courses. I met so many interesting people and learned so much about interpreting art from studying *Paradise Lost*, the poems of John Donne and W. H. Auden, and Dostoyevsky's *The Brothers Karamazov*, that I felt bored and restless when graduation sent me swiftly into the daily humdrum of a job editing legal documents for Seattle's Department of Construction and Land Use.

I wanted to get back into those heated discussions and explore the meaning of art's mysteries.

It was hard to find people who were reading the same books that were catching my attention, so I found myself discussing movies much more frequently. Everybody was going to the movies. Everybody wanted to celebrate their favorites and argue about which titles were a waste of time.

The Internet began to open up around the same time, allowing anyone to publish rants and raves. Right away, I went searching for thoughtful Christian perspectives on film. But it was tough to find anything beyond those "Christian reviews" in which catalogues of cuss words and warnings about violence and sex greatly outweighed any actual interpretation or consideration of excellence. Frustrated, I decided that I would write the kind of movie reviews that I wanted to read. That is to say, I wanted to try writing about film the way C. S. Lewis wrote about books.

It seemed possible for a Christian to consider a movie's craftsmanship and storytelling the way I had been taught to study Shakespeare—considering more than which character committed what sin.

Hence, my review, Looking Closer, was born. A crowd of torch-wielding believers soon showed up at my door, ready to burn down the house. Okay, that's an overstatement. Let's just say that checking my e-mail box became a much more exciting endeavor. I learned that Christians were skilled in the parlance of hate mail. Many seemed convinced that my engagement with the art of contemporary culture was a how-to guide for a life of sinful revelry.

Thankfully, there were others who felt differently. After about two years of rambling about films online, I received an invitation from *Christianity Today*'s Ted Olsen to carry on "Film Forum" on the magazine's website, a weekly column originated by Steve Lansingh. Flattered and grateful, I quickly accepted. And the angry mail addressed to me increased tenfold. Shortly after, Mark Moring, editor of *Christianity Today*'s music-review website, presented his bold vision to create ChristianityTodayMovies.com, a website filled with film reviews, interviews and features. Soon, a whole family of critics was examining films from a Christian perspective, trying to blaze new trails.

And this led to the junket invitations.

* * *

Movie junkets are feeding frenzies for entertainment journalists—press conferences in which reporters, bloggers, radio personalities and critics gather to see advance screenings and then interview the actors, the director, the screenwriter, the producer, and others. I never expected that my online rants and raves would earn me opportunities to meet filmmakers. So it was a pleasant surprise when I began receiving invitations to New York, Beverly Hills and downtown Seattle for special screenings with other reviewers. Suddenly, I wasn't just talking to fans of Nicolas Cage, Spike Jonze and Charlie Kaufman. I was at a table with Cage, Jonze and Kaufman themselves.

These cinematic feasts have ranged from extraordinary to regrettable, but the company at the table for religious-press film critics has always been interesting. After growing up wondering if there were any other Christians as preoccupied with the trivia of filmmaking as me, it has been fantastic to sit down with a talkative collection of Christian journalists fluent in the films of Steven Spielberg, Stephen Frears, Stephen Sommers and Steven Soderbergh.

Christian film critics are recent additions to the junkets, and I'm sure our presence there has raised a few eyebrows among the mainstream journalists. Thanks to the success of *The Passion of the Christ*, *The Exorcism of Emily Rose* and a popular story about a lion and a witch, Hollywood has begun to realize just how much of their audience is made up of churchgoers. This has changed the studios' marketing strategies and even inspired the establishment of new film divisions like FoxFaith. The task for my fellow reviewers and me is to remain clear-eyed and level-headed. We must resist allowing the hype and the generosity (a nice hotel stay, sumptuous meals) to sway our opinions of the films on exhibit.

On the morning after the screening, we carry our notebooks and voice recorders into a conference room, sit and chat in quiet anticipation, and then welcome the studio's special guests to the table for the interviews. All of this excitement has been brought to us by Grace Hill Media, a film publicity company founded by Jonathan Bock, a former sitcom writer. Jonathan's got a sharp sense of humor, but he's completely serious about giving Christian writers the opportunity to engage in these discussions with filmmakers so that they can present their readers with more engaging features and reviews.

Thanks to the hard work of Jonathan and his team, actors and directors are learning that their film promotion responsibilities sometimes involve a visit to "the God Room," where we all wait with our unconventional questions. We ask them about the themes of the film. We inquire about the spiritual leanings of the characters. We surprise them with our lack of interest in gossip and the private lives of the actors.

In this context, I've learned that Christian film critics come in as many shapes and colors as mainstream critics. We arrive to get interviews and information for radio shows, blogs and conservative evangelical periodicals. I've seen a Catholic priest at the table looking forward to an interview with Rachel Weisz. I've seen an evangelical media writer gush to Alison Lohman about her beautiful eyes. My adrenalin has accelerated at the chance to interview John Rhys-Davies, a big screen giant from my childhood. I watched one of my favorite critics lose patience with *The Lord of the Rings: The Return of the King*. Exasperated by the multitudinous characters, she walked away from the interview table where we had just spoken with Dominic Monaghan and Billy Boyd, saying, "I still can't tell the difference between Trippy and Flippy!"

As varied as we are in our histories, perspectives and audiences, this is a community of Christians who feel no shame in admitting that we love movies. My appreciation of filmmaking has grown considerably from reading reviews by, and conversing with, writers like Steven D. Greydanus of DecentFilms.com, Peter T. Chattaway of *Christianity Today*, Terry Mattingly of GetReligion.org, Greg Wright of a website called Past the Popcorn, and Barbara Nicolosi, founder of the Act One: Writing for Hollywood screenwriting program.

And there is another common thread that binds us: Angry backlash is a fact of life for the Christian movie critic. As we discuss the letters we receive, it's clear that a Christian audience is a vast and complicated entity. No matter what I say about a movie, I'm bound to step on somebody's toes. Almost every week, I get a letter informing me that I'll be judged by God for not condemning movies such as *Titanic, Million Dollar Baby* and *Brokeback Mountain,* while others contribute equal and opposite sentiments, distraught that I have dared to find any fault at all with these films. You would think from their intensity that they subscribe to God's own movie reviews, yet their letters contradict one another. (I often wonder what we could accomplish if we could convince some of them to spend half the amount of energy writing to their congressional representatives as they do writing to lash out at film critics.)

Thus, the junkets have given us a chance to commiserate and share laughs over the tantrums we've witnessed. Yet even our mutual love of cinema isn't enough to keep us from clashing over complicated films and controversial issues. After a screening, as I wander through the crowd, I can hear the genesis of the differing reviews that I'll collect for the Film Forum column. "Trash!" "The filmmakers clearly couldn't tell a Catholic from a Pentecostal." "I loved it!" "There was a subtle redemption story at work." "It was entertaining." "Are you kidding? It was so clearly anti-Christian." "It was heresy!" "Yes, but it creates a great opportunity for us to dialogue with our culture." "Well, we should be talking to culture about pornography too, but that doesn't mean we should rush out and buy some." "Why are you making such a big deal about it? It's *just* a movie!"

It's unlikely that any of us have arrived, immediately, at the "right" response to a movie. In our heated exchanges, we've only just begun to sort through what has happened on the screen. I often find that writing the review changes my opinion of the film. What seems at first to be daring, profound and original suddenly seems merely audacious, shallow and derivative when compared with a related work. Or a film that seemed oppressive in its troubling imagery reveals itself to be a redemptive tale *about* evil rather than an irresponsible film *condoning* evil. Post-viewing conversation and examination can lead to whole new discoveries that were out of our reach when we were caught in the current of that first experience.

There are so many different lenses through which we can examine a film. We benefit when we bring into focus each movie's writing, editing, lighting, performance, direction, the intended audience and the film's political, spiritual and cultural perspectives and agendas. Questions about these aspects can lead us to discover strengths, weaknesses and new insights. For some filmmakers, movies are just illustrated narratives. But others aim higher. In treating film as art that is no less profitable for study than great literature and painting, they organize what we see and hear in such a way as to encourage the viewer to examine relationships between character, image, color, music and camera angle. If they do their job well, the viewer comes away wanting to see the film again to take a closer look.

"Layers," Shrek would probably say. "Movies have got *layers*."

In this way, film is uniquely qualified to explore spirituality. More than any other art, it mirrors our experience in time and space. Reflecting our world back to us, it gives us the opportunity to explore and revisit moments. Offering imaginative visions of alternate worlds, it helps us glimpse aspects of our own that we might otherwise have missed. Slowly, we begin to discover the universal in the particular, the timeless in the temporal, the miraculous in the mundane.

When the critics in the God Room pose their questions about the spiritual implications of the films, the filmmakers often blink in surprise as if they hadn't even thought beyond the narrative to what it suggests about choices and consequences. But sometimes, they surprise us with deep spiritual convictions.

Jonathan Bock tells me that he has received compliments and praise from the filmmakers and actors who have visited the God Room. He says they have been startled and impressed with questions that reach beyond the normal mainstream buzz. It is exciting to be a part of this new surge of interest among Christians regarding the art of filmmaking. Hearing so many believers speaking freely and passionately about film, I believe that the dark clouds of fear are lifting at last and that we have stepped into an exciting new era of engagement with art beyond the borders of Christian culture. We are joining our "worldly" neighbors at the table as Christ did, ready to demonstrate discernment and enjoy the feast.

How to Chew Your Movies

Any teacher who tried to show a movie at our small Christian high school was taking sizeable risks, and Mr. Demkowicz knew it. There was one clear law: Keep it clean.

This was much more difficult for the teachers than it might sound. The list of possible offenses was long. If a student went home and complained that he or she had been shocked by a word or an event in a movie or a book, an angry principal might reprimand the teacher who made the assignment. Most teachers lived in fear of a phenomenon that Mr. D called "the mothers reaching for their phones."

Don't get me wrong, Mr. D took seriously Christ's exhortation in Matthew 18 and Paul's instruction in 1 Corinthians 8 that we should not indulge our liberty in a way that causes our weaker brother to stumble. But he also understood Scripture's instruction, in Hebrews 5:13-14, that we should mature in our spiritual understanding, moving from milk to meat. What we find comforting and familiar is often very different from what we really need.

Mr. D knew that my senior class was ready to take a step up and engage in a type of art that we had not yet experienced. We were going to watch a movie together. In fact, we would later watch the same film again.

*   *   *

At class parties, teachers kept the students occupied with videos they considered acceptable entertainment for Christian youth. This narrowed the field down to innocuous Disney fare or the occasional "Christian movie"—usually a dramatized Bible story such as *The Ten Commandments* or a story about missionaries, the Last Days or conversion. Only occasionally did we come across a PG-rated film that was clean enough to keep all of the parents happy. I lost track of how many times I had seen *The Princess Bride* by the time I graduated in 1989.

All of these selections were intended merely as recreation. They were entertainment. It's a word used broadly to represent serious art, frivolous play, video games, dancing, singing, comedy, tragedy and various "adult" diversions. In this book, when I refer to entertainment, I'm talking about films that are intended as a sort of casual pleasure or temporary escape. Entertainment doesn't require us to invest much intellectual energy in the experience. It's *performing* for us. We'll probably get what we paid for—90 minutes of light-hearted laughs, suspense, adventure, scares or whatever conventions we prefer—whereas higher forms of art will offer experiences that are beyond price, and sometimes even costly to avoid.

Most entertainment is assembled for the purpose of satisfying common audience appetites. A lot of these movies have been commissioned and assembled by a committee, not an artist, with more than a little thought invested in what will sell the most tickets. Think of entertainment as the kind of food you'd get at a party or a fast-food joint: pizza, burgers, hot dogs, Jell-O salads, soda pop. Easy to make, easy to consume, fairly predictable. Some ingredients probably came from a can or out of the freezer. Nutritional value? Minimal. And watch out—some varieties contain chemicals and artificial ingredients that nobody should knowingly consume.

The best entertainers appeal to healthy appetites. Moreover, they challenge us with something more than we expect.

Danny Boyle is an internationally acclaimed director of big screen entertainment. He cast a young Ewan McGregor in a suspenseful thriller (*Shallow Grave*) and a memorably disturbing comedy about drug addiction (*Trainspotting*). Later, he delivered a bizarre romantic musical (*A Life Less Ordinary*), a riveting horror film (*28 Days Later*) and a brilliant, whimsical family film (*Millions*). While some of these films worked better than others, all were memorably eccentric. Some were extraordinary.

Boyle told me during an interview for *Christianity Today* that a director has to be cunning. By making films that are relentlessly entertaining, he or she can surprise audiences with something more than they expect from popular cinema. "You've got to smuggle good ideas into something that attracts [people] to the Friday or Saturday night film," he explained.

Mr. D presented *Babette's Feast* in a way that told us this was not just a centerpiece for a class party. It was going to be more than entertainment. It was an experience to share. We would be invited to discuss our impressions of it, just as we had "The Red Wheelbarrow." There was a sense that we would learn from the experience.

Then, the following spring, Mr. D had us watch it *again* in order to realize just how much we had grown in our ability to engage with art. This very thing was on C. S. Lewis's mind when he wrote, "An unliterary man may be defined as one who reads books once only." Sometimes, if you look at art a second time, you start to see the meaning in the method. Many of my favorite films—Krzysztof Kieslowski's *Blue* or Thomas McCarthy's *The Station Agent,* for example—didn't really grab me the first time I watched them. But with repeated viewings, looking at the film through different lenses, I found layers and layers of meaning.

Once in a while, I'll put up my feet and laugh my way through a cheap Adam Sandler comedy. It's clear that he's following a formula, a motion-picture paint-by-numbers game. *Punch-Drunk Love,* on the other hand, is a Sandler film that I go back to again and again because of the many layers of intentionality and imagination that are at work. It's more than entertainment. It makes me think and leads me to new discoveries every time.

Scripture exhorts us to be courageous, to test all things and hold fast to the good stuff (see 1 Thess. 5:21) and to dwell on what is worthy of praise (see Phil. 4:8). By focusing on what is honorable, lovely and excellent, we learn, grow and inevitably mature.

*   *   *

The term "art" is often used to describe the whole realm of creative endeavor. But for the purposes of this book, when I refer to art, I'm keeping in mind what Mr. D taught us was the first rule for artists—a rule that most artists have heard a thousand times: *Show, don't tell.* Or, as William Carlos Williams urged, "No ideas but in things."

When an artist narrows his craft to *telling* us his opinion or perspective, the audience responds by accepting or rejecting that message. But when an artist *shows* us something, he or she is participating in the work of incarnation, making something manifest that is open to our own interpretation. Like Babette's presentation of an extraordinary feast, artists refuse to settle for standard fare and avoid explaining their work. They trust each one of us to have an individual experience and develop a unique relationship with the work.

Art can't be swallowed whole. It takes a fork and a knife. We have to chew on it. But don't get me wrong. To think of it as *work* is to miss out on the pleasure of such exciting play.

For those frustrated poetry students who were accustomed to getting the "right answer" quickly, Mr. Demkowicz offered a patient smile and some perspective: "If you want the meaning of a poem right off, you should end a game with a roll of the dice, and not waste time playing the game."

In her book *Nine Gates: Entering the Mind of Poetry*, Jane Hirschfield examines two poems by Bertolt Brecht and Sharon

Olds and considers the contrasting methods of each poem. She reveals the secret of their lasting and revelatory power, which she states has everything to do with reader participation. Hirschfield writes:

> In each poem, the reader is given the data or image and only enough information to understand what terrain he is in, then left to complete the work himself: to furnish what has been left out with his own awareness, poetic concentration, and knowledge of inner and outer worlds.[1]

This is not to say that the poet left anything out. Rather, the poet knew what was essential and trusted us to explore and discover the rest of the thought—the pieces that couldn't be reduced to words. It is striking how Hirschfield's idea of a poem is similar to the way that British theologian C. H. Dodd, in *The Parables of the Kingdom,* defined a parable:

> At its simplest, the parable is a metaphor or simile drawn from nature or common life, arresting the hearer by its vividness or strangeness, and leaving the mind in sufficient doubt about its precise application to tease it into active thought.[2]

In Mr. Demkowicz's class, we were not going to watch a movie for entertainment or for a lesson. We were going to "tease our minds into active thought." Mr. D's selection was a foreign film, which immediately demanded some level of concentration. We would have to *read subtitles.* Can you imagine the grumbling?

But art, if we let it, rewards vigilance with insight. By looking at what happens within the frame, we train our senses so that we can perceive what is going on beyond the frame.

Today, I am still watching *Babette's Feast*, the film that Mr. Demkowicz showed to our class. Every time, it is a nourishing, rewarding feast, offering new discoveries. It has become a favorite meal . . . but one that I needed to learn how to eat.

*   *   *

If you want to experience it in ideal conditions, stick a bookmark on this page and go rent *Babette's Feast* before you read my reflections on it. Or you can consider my description of the film as an introduction, knowing that you will have an experience all your own when you watch it. Watch the film twice: once now and then again with some friends a few weeks later.

Suspicious of Grace

A massive turtle with a shiny black shell is riding on one of the carts in Babette's parade. Babette is importing the ingredients for an authentic French meal to this remote Jutland village.

To celebrate the birthday of the minister who established this small puritanical community, Martina and Philippa have decided to host a dinner for those who remember him and his wisdom. They have granted Babette's wish, her first request to them in all her years of service. She wants to make the dinner. She wants to show them her idea of a celebration.

It sounded like a good idea. That is, until the ingredients arrived. Now, the villagers watch in horror as this procession of

imported goods goes by. Accustomed to the bare essentials—
boiled fish and bread—they have never seen such bizarre cargo
or even considered whether such things could be eaten.

Fear begins to seep into their conversation. Some believe that
they are about to be served the product of witchcraft. Sensual
pleasures are perceived as a threat, an evil. Only cerebral, spiritual things delight them—or so they claim.

Film critic Steven Greydanus sees the problem with the sisters and their neighbors very clearly: "What is ultimately lacking in this Jutlander community is *grace*. Their religion has
become abstract and remote, a set of brittle orthodoxies rather
than a lived faith. A woman worries a man with doubts about
whether God will forgive them a sin of their youth; he knows
the right theological answer to the question, but there's no
abiding sense of God's peace, or even of his love."[3]

Babette has something to teach her neighbors about the
blessings of God's extravagant generosity. She knows that she
was put on this earth to give people transporting experiences
through food. Whether she understands it or not, she's showing them that they should not fear the touch, texture and taste
of God's gifts, for these were meant to delight us by conveying
God's glory. They are blessings when they are offered in humility and in the appropriate context.

This is a realization that the villagers may not readily
embrace. They are so focused on piety and self-deprecation that
they have forgotten—or perhaps never appreciated—the joy of
receiving blessing. But you can see the astonishment in their eyes
as fear gives way to rapture, each delicacy unveiling its secrets to
their palate.

A special guest has joined them—Lorenz Lowenhielm, a worldly soldier whose connections to the sisters (and, the attentive viewer will discover, to Babette) stretch back to his days of youth and ambition. Lowenhielm has spent his lonely life pursuing personal glory and influence. This has led him to a melancholy verging on despair, and his lamentation before the feast echoes Ecclesiastes.

As the only man who has seen the world and indulged in its wealth, it is he who recognizes and names each one of these delights, from the expensive wines to the exquisite entrees. Here, on the coast of Jutland, he has suddenly stumbled onto—can it be?—"*Cailles en Sarcophage!*"

Lowenhielm looks around the table, incredulous, as his companions stare stubbornly at their meal. They receive the feast out of a sense of burdensome duty, believing that to admit their enjoyment would be a confession of sin.

Babette would have agreed with Annie Dillard, who wrote, "The extravagant gesture is the very stuff of creation. After one extravagant gesture of creation in the first place, the universe has continued to deal exclusively in extravagances, flinging intricacies and colossi down eons of emptiness, heaping profusions on profligacy with fresh vigor."[4]

Lowenhielm concludes the dinner with a profound speech. But he is not the only one to offer an eloquent response. Christopher, an old man and a simpleton who seems to be receding back into the intellect of infancy, offers the perfect one-word review. (You might want to look up the meaning of his name as well.)

What is it about fools that they become the characters who see God most clearly and respond to Him most honestly?

The Guests at the Feast

I imagine myself at a table with a large crowd of moviegoers. The table is set for a meal. And descending from the sky, why, it's a sheet just like the one Saint Peter beheld in his vision! But this vision isn't full of food. It's heavy with piles of DVDs.

"Eat," says a voice. "None of these things are unclean. You are free to explore. But remember, just because all of these things are permissible, that doesn't mean all things are beneficial for you. What reveals glory to your neighbor may not be something you're able to stomach yet. Proceed with caution."

The sheet settles onto the table. We pick up our silverware. I take one of the DVDs, cut it into several portions, and serve it to the guests.

Some dig right in. Others pick at it, skeptically. A few scowl and grumble. They're as colorful and varied as any Mad Hatter's tea party.

As I chew my movie, I find myself frustrated with the other diners' objections. That is, until their faces, which are vague and blurred, start to come into focus. Then I see that they look a lot like me at various stages of my moviegoing life.

* * *

At first, I was like *the child* at the table of movies.

He reaches for everything that passes in front of him, and whatever he can grab he will stuff into his mouth. But his parents watch him carefully and deny him those items that could cause him to choke. He's not capable of chewing or digesting most of the material on this table. He needs art and entertainment that is simple, nutritious and easy to swallow.

I didn't remain a child. I was taught to desire things that were healthy and to reach for more than the cookie jar. I learned how to separate meat from the bone and to chew carefully.

* * *

Later, I became a *reactionary diner*. I would look at the selections on the table and immediately judge their value based on my assumptions or by cautiously tasting a sample. If a movie was scary, complicated or contained some rather spicy elements, or if the language startled or offended me, I immediately denounced it. Worse, I had harsh opinions of anyone who would partake of those dishes.

As a reactionary, my vocabulary was filled with labels and derogatory adjectives for anything that seemed threatening. I didn't engage in thoughtful interpretation. I approached the table with a checklist, and if I saw anything that my fellow churchgoers considered offensive, I would demand that the corrupt dish be removed from the menu. Or if a movie's meaning was not obvious, I wrote it off as boring and pretentious.

If I had continued down the road of reactionary dining, I might have ended up like those who use strong, condemning language against certain films, and who ascribe nasty labels to people who disagree with them. I might have gone from judging movies to judging people.

* * *

By 1987, I had become a *casual diner*. I had spent my teen years enjoying the freedom to see PG-rated movies without much concern for what I was served. I liked the communal aspect of the meal—my friends filled up two rows at Portland's Village Theater, where double features were only 99 cents. Company, conversation, distraction. I had the impression that good films were for all ages to enjoy and that bad movies were R-rated. The idea of going out and discussing a movie in detail was foreign to me.

But at home on the weekend, I tuned in to Siskel and Ebert. I was fascinated by the way they spoke with grave intensity about movies that hadn't been released yet. They took it so seriously. Their tempers flared. I was startled to hear them finding fault with some of my favorites. They discussed the virtues of R-rated films in a way that whetted my appetite. Maybe some of those forbidden dishes had value after all. I began to realize that I was learning about the craft of filmmaking from their combative conversations.

In the meantime, I began seeing as many movies as I could fit on my plate. When I got a summer job at a video store, I became something else entirely . . . a *glutton*.

* * *

As a glutton, I consumed, consumed, consumed. I wanted to be able to talk about everything showing in theaters, from *Rain Man* to *Running on Empty*, from *Dangerous Liaisons* to *Die Hard*. Technically, I wasn't supposed to see R-rated films, but they were being served at classmates' parties now. During my video store shifts, I was free to chow down on anything.

I was only familiar with mainstream movies, so foreign and independent films weren't on the menu. And if I couldn't find my favorite flavors—familiar celebrities, Spielbergian special effects, thrilling chases, sweeping romance and laugh-out-loud comedy—well, I wasn't in any mood to turn big screen dining into something that required preparation, special utensils and actual work.

I wasn't thinking about whether my intake of mediocrity and cinematic junk food was doing any damage or dulling my intellect. After all, I didn't *feel* any damage.

In retrospect, I probably should have avoided video store work at that age. My reckless, adolescent pride led me into dangerous territory. But by God's grace, I developed a deep respect for teachers who were concerned with discernment. They inspired in me a desire to embrace the best and reject the worst. It might have been different. I might have become an *addict*, hooked on something unhealthy that would slowly corrode my imagination. I'm grateful for the guidance I received.

* * *

During my college years, I suffered some *cinematic allergies*. After I was assaulted on the sidewalk by a drug-crazed man, I shied away from portrayals of violence until I had recovered from the trauma and the nightmares had stopped. The wounds were too fresh.

This was not unlike my childhood fear of movies that portrayed plane crashes. A DC-8 crashed in my neighborhood when I was eight years old, killing several people. It took me some years to be able to work through that shake-up. In a post-9/11 world, I find I have to ask myself if I have the time and the strength necessary to put myself through the grueling experience of a film about terrorism.

Today, I know others who are allergic to films in which a character is raped (*Rob Roy*, *The Accused*) or animals suffer injury (*Amores Perros*, *Au Hasard Balthazar*). Just a trace amount of nudity might inspire inappropriate thoughts. Even an incidental, non-exploitative image of bare flesh can lead some people into trouble. I know moviegoers who are as jeopardized by footage of designer clothing as others are by glimpses of nakedness—they are influenced by the film's product placement and materialistic implications. There are all kinds of elements in art that can cause a viewer trouble.

Yet this doesn't mean that there's anything necessarily wrong with the meal or that the cook is cruel. "One man's faith allows him to eat everything," the apostle Paul said in Romans 14:2, "but another man, whose faith is weak, eats only vegetables." The responsibility lies with the diners to attend to their conscience, know their weaknesses and steer clear of damaging choices.

Similarly, each of us must be sensitive to our fellow diners. In the Gospel of Matthew, Jesus says, "Woe to the world because of the things that cause people to sin! Such things must come, but woe to the man through whom they come!" (18:7). Sadly, there are some little ones and weaker brothers who fancy themselves to be the strong ones, readily denouncing rather than just cautioning those interested in meat. Imagine a child lecturing an adult about matters requiring maturity and you might understand why some moviegoers roll their eyes when self-righteous Christians confront them on what they choose to watch. Their selections may be complicated and even dangerous, but that does not always mean that the viewers are spiritually ignorant or rebellious.

It's a challenge for me as a film critic to help weaker brothers avoid films that might pose a threat to them. I need to be extremely cautious, taking care to educate readers about what dangers they might encounter. But it would be an equally damaging response if I were to condemn all films that contain potentially offensive elements or to burden my examination and appreciation with catalogues of things that could trouble someone else.

If your friend has a peanut allergy, don't serve him or her a peanut butter sandwich. At the same time, don't protest stores that sell peanut butter. If we decide that the best way to avoid being a stumbling block is to insist on abstinence from anything that could possibly be a temptation, we bind up the body, confining everyone to the limitations of the weaker brother. The goal should be growth and strength, not mere safety.

* * *

If we focus too much on the dangers of different dishes, we encourage an attitude of fear. And this can provoke people to become *phobics*.

I was once a phobic when it came to rock music. In my early teens, I read Christian publications that warned me about the dangers of rock music and how the rhythms and sounds of rock were related to the music of devil worship in primitive cultures. I became convinced that music by Prince, Van Halen and Huey Lewis (Huey Lewis!) could automatically contaminate me in some way. It wasn't just the music I held in contempt. I grew bitter toward classmates who listened to it, thinking they were on the fast track to hell.

In the epistle to the Hebrews, we are told, "Solid food is for the mature, who by constant use have trained themselves to know good from evil" (5:14). In 1 Corinthians 6:12, Paul tells us, "'Everything is permissible for me'—but not everything is beneficial. 'Everything is permissible for me'—but I will not be mastered by anything."

By learning to attend to my conscience and develop artistic discernment, I was able to overcome my fears and delight in what was excellent. It set me free to explore the world of rock, folk, jazz—yes, even country—with a healthy dose of caution but without fear.

* * *

At the feast of movies, I'd like to leave gluttony, judgment and fear behind me. I know that I am free to eat almost anything, but I want to be strong and fit, disciplining myself to a diet of excellent, nourishing work.

Dessert? Alcohol? In moderation, on occasion.

As a critic, I feel more like the *nutritionist*—doing my best to counsel others on a balanced diet that serves their individual needs and respects their sensitivities. But I also want to be the kind of connoisseur who can speak knowledgeably about the culinary arts. I want to speak with eloquence about Sofia Coppola's sauces, the exquisite wines of Eric Rohmer and the finer points of Martin Scorsese's pasta.

But the more I learn, the more I'm in danger of becoming another character at the table—the *snob*. It would be easy for me to leave behind enjoyment of the simpler sorts of films and demand only the most sophisticated work, sneering at those who don't understand or appreciate it. I have, at times, ranted against the ignorance of others, forgetting that I was once at their place in the journey.

If my enthusiasm for films as cerebral as *Russian Ark* or *Werckmeister Harmonies* makes me pretentious or condescending to those in line for blockbusters, then I have lost my perspective on the purpose of art. The goal is not to see the most obscure movies or even to be the greatest interpreter. If these experiences aren't strengthening my conscience as well as my intellect, what good are they?

Henry Miller once wrote, "Art is only a means to life, to the life more abundant. It is not in itself the life more abundant. It merely points the way, something which is overlooked not only by the public, but very often by the artist himself. In becoming an end it defeats itself."[5]

If dining at the table of movies becomes my primary focus, I am forgetting the purpose of the meal. It is served to give me strength so that I can return to my life stronger, healthier and closer to being whole.

The Turning

Just as I moved from bedazzlement with Disney movies to enthrallment with *The Empire Strikes Back* to feeling convicted by Krzysztof Kieslowski, so the pursuit of more and more challenging artistic visions inspired the expansion of my religious experience as well.

In Sunday School, we sang songs about Jesus' love, and in "big church" we sang hymns about God's faithfulness through trials and tribulations. At home, I put my parents' LPs of The

Bill Gaither Trio on the turntable, until the energy of Amy Grant's Christian pop music provided praise with a youthful rock-and-roll edge. As long as these lyrics were clearly crafted as Christian confession, they were acceptable. But God wanted me to learn that I could venture beyond the boundaries of contemporary Christian radio stations and find glimmers of his glory all over the radio dial.

Christian literature bookshelves, Christian music racks and Christian video selections offer a wide variety of artistic endeavors. Most of them have been crafted with the best of intentions: to minister to our minds and hearts, to lift our attention to worship, to echo the teachings of Scripture. They deliver what that audience wants to receive: devotional meditations, praise choruses, conversion tales or end-times adventures.

The so-called Christian films I watched in school were short and simplistic dramas that portrayed worldly people as snarling, plotting, malevolent devils, while Christians were depicted as brave, kind and gentle saviors. Like the artificially enhanced science documentaries, such films distorted reality in order to make heavy-handed lessons compelling.

A recent film called *Hangman's Curse* delivered Christian entertainment devoid of the profanity and sexual misbehavior evident in many films about high schoolers. If you watch the film carefully, you'll note that the good guys are clean-cut, nicely dressed American middle-class folks. The students plotting trouble wear black, have punk rock haircuts and sport multiple piercings. By the conclusion, when some of the troublemakers have cleaned up their act, they're dressed as blandly as the heroes. Talk about extreme makeovers!

I'm sure the storytellers mean well, but they seem to be as interested in promoting lifestyle and fashion preferences as they are in telling the truth. In my high school experience, the clean-cut students were often the most pretentious and judgmental, and some of the most sensitive and perceptive dressed like the troublemakers of *Hangman's Curse*. When storytellers make such generalizations to an audience familiar with the territory, the audience will stop listening.

Entertainment with such obvious messages tends to please viewers who already agree, but art driven by such transparent agendas can be as clear and off-putting as a sales pitch. If the craftsmanship is anything short of excellent, that can make the endeavor even more counterproductive. Instead of cultivating healthy questions, such message-driven media can make seekers less likely to ask.

This contrived form of "persuasive" entertainment began to insult my intelligence long before *Hangman's Curse* opened in theaters. It was already prevalent in popular Christian music.

The more I learned how to concentrate on poetry, the more the lyrics of contemporary Christian songwriting began to bother me. The range of subjects explored by Christian musicians began to seem restrictive. Sure, the songs were full of honorable sentiments and fundamental truths. But is this all that Christian music could address? Did I really need every album to tell me things I knew by heart? Should every song be clearly linked to the Scripture that inspired it? Much of this music began to feel more like advertising than art, constantly persuading me to give myself to Jesus by aggressively exaggerating the pros of being a Christian and the cons of running from God.

I began to hear myself murmuring, "Okay, I've covered this. I have what I need for the journey. When does the journey begin?"

*　*　*

In the early 1980s, a recording artist named Leslie Phillips played an important part in leading me into more rewarding encounters with art. She cooked up an entrée that most Christian music fans rejected, but it led me to comfort, challenge and hope.

During that decade, Phillips was second only to Amy Grant for the title of Christian pop diva. She recorded a few successful albums, including *Dancing with Danger* and *Black and White in a Grey World*. But later, she approached her Christian music label with new songs drawn from her journals. These songs made it clear that she was no longer sure that the Christian life was a matter of black and white.

In fact, the new songs, like so many psalms, reflected struggles with doubt, questions about God's mysteries and disappointment with the Church. The record label executives were displeased. This was not what they expected from their premier pop star. It wasn't what Christian audiences would spend money to hear. And the industry is, first and foremost, a business.

Phillips told CCM Magazine, "I felt strangled as a writer." But when her producer, the legendary T Bone Burnett, encouraged her to record that passionate poetry, she realized that she wanted to be more than just a Christian entertainer. She wanted to grow, explore her questions creatively and invite listeners to join her on her journey through the tougher chapters of faith. Rather than reshaping Christian lessons into catchy choruses, she wanted to express her own questions and experiences. She wanted to be an artist.

The album she released in 1986 was entitled *The Turning.* When Phillips performed this material live, some Christian listeners, expecting to see a pop star singing and dancing her way through praise songs cast in a dazzling fog-and-light show, walked out.

But that's when the rest of the world suddenly began to take notice. *Rolling Stone*, which rarely ever acknowledged Christian music, praised *The Turning* as an impressive and inventive work of art. Phillips's lyrics resonated with those who were willing to admit that the Christian life was not a journey free from doubt or struggle—those who often found the expectations of fellow Christians too strict and unforgiving. *The Turning* remains, to this day, a lasting, influential and celebrated work.

Leslie changed her name to Sam Phillips, moved to a mainstream music label, and began one of the most critically acclaimed recording careers in contemporary rock. Her songs have been consistently poetic, challenging, inventive and mysterious. For this Christian music listener, her work has been a revelation. She is an example of what is possible when a Christian courageously steps outside the box of what Christian audiences expect and follows where the Spirit leads, acknowledging both the ache of doubt and the glory of grace. Now, Phillips's lyrics read like the travel journal of a brave pioneer forging through tough spiritual territory. Most of what she sings is rich with metaphors drawn from the journey.

"God took the taboo off of things," she said when I interviewed her in 2005, almost 10 years and 7 albums later. "I feel that way about metaphor because, as Jesus said, 'Man does not live by bread alone, but by every word that comes out of the mouth of God.' And I can even take that to mean *metaphors* . . . or *art*. That's available to feed us. A lot of the things we might have thought were forbidden for one reason or another . . . I don't think they are."

Phillips's albums have included melancholy love songs (*The Indescribable Wow*), witty and wry observations on materialism and culture (*Cruel Inventions, Omnipop*), clever political commentary and diatribes against religious hypocrisy (*Martinis and Bikinis*) and, more recently, meditative and poetic explorations of her own failures and longings (*Fan Dance, A Boot and a Shoe*). Outside of the Christian music industry, she is allowed to represent herself honestly, sing about whatever interests her, and share not only observations but also questions. While she no longer limits what she'll explore in song, her expressions of faith have become more personal and particular—and more resonant. She's landed some surprisingly high-profile gigs as well. If you've ever seen an episode of TV's *Gilmore Girls*, you've probably heard Sam strumming her guitar and singing the show's soundtrack music.

Like Bob Dylan, U2, Bruce Cockburn, T Bone Burnett, Over the Rhine, Sufjan Stevens, Sixteen Horsepower, Bill Mallonee and The Innocence Mission, Phillips has frustrated those who want art to remain safe and comfortable. These artists followed their faith to deeper forms of poetry that require our close attention, leading the way for a new generation of courageous artists who draw inspiration from their faith.

I still enjoy some of Phillips's early praise choruses. Worship music offers us avenues of prayer and essential resources of encouragement and counsel. But if we build a fence around worship music and act as though anything beyond it is secular rather than sacred, we cut ourselves off from much of the revelation of God.

The image of that sheet descending from heaven comes to mind again, and the voice returns: *Don't limit yourself anymore to the fish and the bread. With discernment, you'll find nourishment in the whole feast.*

Searching for the Next Feast

Recently, I sat in a huge shopping mall cineplex north of Seattle, preparing myself for a seven-course meal prepared by Terrence Malick called *The New World*. This was my third visit to the feast. I wanted to experience it one more time before it disappeared entirely.

Some of my friends think I'm crazy, because to them this 135-minute film feels like one of the slowest-moving epics ever made. I would also find it an excruciating two hours if I found no pleasure in birdsong and poetry, if I was bored by the sight of sunlight pouring through the high boughs of trees, or if I eschewed the company of John Smith and Pocahontas as they slowly stroll together in silence.

But I am enthralled. Malick is not entertaining us. He's in no hurry to show us what happens next. Instead, he's giving us the privilege of walking for a while outside of time along paths that have long since been paved over. He's sharing impressions with a zeal that tells us he has been somewhere extraordinary, breathed air pungent with history and life, and seen things that make his heart break. His intensity makes me sit up straight and pay attention. I want to taste what he has tasted.

A group of teenagers sat behind me during the screening in this almost empty theater. I don't know why they chose *The New World*. Was it because the infamous Colin Farrell and the latest big screen Batman, Christian Bale, were in it? Normally, these kids would have driven me insane with their whispering, their cell phones and their ongoing commentary, but the film was so transporting that I was able to endure.

After two hours, just as the story was reaching its crucial turning point, the teenagers sighed in disgust and stormed out of the theater, grumbling in exasperation. They hadn't come for a feast of challenging new sensations. They had come for entertainment. Just as I can remember being young and appalled by the taste of coffee or wine, I can relate to those who haven't yet discovered pleasures that come through discipline and discernment. But I remained in my seat, savoring the subtle flavors of color, the sound of the waves on the shore and the birds in the grass, until the last line of credits passed.

As the lights came up, I walked down the stairs and realized that there was one other person in the theater with me. I turned and saw a silver-haired woman, all alone, bundled in a big brown coat. She had brought a plaid wool blanket with her, which I assume she had wrapped around herself for the journey. She smiled at me, a gleam of pure delight in her eyes. It was the light that shines in the eyes of the villagers at the conclusion of *Babette's Feast*. We didn't need to say anything. What words could have expressed our gratitude?

We were satisfied. Dazzled. Full.

I walked into the lobby and through the clouds of vaporized butter flavoring, through crowds of congregating moviegoers, anxious to escape into a quieter place, to preserve the echoes of crickets and birds, to hold on to that stillness and harbor that feeling of awe.

I wanted to sing a hymn of blessing for the feast.

Notes

1. Jane Hirschfield, *Nine Gates: Entering the Mind of Poetry* (New York: Harper Collins Publishers, 1997), p. 22.
2. C. H. Dodd, *The Parables of the Kingdom* (New York: Charles Scribner's Sons, 1961), p. 16
3. Steven D. Greydanus, *Babette's Feast* film review, DecentFilms.com. http://www.decentfilms.com/sections/reviews/babettesfeast.html (accessed November 2006).
4. Annie Dillard, *Pilgrim at Tinker Creek* (New York: Harper's Magazine Press, 1974), p. 9.
5. Henry Miller, *Wonders of the Heart* (New York: New Directions Publishing, 1960), p. 24.

Wonders of Heaven and Earth

*Every child is an artist. The problem is how to
remain an artist once we grow up.*

PABLO PICASSO

Art does not reproduce what we see; rather, it makes us see.

PAUL KLEE

Close Encounters of an Artist's Kind

In a scene in Steven Spielberg's *Close Encounters of the Third Kind,*
Roy Neary wants to take his children to see a big-screen revival
of *Pinocchio.* He hasn't outgrown his appreciation for the things
he loved as a kid. But his eagerness is not catching on.

Roy's oldest son, Brad, needs help understanding fractions
so that he can finish his math homework. Speaking of mathematics, little Toby is behaving like the toddler he is, trying to
smash his baby doll into fractions against the edge of his
playpen. Roy's wife, Ronny, doesn't notice Roy's excitement
either. She's too busy being ticked off that Roy's tools are scattered across three-quarters of the dinner table. On the television

screen, God is parting the Red Sea (with a little help from Charlton Heston), but the Neary family doesn't even notice.

If the Almighty's intervention plays out on television without getting the Neary's attention, how will Roy ever inspire them to go out and sit still for a movie? It's a wonder that he's still capable of feeling awe himself with the world turning against him like this. Perhaps that is why he's one of the first to see the visitors.

In the middle of this family chaos, the power suddenly goes out. And when the lights in Muncie, Indiana, go off, it's Roy's job to head out and look for the cause. So he takes his truck on the road, hoping to find the problem and restore the power. Then, before his very eyes, the lights come on—lights quite unlike any he's seen before.

Space ships. A parade of kaleidoscopic aircraft are gliding along, casting spotlights here and there inquisitively.

But Roy is not the only person in Muncie to see the visitors coming. A child has already responded to their call—a wide-eyed youngster named Barry. A bright light in the middle of the night lured him straight through the front door.

Unable to find any other words to describe his feelings, Barry shouted, "Ice cream!" and disappeared into the night.

*   *   *

Close Encounters of the Third Kind is just one of several films in which Steven Spielberg demonstrates his ability to kindle sensations of awe in his audience.

Sometimes in his zeal, he can overdo it. In *Hook*, he and Robin Williams worked so hard to wake each viewer's inner child that they caused something similar to shaken-baby syndrome. The music, the dramatic swoops of the camera, the dialogue, the characters' teary-eyed epiphanies—*Hook* demanded so much emotion that I quickly grew weary of the ordeal.

But when Spielberg captures a tangible sense of mystery, he can thrill an audience like no one else. *Close Encounters* is crafted with such restraint—the long silences, the lack of explanations—that it remains his most beautiful and mysterious work. The way he gathers us into collective anticipation and, eventually, amazement suggests that he has an intimate understanding of the feeling.

During an interview on the television talk show *In the Actor's Studio*, Spielberg told host James Lipton about an unforgettable childhood experience. He had been abruptly awakened by his father and told to get dressed. A few minutes later they drove to an open field where several other people had congregated. They lay down on a picnic blanket to stare at the dark night's canvas where, to his bedazzlement, a meteor shower lit up the sky like the Fourth of July.

He mentions this event again on the DVD commentary for *Close Encounters of the Third Kind.* "I think that was my first introduction to the world beyond the earth. [And] that probably first impregnated me with wanting to tell stories not of this world." He came away with a conviction that we are not alone, and he wanted to share the experience.

But the film is about more than just encountering wonder. After Roy Neary and the people in his neighborhood watch a parade of splendor from outer space, Roy imitates Spielberg's own need to transform his experience into a work of art. He responds to his experience like a madman, sculpting an absurd mountain out of clay right there in his family's home. Like Noah building the Ark,

Roy is branded a fool. But eventually, the secret of his enigmatic sculpture whispers its significance to him, revealing the next step of his spiritual journey. It leads him to a sort of holy mountain where he will encounter an even greater level of mystery.

Roy, *E.T.*'s Elliott, Indiana Jones, *Empire of the Sun*'s Jim Graham, Oskar Schindler—in fact, most of Spielberg's central characters—undergo monumental paradigm shifts, learning that there is much they do not know about life. Moved by mystery, their egos recede to humble proportions.

This is one of the rewards of Spielberg's work that is so often disregarded by critics as merely sentimental indulgence. His stories sometimes restore us to a state of childlike faith, encouraging us to see miracles in the mundane.

* * *

Of course, the audience's experience with his films depends partly on their own background. I've never seen an alien. And yet, watching Steven Spielberg's *Close Encounters of the Third Kind*, I know what Barry and Roy are feeling.

On Friday nights in the mid-'70s, while other families went out to expensive dinners, movies or amusement parks, my parents took my brother Jason and me on a low-budget adventure. We'd drive to the edge of the runways at Portland International Airport. There, we thrilled to the flash, rumble and roar of descending 747s. That was my idea of *awesome*.

But nothing prepared me for the night my home address received an unexpected visit from the sky. My mother pulled me out of my Charlie Brown and Snoopy bed sheets and shook me, trying to wake me. I resolutely refused. She held me upright and kicked the backs of my feet so that I would walk down the hall, through the living room, onto the kitchen linoleum, out through the sliding glass door and then into the backyard. My bare feet scuffed across the cool, rough cement of the patio, and still I did not wake up. She lifted my chin and pried my eyelids back with her fingertips. "Jeff. *Look.*"

There, hovering right above the apple and birch trees of our ordinary Northeast Portland backyard, like E.T.'s spaceship descending before Elliott's wide eyes, was the Goodyear Blimp, its motors roaring and seething like a dragon, its bright display screen flashing friendly messages to the neighborhoods below about the upcoming Portland Rose Festival. It hung in the cobalt sky, an enormous cylindrical shadow, outlined by tiny pinpoints of light. Our windows rattled. The ground vibrated.

My mother loves to imitate the groan of fear and amazement with which I marked the occasion: *Orrrrhhh!*

It happened again, 20 years later. My college roommate, Wayne, and I spent a weekend in Portland where we visited Todd, another friend from school. We had just crashed for the night at Todd's family home. Within minutes of falling asleep, all three of us were jolted to our senses by a booming voice that said, "Todd! Guys!"

We rose from our sleeping bags as if in obedience to God Himself. Adrenalin took hold. Emergency? I half expected to see black smoke billowing down the hallway. But no, there was Todd's father, clad in a thin T-shirt and boxer shorts, storming past us out into the late summer breeze. We followed him without hesitation and stood barefoot in the grass on the front lawn.

It looked like a comet, fierce and bright, neatly disseevering the clear summer sky with a peach-colored stripe of billowing smoke behind it. Watching the late newscast, Todd's dad had caught the televised alert and jumped to attention—the Space Shuttle was passing over Portland, Oregon, visible in the night sky, headed for Cape Canaveral on the other side of the continent! The Challenger disaster was a not-so-distant memory, so there was a terrifying, fragile brilliance to the sight of that shuttle gliding gracefully through the cosmos. There were *people* in that ball of light. It made me feel so small and yet so exceedingly grateful to be alive.

Enthralled, we didn't stop to think about the fact that the neighbors were probably looking out their windows in similar bewilderment, seeing four men in underwear gaping at the heavens.

*   *   *

Few memories from my past are as vivid as these surprises in which something completely unexpected drew me up out of my immediate context. That blimp expanded my imagination, and the sci-fi adventure stories that I wrote in my bedroom were often propelled by adventurers in spherical starships. The experience of awe prompted a creative response, an attempt to recapture that feeling and record it. But my writing was also driven by a desire to pass the same kind of experience to others through their imaginations.

If we are not cautious and thoughtful, our criticism of a work of art can become twisted into presumptuous comments about the artist's intentions. If we attack the ideas they're conveying without understanding that those ideas may have come from experience, we expose our own arrogance and unwillingness to listen. Perhaps we'll understand the work differently a few years down the road. Or perhaps that work belongs to a different audience entirely.

Equivalents

I'm standing in the Seattle Art Museum, marveling at a black and white photograph of a particularly dramatic cloud that sweeps across the sky like an angel wing. Perhaps this is what the photographer, Alfred Stieglitz, felt when he took the photograph back in the 1920s. A few years ago, I would have glanced at this picture, shrugged and moved on. What's the point of looking at a snapshot of a cloud? Nothing's *happening*. There's no *story* here.

Stieglitz might have corrected me. This photograph isn't telling a *story* so much as offering me an *experience*. Stieglitz photographed this cloud so that I could feel what he felt as he gazed upward in awe. It was an endeavor of translation, delivering a sensation from one context to another. *Look, there's something interesting about this experience. I can't explain it to you in any other way but to show you.*

The cloud is part of a series that Stieglitz called "Equivalents." Placing a frame around these natural wonders, he communicates a word . . . a metaphor . . . a mystery . . . to provoke in us the equivalent of his own experience. T.S. Eliot called this concrete image an "objective correlative"—something to evoke a particular emotion or thought that cannot be achieved through direct communication.

Perhaps this is what the psalmist was thinking about when he said that the heavens declare the glory of God. The heavens don't speak English. But pay attention. They do speak in their own particular way.

*   *   *

The artist's response to the ecstatic experience is a way of making sense of what he or she has encountered. That desire is built into us: to take something imprinted within us and make it manifest. To *incarnate*. Made in God's image, we share His compulsion to create. J.R.R. Tolkien wrote that we are "co-creators" with God.

Once we have crafted experience into expression, we want to share it. When we are drawn out of ourselves, humbled and thrilled by greatness, we have this instinctive notion that the process is not over until it is shared. It brings us together with others, our connections strengthened, our separateness healed . . . to an extent. And so we yearn to find an audience, ready and willing, with whom we can bond through the "news" of the experience, whether that is an encounter with grief or mystery or blessing.

Christ's disciples witnessed appearances of long-dead heroes of the faith. They watched a few loaves and fishes become a feast for a crowd. Lazarus staggered out in his smelly burial clothes and embraced his flabbergasted friends. Later, the man who had raised him rose from the grave Himself. Imagine the bonds that must have formed among these men, having witnessed so much together. God knew how to cultivate a close-knit, zealous team to carry on His ministry in the face of devastating trials. The formation of the Church became their creative act, their obedient response to all they had experienced. They took the example of the ritual of incarnation introduced by their teacher, developed ways of preserving their sacred union, and then passed on what it all meant to future generations that needed the same redemption.

As a ceremony of bread and wine unites them with us in defiance of time, so the sacramental work of artists, when their work is done with excellence, connects them with an attentive audience in a shared discovery, a journey or a sensation. We can receive some faint glimmer of that original inspiration.

That particular moment Alfred Stieglitz enjoyed under a particular sky, looking at a particular cloud in an instant of arresting display, spoke to me in that museum. He was serving and celebrating the subject by preserving his impression of it.

When we read a poem, the same thing can happen. One of my favorite poets, the insightful and extraordinarily gifted Jane Hirschfield, observes that saying a poem out loud can draw the reader into the same rhythms and state of mind that the poet experienced at the moment of conception. In her book about the art of poetry, *Nine Gates,* she says:

> We breathe as the author breathed, we move our own tongue and teeth and throat in the ways they moved in the poem's first making. There is a startling intimacy to this . . . Shaped language is strangely immortal, living in a meadowy freshness outside of time.[1]

When we look at a movie screen, if the artist is gifted and successful, and if we are in the right frame of mind and experience to understand, we see what the director wants us to see. Sometimes, we don't "get it" in the first viewing. But as we concentrate, we learn something about how the artist experiences or imagines the world.

Close Encounters of the Third Kind unites its viewers in the perspective of its creator for something a few steps shy of a religious experience. For general audiences, this speaks to that indwelling sense that the cosmos is full of mysteries and meaning yet to be revealed. Hamlet, upon the intrusion of his father's ghost, said to his friend, "There are more things in heaven and earth, Horatio, than are dreamt of in your philosophy." For Christians, the experience can humble us in the reminder that there is so much we do not yet know about what God is doing with the universe. The fact that there is benevolence in the visitation also resonates with us. We know that, for all of the evil in the world, an immeasurable love is evident even in the stars.

Whatever our interpretation, we feel something of what Spielberg felt lying on a picnic blanket beneath a meteor shower. The illusion that we are on our own, separated from everyone around us, is shattered through the shared experience of art.

* * *

A decade of war movies has shown us that battlefield combat can look terrifying, comical, chaotic, disgusting, or cool, depending on how it is filmed. The artist's choices can determine not just *what* we see but also the *way* we see it. Some artists place the camera down low and look up at the characters, making human beings seem like giants. (Orson Welles used this technique in *Touch of Evil* to make characters seem powerful and intimidating, and he used it with sharp irony in *Citizen Kane* when Kane was defeated in the gubernatorial race.) Others exaggerate and enhance characters' abnormalities and misbehaviors so that we can share in a sense of superiority and condescension. But some portray humanity in a more naturalistic style, and we have a greater sense of "being there" as an observer.

Perhaps that is why so many people respond when meeting a celebrity by saying, "He was much shorter than I expected." I remember standing alone in a Beverly Hills elevator and watching the doors slide open to reveal Robert Duvall, who stepped in next to me. The astonishment of seeing him—and of seeing that he's no taller than my dad—was strangely surprising. I was finally seeing him in the context of reality.

The transforming ideas in the films of Yasujiro Ozu, who made *Tokyo Story*, may delight a few viewers here and there during their initial encounter with his work. But for most of us, those rewards only come through patient attentiveness.

The films of Ozu and Spielberg are as different as fine wine and soda pop. Instead of stimulating a child's awe, Ozu's work appeals to adult powers of discernment. It doesn't pull us out onto the patio and aim our eyes at the sky, shouting "Look!" It invites us into a room and makes no extra effort to focus our attentions on anything in particular. Ozu trusted us to be awake, watchful, contemplative. The wonders in his world are subterranean, subtle, written in traces of emotion, absences and silences.

He positioned his camera to film his subjects from the level of a person seated and meditating—which allows us to see human beings in a more natural scale than the way we're accustomed to seeing them onscreen. Further, the camera did not move from its fixed place during a scene. When I started watching Ozu's films, I felt confined and frustrated by this approach—that is, until I realized that such stillness offered me more freedom to look around on my own.

Many find themselves bored when they don't have fast-paced camerawork and rapid editing or when there isn't music to tell them which emotions to feel during a scene. But a viewer's boredom may not be the fault of the director. It may be that the viewer has not learned how to look and think for himself. Typical camera movements prevent our curiosity and condition us to be lazy—they tell us outright what we should notice. The face. A shadow behind the door. The telephone that is about to ring. Ozu rarely directs our attention this way. He is interested in letting us decide for ourselves what is important about a moment. And thus, everything becomes important.

The more we watch Ozu's films, the more opportunities we have to discover new aspects of scenes, new changes in characters and even new stories being told. When we seize those opportunities, our senses become trained to discern the quiet dramas going on in the silences of others.

* * *

The wonders preserved in a film may not concern extraterrestrial activity or a cosmic wonder. They may be something delicate and almost imperceptible, such as a fleeting glimpse of emotion that reveals a hidden agenda or a secret wound. They may be a grand observation about the universe or a quiet admission of our common failures.

Whatever the case, when the elements of art combine to become more than the sum of their parts—that is, when a mystery is conveyed through a photograph, a painting, a poem or a film—it should encourage us to suspect that there may be more to the world than science can discern. Perhaps nature itself is pouring forth speech about something beyond itself. There just might be method in what seems madness. The world's aesthetics suggest that Someone is making these signs, Someone who cares enough to share.

Looking at those cloud photographs, I feel something of a kinship with Alfred Stieglitz, just as I feel close to his beloved Georgia O'Keeffe when I stare into the vivid treasures of her paintings. In that marvelous O'Keeffe museum full of masterpieces in Santa Fe, I peer through a gap in a white pelvis bone at the faint ghost of a New Mexico moon as it floats in the turquoise of a morning sky. Light, space, balance and proportion, even death . . . they all work together to a good and powerful effect.

O'Keeffe's perspective gave me such a love for the quality of New Mexico color, light and land that it may have inspired my attraction to a woman from that territory—one who dearly loves the high plains. (Of course, *Close Encounters* might have influenced me as well. My wife, Anne, is from Roswell, where, as everybody knows, the aliens landed.) We've been married now for more than a decade.

Oh, the consequences of art can be sweet.

*　*　*

It is easy to appreciate the visual spectacle of wide-eyed commercial filmmakers such as Spielberg, George Lucas and Peter Jackson. But the rewards to be found in the work of Yasujiro Ozu, Robert Bresson, Andrei Tarkovsky, Abbas Kiarostami and Krzysztof Kieslowski can go completely unnoticed if an audience does not make the effort to *receive* those gifts. The Space Shuttle might cross the sky unnoticed if no one knows where to look or what to look for.

I'm learning to let an artist lead me for a while. He may disappoint me, but it often pays when I give him a chance. I have to patiently follow, learning the artist's pace and point of view. I have to go out of my way. I have to run out onto the lawn in my underwear, no matter how ridiculous I look.

Most of the profound discoveries I've enjoyed have come from learning to recognize which movie buffs and film reviewers have the keenest sense of where to dig for gold. We learn by example until we're equipped to go out on our own.

I continued to meet with Mr. D and a group of my classmates after graduating from high school. We'd gather and sit in a circle in his apartment to read Shakespeare, short stories and poetry to each other. We were discovering so much together, and I was reluctant to strike out on my own just yet. But one night as I was leaving, Mr. D recommended a German movie to me called *Wings of Desire*. This was the first time I ever heard the name Wim Wenders.

"You wouldn't have been ready for this movie a year ago," Mr. D said. "But I think you'd find it interesting now."

Did this mean I was maturing?

On the Wings of Angels

Deep, resonant notes of a bow drawn slowly across the strings of a cello accompany the opening title cards of *Wings of Desire*: white letters etched on scratched black frames, suggesting that this is a canvas on which an artist is sketching his impressions for us.

For many, the challenge of a first encounter with Wenders' film is to stay awake. I've seen people lose that fight. When I brought *Wings of Desire* with me to the apartment of some friends, intent on introducing them to the movie that had changed my life, I was dismayed to discover that their television screen was only 12 inches wide. The detail and complexity of Wenders' imagery would be lost, minimized to the point of invisibility. We'd have to strain to read the subtitles. The set's one speaker had the quality of a transistor radio, eliminating the resonance of the music. Sure enough, a half hour into the film, one of my friends was asleep and the other had become distracted by the newspaper.

Even on a big screen, *Wings of Desire* is a challenge. For more than half of the film, it is less like a drama and more like wandering through a gallery of photographs or listening to a series of journal entries. Wenders takes us down into Berlin when the Wall still separated East from West. It could easily become a dispiriting, dismal display, but it is arresting because we're looking at Berlin through otherworldly eyes. Wenders' first stroke of genius is to place us in the vantage point of heavenly beings who live in God's presence and soar down to investigate the experience of humanity. They move gracefully, gliding through walls, in and out through windows both open and closed.

It's hypnotic.

*   *   *

Damiel, the central character of the film, is a deep-thinking angel. He doesn't *do* much . . . at least, not at first. His primary purpose is to give us new eyes. (The great German actor Bruno Ganz is perfectly cast here due to his gentle demeanor and his kind, smiling eyes. How is it that he ever overcame these appealing qualities to portray such a convincing Hitler in 2005's *Downfall?*)

Damiel eavesdrops on the thoughts of a child-weary mother, a wise old man teetering on senility's edge, a despairing bus rider reflecting on a wasted life, and a taxi driver who has seen dramatic history change the city's sights and sounds. At the scene of a motorcycle accident, Damiel touches the shoulders of a dying man, coaxing his thoughts toward comforting memories.

Watching Henri Alekan's enthralling cinematography—some of the most beautiful black and white images ever captured (Alekan also filmed the gorgeous 1946 version of *Beauty and the Beast*)—patient viewers will relax into a sort of angelic groove. The scenes seem almost arbitrary and haphazard at first. But the more we watch them, the more we see how some pictures echo others and how different characters' perspectives contrast in revealing ways.

In one extraordinary sequence, we glide from chamber to chamber of a family's high-rise apartment and listen to their thoughts about each other—each one separate, each one judging and presuming about the other—and then the camera continues without hesitation right through a window and into space, glancing down, down, down to the alley below where children pause to look up. A little girl smiles. We realize, with a delightful chill, that she can see the angel.

As this continues, we become accustomed to this detached observation, crossing the natural boundaries of silent expressions into the private thoughts of the Berlin residents. Wenders demonstrates the ways in which the presence of the Berlin Wall has damaged German psyches. That historic barrier comes to represent not only the political divide but also the divide between angel and human, observation and engagement, restraint and indulgence. Crossing intersections, a taxi driver thinks to himself, *Germany has crumbled into as many small states as there are individuals. And these small states are mobile. Everyone carries his own state with him, and demands a toll when another wants to enter.*

Yet Wenders has given us the privilege of drifting through these barriers to acknowledge just how close these people are, not only to each other, but to us as well. As in Lars Von Trier's film *Dogville*—in which the actors play out the story of small town life on a bare stage, pantomiming as if the walls of their houses divide them—we can see that they have succumbed to an illusion of separateness. The movie becomes a revealing lens, allowing us to see beyond abrasive exteriors to the common needs and fears in their hearts.

I don't mean to imply that *Wings of Desire* is about voyeurism. It's not. Voyeurism is about indulgently enjoying one's invisibility without any care to become involved in what is going on. These angels do not look at others out of self-interest. Nor do they behave with mischievous motives, like the heroine of *Amelie*. These angels, like biblical angels, long to understand what they are watching. Loving God, they look with love on the people around them. What they see pains them. Occasionally, with what powers they are allowed, they tenderly coax people to observe the evidence of God right in front of them, whispering rumors of meaning, giving them cause for peace.

When we were children, we were sometimes unnoticed by the grownups around us. We had a somewhat insulated world; we could pretend that we were invisible, investigating the world around us incognito. We could listen to adults talk to each other, oblivious to our discernment. *That* is the same way in which the central characters of *Wings of Desire* observe human beings.

Is it any wonder, then, that Damiel sits ecstatic in the company of children at the circus? The children in this film take delight in the simplest activities, such as fishing for coins down a gutter with a magnet on a string. Watching the children through the eyes of angels, we feel our sense of wonder begin to burn again.

Crossing Over

Damiel and his angelic friend Cassiel, the angel of sorrow (solemnly played by Otto Sander), are sitting in a car in the showroom window of a car dealership. The camera glides in front of the car. The fluorescent lights on the ceiling create a fantastic reflection on the windshield. We can see the angels, but also the light, which stretches and bends like a manifestation of their thoughts projecting heavenward.

"Well?"

Cassiel opens a little black notebook. He begins to read his observations of humanity and recollections of history. But Damiel soon interrupts him, pointing through the display window to the street. Historical musings are all fine and good, but lovers dancing, embracing and making out on the sidewalk— that's *fantastic*. Damiel is preoccupied with this display of love between humans. It's a beautiful mystery, and it distracts him.

"In the hills, an old man was reading *The Odyssey* to a child," Cassiel continues, "and the young listener stopped blinking his eyes."

Damiel takes a turn, reading what he has observed: A pedestrian folded up her umbrella and was soaked by the rain.

A schoolboy astonished his teacher by explaining to her how a fern grows. A blind woman, sensing the nearness of the angel, reached for her watch.

"Sometimes," Damiel sighs, "I'm fed up with my spiritual existence. Instead of forever hovering above, I'd like to feel a weight grow in me, to end the infinity and to tie me to Earth."

Damiel doesn't have grand ambitions to beget a child or plant a tree. But he wants to know what it feels like to be Philip Marlowe—to come home at the end of the day and feed the cat, to have fingers smudged with newspaper ink, to be excited not only by the mind "but by a meal . . . by the line of a neck, by an ear."

In that moment, through Wenders' splendid sense of absurdity and comedy, an old man in a business suit, his jacket folded over his arm, stares through the window at the car occupied by the angels, excited by its finely sculpted lines.

* * *

Later in the film, Damiel becomes preoccupied by a very human set of curves . . . and everything that comes with them. Marion (played by the angelic Solveig Dommartin) is a sexy circus trapeze artist, but she's far more than that. She's spiritually inquisitive, and that's what really gets Damiel's attention.

Marion longs to enjoy spiritual communion with a kindred spirit. She spends her days swinging between heaven and earth on a circus tent swing and whiles away the hours between performances by daydreaming, longing to find the love missing from her life.

Unable to keep his distance any longer, Damiel takes the plunge and becomes a human being.

Wenders had left his church upbringing behind, so he felt free to treat the angels of *Wings of Desire* like mythological creatures, inventions he could craft to his specifications. These pony-tailed, overcoat-clad characters aren't bound by the definitions of biblical angels. They can choose to cross over and become human, living among people in order to satisfy their curiosity about human experience.

Some Christian viewers have found this to be somewhat blasphemous. But Damiel and Cassiel are not meant to be *literal* angels. Like the angel in *It's a Wonderful Life,* they are whimsical metaphors, characters who have lost the joy of sensual human experience.

They serve his purpose powerfully. When Damiel takes the plunge and becomes a human being, activities that seem mundane to us suddenly become exquisite, sensual undertakings. Damiel gives up his practical observance of human beings—his detached attention in service of *agape* love—and takes on the form of a man in search of something more *material* . . . something *erotic,* in the healthy sense of the word. He wants to get beyond objective observance and to start knowing creation intimately.

To represent Damiel's entry into five human senses, the screen shifts from black and white into color. Viewers sometimes gasp in surprise and delight as they are restored to the world as they know it.

Giddy with his new heaviness, Damiel finds everything intoxicating—from the heat and weight of a hot cup of coffee, to the taste of his blood from a minor head wound, to the pizzazz of a colorful plaid jacket buttoned against the cold, to the ecstasy of physical intimacy. His awe and wonder grow exponentially.

Peter Falk, playing himself, inadvertently becomes Damiel's tutor in the simple pleasures of human life. "To smoke and have coffee," he says with relish, "and if you do it together, it's fantastic."

I usually walk away from *Wings of Desire* craving the beautiful simplicity of an ice cream cone, or wanting to go to the circus, or desiring to spend time with my 20 nephews and nieces. When Damiel takes that first cup of coffee into his cold hands and brings the steam up to his face, I suddenly crave a hot beverage as if it is a new and exhilarating privilege.

So I go and order a triple Americano at the Hotwire Online Coffeehouse and savor every sip.

* * *

To look at art by people of different experiences—whether cultural, religious, economic, or otherwise—is a way of stepping outside of what is comfortable and familiar in order to become more compassionate. It cultivates understanding, and thus sympathy, with people who are different than us. This is an especially powerful endeavor if we are willing to consider how our enemies experience the world—what a giant step it takes us toward loving them as Christ requires.

Wings of Desire is not about understanding our *enemies,* per se, but it does enable us to forge those bonds of sympathy because Wenders is a veteran of crossing borders and learning to see life through the eyes of others.

When I interviewed Wim Wenders, he explained, "It could be the story of my life as a German born after the war in a politically unreconciled country, and then . . . as somebody who set out very much as a loner." When he left his homeland for America, the director's life split into two different worlds of experience. Similarly, he has known life within the vocabulary of the Church and in the parlance of secular culture.

In each film, he builds bridges between differing worlds, and his characters travel back and forth for life-changing realizations. He seems preoccupied with reconciling characters separated by chasms. "They are longing to belong to a different context, both physically and spiritually," he told me. "As I look back at my movies, I think that is the story of my life right there."

Damiel's Gaze, Marion's Beauty

For a guy who grew up in a Baptist church where the pastor advised us against using trace amounts of alcohol in our cooking and where there was little distinction between sinful lust and the mature admiration of physical beauty, *Wings of Desire* was a liberating revelation of the glory of God in creation. Through an angel's eyes, I could see that while the world of the flesh *can* lead us into temptation and even to destruction, it is attractive because it manifests God's glory, and thus it *should* be enjoyed for its wild majesty.

Enjoying God's gifts responsibly is a way of showing gratitude to the Giver of all good gifts. I am occasionally criticized—even condemned—for approving of *Wings of Desire*, because some see it as a celebration of lust. They believe this because of one particular scene in which Marion leaves the circus tent, retires to her trailer with Damiel the angel invisibly following, and quietly disrobes. Damiel is awestruck. The camera shows us his face, and it also shows us the elegant lines of Marion's shoulders and back. This may be more flesh than some viewers are accustomed to seeing on the screen, but Wenders holds back, maintaining a respectful distance, and she has her back to the camera.

Still, the scene causes discomfort for some, and it is entirely possible that a viewer who is easily tempted to lustful thoughts will be provoked by such a moment. I must recommend the film with precautions to certain viewers. (You probably know who you are.) But is this evil? Is this a celebration of lust?

In response to this, I must remind viewers that Damiel is an angel, not a man. We are meant to see the world as he does . . . as an otherworldly observer appreciating a great mystery—the grace of the female form. It is entirely natural for guardian angels to be present when we are alone, in private moments.

But we are human, of course. If Wenders is to be a responsible artist, he must show us these moments carefully. And he does. He does not zoom in to exploit Marion or turn her into a sex object, but frames her as if presenting a fine sculpture, a black-and-white statue crafted in God's image, something alluring in the purest way.

Because Wenders takes great care to develop Marion as a three-dimensional character, only a viewer's weakness can result in her objectification. The artist is behaving responsibly and delicately. It is a moment of deep respect, awe and reverence, not a crass indulgence meant to provoke cheap, greedy responses. Remember, the viewer has a responsibility, too. To accuse Wenders of pornography is to deny that personal responsibility.

Many viewers will already feel a care and compassion for Marion, because they have resonated with her spiritual longings.

She has been chided by her show-business colleagues for not making an effort in her trapeze work. But she is making an effort. Her whole life is effort. The circus keeps failing. She has lost the joy of life. Everything is a steep uphill climb, and she's making the journey alone. When her career takes an unfortunate turn, she notes that there will be a full moon on the night of her last performance and wonders if she might fall and break her neck. The idea seems almost appealing to her.

In this moment of vulnerability, her nakedness represents her fragility, vulnerability, and openness to the spirit. It is in that moment that Damiel's admiration turns into a deep passion to provide the love and care she needs so badly.

* * *

Perhaps that is one of the reasons my teacher told me that I had to be ready for such a movie. Perhaps he trusted that I could receive the scene as it was intended—as meaningful imagery, not as a provocation.

Wenders is showing us a beautiful woman in this scene, but the meaning of the image lies in *how* he creates the image. Great artists such as Michelangelo, Rembrandt and Rodin knew that one of the greatest challenges lay in representing the human form, and it was in this that they demonstrated their genius. Their work presented a stunning manifestation of God's imagination and design, sculpted to remind us of God's glorious power.

Through the experiences of Damiel and Marion, Wim Wenders has given me some of the most sacred moments I have ever encountered in film. Damiel is intent on the mystery of the human experience—on what it means to be embodied and touch another human being. Rather than striving to possess, Damiel is enraptured by a marvel. Rather than entertaining shallow sexual fantasies, he is intrigued by Marion's whole person, her meditative questions about existence and whether or not there is any benevolent presence looking down on her. Damiel wants to answer her questions, and he wants her to answer his.

The film culminates in a monologue from Marion during which she seems to have stepped outside the bounds of real time, offering a poem about her sense of hope. Her poetry inspired in me a greater ambition for my own marriage—a desire to complete, and to become more complete, in greater measure than I had imagined before.

* * *

That is the gift *Wings of Desire* offers. With each concentrated viewing, we discover more poetry in its images, more understanding of its characters. Even incidental characters become fascinating mysteries. This is a worthy practice that we can apply when we turn our attention from the screen to the world around us, where every woman filing out of the theater has a story in her face and every man has mysteries in his head.

During his special appearance in the film, Peter Falk sketches the portrait of an old woman waiting on a movie set for her turn in front of the cameras. He silently exclaims, "What a dear face! Interesting. What a nostril. A dramatic nostril. These people are extras . . . extra humans."

I've found that bus rides have been much more interesting ever since.

Seeing More Than the Artist

Sometimes, we film critics get it all wrong. We think we know what a movie's about, but we ain't seen nothin' yet.

During a film seminar, a lecturer looked at me and declared, laughing, that he was always astonished when people didn't understand that J.R.R. Tolkien wrote *The Lord of the Rings* as a protest against the nuclear arms race. But Tolkien himself denied this, saying that he wanted to create an original mythology for England. While the story can offer meaningful insight into the debacle of atomic power, it also echoes Tolkien's own experience with industrialization, which tore apart the beautiful neighborhoods he knew as a boy, and the stories also give voice to the deep sadness he experienced when he lost his parents during his childhood. Moreover, as he wrote the saga, he sent the chapters to his son who was fighting in World War II, hoping they would provide both an escape from the toil and encouragement in the chaos.

Great art reveals its significance by its ability to show us new surprises every time, speaking to more than one culture, more than one age. Sometimes, even the artist doesn't know the significance of what he's done. In his impulsive response to an experience, he creates another experience that communicates more than he could ever realize.

Wim Wenders is still amazed by the rapturous reception that *Wings of Desire* received two decades ago. He was caught by surprise when it received outpourings of appreciation and gratitude in the form of film festival awards and fan mail. The experience had a direct influence on his decision to return to the Christian faith.

"I had no explanation for the fact that the film had actually succeeded in showing what it wanted to show," he told me. "And there was no explanation for the powerful impact that these figures had on audiences." The only way he could respond to the film's impact was to acknowledge that there were powers beyond himself at work and that the camera had captured more than he had sought to portray.

"This is one of the amazing achievements of films," he told me. "They can reveal something that you can't actually see. When I started out, because I started out as a painter, I strictly believed in the visible, and . . . that was *it*. [But] in the course of making movies, I realized that something I hadn't actually seen in front of my camera was then there in the movie."

This was especially true in *Wings of Desire*. The invisible angels that Wenders had made visible in order to provide a metaphor had, he now believes, actually been present. "I never really thought that a film could deal with anything metaphysical, and I had started this almost against better knowledge. And [yet] when we finished it, I thought, *How much help can I possibly get?* It felt like I had almost made the film completely unconsciously, and that the angels that I had sort of 'called' had actually been there to help me. So, as much as they were more of a metaphor when I made the film, I realized that somehow they had actively supported it. What I had taken for a metaphor had, sort of miraculously, materialized. So I came to terms with the fact that the invisible was powerfully working in movies. I just had to let it happen. You can't make it happen. I don't think you can consciously evoke that. At least, I didn't."

Like Roy Neary, who was mysteriously inspired to sculpt a mountain in response to an encounter with extraterrestrials, Wenders was inspired to tell a story of extraterrestrial—and angelic—intelligence in response to his experience of Berlin. In both cases, the artistic process led to further revelation.

* * *

Once you start to listen for these confessions of artistic bewilderment, you can find them everywhere. J.R.R. Tolkien once wrote, "I met a lot of things on the way that astonished me. Tom Bombadil I knew already; but I had never been to Bree. Strider sitting in the corner at the inn was a shock, and I had no more idea who he was than had Frodo. The Mines of Moria had been a mere name; and of Lothlórien no word had reached my mortal ears till I came there."

In an interview with Kevin Smith, director of the *Clerks* movies, *Chasing Amy* and *Dogma*, I told him that I interpreted *Jersey Girl* as a tale of a father's redemption. I asked him if that was what he'd hoped to achieve? Smith replied, "Well, that's all pre-supposing that I gave it that much thought ahead of time. I'm flattered that you would feel that I did. But I'd be lying if I said, 'When I sat down to write years ago, I wanted to write a tale of redemption.' It doesn't work like that . . . That's why I like it when people write about film. You suddenly see film from a different point of view."

As I sat in the God Room at a press junket for *Constantine*, a journalist asked the young actor Shia LeBeouf if he thought the film had any sort of redemptive message. He replied, "It's a fun ride. It's purely for enjoyment purposes. . . . I understand that it's dealing with religious philosophies, and there's probably a lesson in the film. But . . . I don't think that was the purpose of making the film. It's not *The Passion of the Christ* that we've made."

A few minutes later, Rachel Weisz joined us. When I asked her a similar question, she struck me silent with those fierce, beautiful eyes and declared, "It's about the capacity that we as human beings have to do good or to do evil. Good and evil occur on the earth, and we have free will. We can choose. But there is also a question of predestination—God's will. There's a tension between these two things, and it's in a state of flux. It's one of the biggest questions you can ask. For me, it's a question that is unanswerable. We can't say to what degree we're in charge. We don't know these things. It's a mystery."

In an interview for *Paste Magazine* with Patrice Leconte, the intriguing French director of *Man on the Train, The Widow of Saint Pierre* and *The Hairdresser's Husband,* I asked him one question that always haunted me after watching his movies: "Why are you so preoccupied with stories about temptation and about characters who must decide whether or not to transgress an ethical boundary?"

Through a translator, Leconte replied, "There is something very curious and interesting in what you are saying. There is nothing more interesting than meeting someone who casts a new light on your work. I have never thought about it, but you're absolutely right in what you say about the obsession in my movies' main characters. It's true that the situations revolve around the temptation of transgressing something that is forbidden." Leconte sat quietly for a moment, deep in thought, and then nodded. "I really thank you, because it's something that I've discovered, thanks to you."

After the interview, he shook my hand and said again, "*Merci beaucoup*! Thanks for shedding some light on my work. So, now I know." Beaming with pleasure, he exclaimed, "I am a filmmaker of transgression!"

* * *

As Steven Spielberg continued to speak with James Lipton on *In the Actor's Studio,* addressing a live audience of film students, he spoke more about his childhood. He had grown up quite happy, until his parents divorced and his world split in two. In one world, his mother was a concert pianist. In the other, his father was a pioneering computer scientist.

Lipton, keeping this in mind, smiled and observed that the culminating moments of *Close Encounters* were clearly a manifestation of Spielberg's dreams. "How do the scientists communicate with the spaceship? Through *music* made on their *computers.*"

I gasped. I'd never thought about that. Was the movie really about Spielberg's longing for his parents' reunion? Spielberg nodded, smiling, and then I saw emotion well up inside of him—that moment of realization art can provide even decades later to the person who crafted it.

"You know," the filmmaker said, astonished, "I would love to say that it was all conscious and that I planned that—but honestly, I had no idea. Until this very moment!"

Somehow, the audience understood the gravity of what had just taken place. Laughing, they applauded for joy. "Thank you so much for that observation," Spielberg added later. "Thank you so much. I had no idea that's what I was trying to get at. I had no idea. Thank you."

Watching this tape again, I'm reminded of something Wim Wenders told his colleague Scott Derrickson in an interview for *Image* journal: "It's strange, especially for a director, to find out that you are not the creator. You are instrumental in creating something, but even if you fancy the idea that you pulled it out of yourself, you have to acknowledge that you could not have done it alone."

In opening ourselves to the experience, we make contact not only with intelligence beyond the art but also with those who share the experience. In doing so, we make the experience more complete for the artist, and for each other. And then it's on to experiencing the world around us, better trained to complete the design, to apprehend the mysteries of heaven and earth that are there waiting to be discovered.

Note

1. Jane Hirschfield, *Nine Gates: Entering the Mind of Poetry* (New York: Harper Collins Publishers, 1997), p. 8.

PART TWO

Saving the World

CHAPTER
FIVE

Coming to the Rescue

*Han Solo: "There's no mystical energy field [that]
controls my destiny."
Obi-Wan Kenobi: "Then what does?"*

STAR WARS

*[You] create a world in which some sort of faith seems to be everywhere
without a visible source, like light from an invisible lamp.*

FROM A READER'S LETTER TO J.R.R. TOLKIEN REGARDING
THE LORD OF THE RINGS

The Hero Fix

Chances are that somewhere, right now, viewers are watching in
rapt attention as a hero tries to beat a countdown, which is probably displayed on a red digital readout. If the guy doesn't cut the
right wire in time or press the right button, it's a nuclear disaster.

In the next theater, you can bet that mysterious deaths are
kindling a heroine's curiosity about a corporate cover-up. Others
are puzzling along with desperate detectives, trying to decipher
cryptic messages from gloating serial killers. Elsewhere, they're
watching another hero who witnessed a crime as he becomes

frantic to save his family from the clear and present danger of what lies beneath. It's more than likely that the villain will turn out to be someone we've presumed innocent.

We're drawn to heroes because they embody the values we hold dear. They protect our families. They defend freedom. They seek to expose lies. In *To Kill a Mockingbird,* Atticus Finch dares to take a stand against racism, making the courtroom cringe in fear. His plea is unforgettable: "For God's sake, do your duty!" We cheer.

And heroes do more—they make bold statements about convictions we did not even realize we held until we heard them spoken with such eloquence and conviction. In *Sophie Scholl: The Final Days,* the heroine dismantles her interrogator's Nazi agenda with her piercing intellect and eloquence. Who would have thought that a scene in which two people sit and stare at each other across a desk could stretch on for so many minutes and remain absolutely riveting? But as you compare one hero to another, it becomes clear that there are stark differences between their concerns and perspectives.

James Bond risks his life regularly to defend England—and sometimes the world—for Her Majesty's Secret Service, but he doesn't seem to value much beyond sensual indulgence in sex, smoking, liquor and cars. He's the hedonist's hero. By contrast, in *The Matrix,* Neo's quest becomes a spiritual journey concerning matters of doubt and faith. The film's popularity confirmed that while we enjoy martial arts and mayhem, we also value spiritual exploration. As the trilogy progressed, the Wachowski brothers dumped a whole box of religious and philosophical vocabulary over our heads, sending us scrambling to understand what it all meant. Two sequels later, we were still trying to make sense of it all.

When Peter Jackson brought J.R.R. Tolkien's meaningful mythology of longsuffering, sacrifice and hope to the screen, people were deeply moved and passionate about portrayals of such unusual selflessness. Somehow, Tolkien's "Catholic work" resonated with viewers who flinch at the word "religion." They were introduced to representations of faith and love that allowed them to approach without fear, and they responded to the "ring" of truth.

* * *

Unfortunately, heroes with this sense of a higher calling are few and far between. Judging from the weekly box office totals, we're stuck with the lesser thrills of watching human beings rise up, load their guns, solve the puzzle, force a confession, and save the day through their own might and cleverness.

I must admit that after a long day of living through unresolved conflicts, I find prime-time justice to be rather satisfying. This is especially true if I've watched the evening news beforehand. On the news, yesterday's real-world crimes go unsolved, and today presents a whole new list of problems. Would-be heroes in the real world rarely cut the blue wire in time. Bombs go off. Innocents die. The bones of the missing girl are found just a mile from her mother's house.

To indulge our appetite for justice, Anne and I occasionally skip back and forth between three televised crime dramas in the same hour. It's surprisingly easy to keep up with the plotlines of each. Before we're off to sleep, we've watched investigators connect those grisly dots, reveal the whole horrible picture, and then ensnare the bad guys with words and weapons. Several crimes foiled, several threats locked up or shot dead. If one of these shows fails to supply that justice buzz, another will succeed. It's a fantasy world, but it's comforting to live there for a while, where things don't fall apart, where the center holds.

We want to be assured that someone heavily armed—Sidney Bristow or *Walker: Texas Ranger* or Jack Bauer, perhaps—is watching over the world. It suggests that there's still hope for us humans to solve these problems on our own. In an era when so many insist that there are no moral absolutes, it's encouraging to know that our society sits down every evening to unite against common televised enemies. We agree that the truth should be told. We cheer when the vulnerable and innocent are saved from disaster.

It usually plays out like this: The hero realizes—just before it's too late—who the killer is. Or he seizes the moment to finally confront his longtime nemesis. During a desperate struggle, the villain gets the upper hand, corners the hero, and feels suddenly and strangely compelled to explain his wicked deeds in detail. Gloating, he lunges for a killing blow . . . only to find himself skewered on a sharp object, or falling from a great height as the hero manages one last, desperate surprise. The "good guys" all live happily ever after. We celebrate and avoid thinking about the villain. Or his victims. Or their families.

It's comforting, really, that people still resonate with a triumphant conclusion. It's enough to strengthen our faith that God has, as Scripture says, placed "eternity in our hearts" (Eccles. 3:11). On some level we all know the truth: Evil is prowling like a lion waiting to devour us. We all need a hero, and we're right to suspect that one has been provided. But history's great hero stands in stark contrast to those we, in self-centered wishful thinking, have imagined.

Judgment Junkie

I confess, I have been a junkie for watching the bad guy fall into the fire, get pureed by a giant propeller, or discover that the pin on his grenade has been pulled. When I was very young, I relished that thrill in story after story as I sat and listened to the narrator's scratchy voice emanating through the speaker of my Fisher-Price children's record player.

The turntable had a picture of Mickey Mouse on it. Mickey's arm was heavy and plastic, with a needle situated under his index finger. That needle wore out the grooves of my records, especially my favorite ones. My mother remembers—and probably wishes she could forget—just how frequently I dropped the needle down onto Walt Disney's version of *The Three Little Pigs*. She remembers because I played the record continually.

The pigs' signature song, "Who's Afraid of the Big Bad Wolf?" must have driven her close to the edge. But how I loved that story. When the pigs taunted that black-furred predator in the suspenders and the hat, I laughed. When the wolf huffed and puffed and blew down the little pigs' houses, I huffed and puffed along with him. And the whole time, I was counting the seconds, reciting the words like a liturgy, right down to the moment when the wolf finds himself incapable of blowing down the smart pig's brick house and, as a last resort, tries to sneak down the chimney. The fiery surprise awaiting him made the whole story worthwhile. End of wolf. End of story. I joined the pigs in a triumphant reprise of their theme song, lifting up Mickey's arm to start the record again.

There were other Disney stories I loved—stories of friendship and honor and honesty and foolishness. Some of these stories even suggested higher powers that would make our dreams come true if we would only wish on the right star. But the stories that satisfied me most were those in which the Great Goblin was slain by a hero with a sword or Peter Pan sent Captain Hook to an ugly demise in the jaws of a ticking crocodile. Thus, the first definition of "hero" that made sense to me had a great deal to do with desiring a savior.

To me, a hero was a character who stood between a mean-spirited monster and vulnerable, suffering innocents. He loved a princess. Maybe he was threatened by an egotistical, broad-chested, evil-eyed suitor. In the big moment, he fired arrows into the monster or sent the arrogant swain plunging over a cliff and claimed the girl. Eventually, my enjoyment of heroic showdowns became so great that I started making up my own adventures just to see if I could concoct clashes and victories more spectacular than those in my fairy tale anthologies and Disney read-along records.

At age five, I sketched my very first picture book: *The Sea Monster*. In purple crayon, I illustrated the desperate plight of a tiny stick man as he swam for his life to escape the massive fanged jaws of a sea monster. In the first picture, the little man is swimming only inches away from the snapping jaws. Then the teeth of the monster close around him, pinching the single line of his torso, and—horrors!—all seems lost! But then, turning the page, we see that our nameless hero has suddenly acquired a sword, which he uses to poke the sea monster in the eye. The eye is replaced with an ugly *X*. Our champion triumphantly swims to the surface as the slumping form of the sea monster sinks into the murky depths.

It can't be just a coincidence that I drew these pictures in 1975 when advertisements for Steven Spielberg's *Jaws* first began to appear in newspapers. That frightful image of a sea monster preying on a swimmer probably provoked me to resolve the tension I felt by telling a story. That was also the year my parents took me to see my very first movie. No, it wasn't *Jaws*. We caught a screening of Walt Disney's *Snow White and the Seven Dwarves*, which enjoyed a revival during that Christmas season. I'll never forget the ferocity of those climactic moments when the wicked witch was driven to her doom. Victory! Justice!

Afterward, I became obsessed with looking through the movie pages of the daily *Oregonian* to discover new stories about the conflict of good versus evil. Around the age of seven, I even started reading reviews to try to get glimpses of how these stories played out. I wanted to entertain ideas of conflict and resolution that were not addressed anywhere else in my contented, comfortable, love-blessed childhood. As peaceful as my little world was, I wanted adventure. I wanted to see supermen rise up to face the wild things that I suspected were lurking in the shadows so that I could go to bed knowing the world was under guard.

And yet, the popular culture's heroes struck dissonant chords with me. Their lifestyles were so different from my own. My parents modeled for me the belief that we cannot overcome evil on our own. At mealtimes and during evening devotions, we practiced calling for help from a source beyond ourselves, beginning with "Our Father in heaven" and closing with "in Jesus' name, amen." In Sunday School, I learned about heroes who kept talking to God and trusting in Him to deliver them from plagues and persecution.

The heroes of television and movies seemed unconcerned about God. They didn't feel the need for a savior. They planned to save the world themselves, even though they were just flawed human beings with bad habits and bills to pay. I remember reading that worldly storytellers tell stories about human saviors because God has given us all the expectation of a redeemer. I still believe that this is true, but I could see even back then that most of the world's invented heroes overcame the bad guys by using their quick wits and a few explosives. They didn't seem like ideal stand-ins for a messiah. They suggested that the world could be saved and predicaments resolved with a few precise pistol shots. They implied that I could get along just fine in the world if I did good deeds and developed reflexes fast enough to answer violent threats.

Not much has changed. These days, spirituality is more common in commercial entertainment, but it's little more than a sexy accessory, giving a character depth—right up to the moment he gloatingly serves up a cold plate of revenge and asserts himself as the latest smack-down champion. We're not likely to find many big screen adventurers for whom faith is a humbling conviction that plays a vital role in saving the world.

I'm grateful that I found a few important exceptions—characters who demonstrated thrilling heroism, but who did so in partnership with higher powers, realizing that they were playing small parts in a larger drama. These stories showed me a world in which there was hope for all of us insufficiently heroic humans. They captured my imagination unlike anything else. They helped me take those first steps into a larger world of meaningful storytelling.

Redeeming the Dark Lord

It won't surprise anybody to hear that *Star Wars* rocked my childhood world with its mind-boggling effects and memorable characters. Yes, I bought the action figures produced by the Kenner toy company, and I found a sort of poetic justice in the fact that my Darth Vader figure was defective, with one leg longer than the other. This villain would not stand!

But more important, I became fascinated with the idea of The Force. When Luke turned off his targeting computer and opened himself to a mysterious spiritual power, it reminded me of learning to pray for God's help. The whispers of his mentor, Obi-Wan Kenobi, who had given his life to save his friends, reminded me of Jesus, who had done the same. It was heartening to encounter heroes who made a difference by making themselves smaller and opening themselves to something greater.

I especially loved the unexpected twist at the end: The heroes were not completely victorious. Darth Vader got away! The monster hadn't been slain! He was still out there, somewhere, threatening to come back and cause more trouble.

The plot thickened when Vader returned in 1981. Nothing had prepared me for the shock of *The Empire Strikes Back*. The revelation that the Dark Lord of the Sith was actually Luke Skywalker's father astonished me. It threw me off.

My own parents have never been anything but supportive and willing to invest their best efforts in helping me grow up safe and strong. As a naïve 10-year-old, I had never considered the possibility that any of my friends might have reason to flinch when their fathers came home. In retrospect, I'm certain that Darth Vader's revelation was horrifying for some of them because of how it mirrored the truth of their experience. It rang true.

As I mentioned earlier, art conveys truth in mysterious ways, and we interpret it differently because we come with different experiences. But that's not to say we necessarily arrive at conflicting interpretations. We might just be seeing different fragments of its truth depending on where we stand.

It is often presumptuous and premature for a critic to proclaim that a movie is abhorrent or un-Christian. For some, a story about an abusive father may seem like a subversive attack on the idea of family values, while for others it may look like a portrayal of their own life. For some, the idea of an invisible Force may sound like the occult, while for others it might stimulate suspicion of a grand design in the cosmos and a higher power that can intervene in our lives. The *Star Wars* stories ultimately portray a journey out of darkness toward hope and the power of forgiveness.

Growing up, I had become accustomed to villains who disappeared in a flurry of violent justice. Madame Medusa's riverboat exploded and sank in *The Rescuers*. The wicked witch of *Snow White* was driven to her death by dwarves on a dark and stormy night. Rumpelstiltskin was exorcised by the speaking of his proper name. In *The Hobbit*, the grandiloquent dragon was slain by an arrow. I had thought that heroes had every right to shove their enemies into the abyss. But what's a hero to do if his enemy is a member of his family?

The Force was up to something in the heart of Luke Skywalker. Three years later when *Return of the Jedi* arrived and Luke faced his father in a climactic duel, I learned that heroes were capable of something even braver than striking swiftly with their light sabers. As John Williams' dramatic score swelled, what transpired was a victory motivated by compassion and love rather than a demonstration of rage and power. As we watched Darth Vader cast his malevolent master into the fiery abyss, we weren't taking pleasure in the Emperor's demise. We were focusing on the important thing—the redemption of a prodigal father.

A Gleam That "Rends the Web of Story"

As Peter Jackson's *The Lord of the Rings: The Fellowship of the Ring* enters its third hour, we watch Gandalf the wizard guide Frodo the hobbit and their fellowship of companions deep into the Mines of Moria, beginning their stealthy quest to destroy the enemy's weapon of mass destruction—the Ring of Power.

What ensues is the most spectacular half-hour of adventure moviemaking I've ever seen. Swarms of orcs and trolls rush down upon the heroes, but they're restrained by the light of Gandalf's staff. He stands like Moses holding back the waves of the Red Sea. And then, the monsters suddenly turn and run, thrown into terror of something far scarier than themselves.

As they recede into the cracks and crevasses of the mines, a hellish Balrog rises up from the abyss to challenge Gandalf.

This all plays out just as I had imagined when I read J.R.R. Tolkien's *The Lord of the Rings* for the first time at the age of eight. Yet for all of this frenzied action, what precedes the spectacle of the fellowship's flight is even more important: a quiet conversation between Gandalf and Frodo as they pause, weary and worried. Frodo has heard the flip-flap of slimy feet on the stony path behind them, and Gandalf informs him that Gollum—that tormented, treacherous wretch who is addicted to the Ring's power—is following them.

Tolkien's epic trilogy turns our common ideas of heroes on their heads. Gollum is a murderer, a thief and a fool. If he gets his sticky fingers on the Ring, he could deliver the world into the enemy's hands. Frodo remembers that Uncle Bilbo once had a chance to eliminate this creature once and for all (a scenario played out in *The Hobbit*). But Bilbo's mercy kept Gollum alive. As a result, this menace is still on the prowl.

Frodo tells his wizardly guide, "It's a pity that Bilbo didn't kill him when he had the chance." Gandalf, his thoughts so ponderous that his beard appears to be weighing his head down, replies, "Pity? It was pity that stayed Bilbo's hand. Many that live deserve death. Some that die deserve life. Can you give it to them, Frodo? Do not be too eager to deal out death and judgment. Even the very wise cannot see all ends."

These sentiments take on definition later when Frodo eventually puts Gollum on a leash and employs him as a tour guide through enemy territory. The wary, weary hobbit coaxes the monster's former, more lucid self to the surface. Might Gollum be redeemable? Are we capable of feeling sympathy for him? When the ever-vigilant Samwise senses Gollum's treachery and beats him, Frodo, who is coming to understand Gollum's weak will, steps in.

Reading this, I understood what was happening. The more I learned about the poor monster's history and misery, the more I, too, felt pity for him.

*   *   *

When I joined a number of religious press journalists to interview the cast and crew of Peter Jackson's *The Lord of the Rings* films, I was surprised at how differently people interpreted Tolkien's work. The story bears a strong subtext about the corrupting nature of power, and Tolkien teases the reader with hints of "another will" that intervenes in the affairs of men, hobbits, dwarves and elves. Nevertheless, the actors and their director found the films to be a humanistic tale about the ways in which men and women can save the world through determination and cultural diversity. Dominic Monaghan and Billy Boyd spoke of it as an environmentalists tale.

Perhaps the most confounding response to our questions about Tolkien's worldview came from Sir Ian McKellen, who played Gandalf. When Steven Greydanus asked McKellen what it was like to put himself inside the imagination of a devout Catholic and personify a spiritual hero, McKellen made it clear that he did not share Tolkien's faith. "I note with delight that Hobbiton is a community without a church," he said. "There is no pope in this story. There's no archbishop. There's no set of beliefs. There's no credo. I think what [Tolkien's] appealing to in human beings is to look inside yourself, and to look to your friends, and to join a fellowship."

All of these interpretations carry elements of truth. Yes, Tolkien believed in the power of friendship, and he was passionate about defending the natural world from the destructive advance of industrialism. But these views fall short of real insight and fail to take into account prominent themes and events.

Tolkien's Hobbiton reflects his enjoyment of earthly pleasures, but it is also a place of profound ignorance. It is a society that would have been wiped off the map by Sauron if Frodo had not discerned the importance of Gandalf's highly "religious" view of the struggle between good and evil. No, the Shire had no church, but this speaks more to its failure than its strengths. Ultimately, it's the intervention of a higher power that saves Middle-Earth from destruction. Any suggestion that *The Lord of the Rings* demonstrates a human capacity to withstand and vanquish evil reflects an incomplete interpretation, especially in view of the story's climactic events.

* * *

Eventually, Frodo finds that his own will is not sufficient to resist the powers of evil. Like Gollum, the burden has weakened him. The constant pull of temptation finally overwhelms his spirit. Reaching the last steps of his journey, where he can cast the Ring into the fires of Mount Doom, he turns against his dear friend Sam and announces, "The Ring is mine!" As Tolkien later explained in a letter, Frodo "indeed 'failed' as a hero, as conceived by simple minds: he did not endure to the end; he gave in, ratted."

Was Tolkien's lack of faith in earthly heroes born out of a general pessimism? No. He knew, as Christ knew, that the force of human will cannot triumph over evil. Our hearts are too weak, too corrupt. Yet this great storyteller confessed that his lack of faith in humankind went hand in hand with his faith in the sovereignty of a higher power who will save the world: "But one must face the fact: the power of Evil in the world is *not* finally resistible by incarnate creatures, however 'good'; and the Writer of the Story is not one of us."[1]

So, who was it then that saved the world in the thrilling resolution of *The Lord of the Rings* if not Frodo? What power intervened?

There are hints all along the way. When Frodo is faltering, he holds up the phial of Galadriel and calls on the power of Elendil, much like the way a devout Catholic might ask for the intercession of a saint. Elsewhere, when Gandalf himself is in trouble, he tells his enemies that he is a servant of "the Secret Fire." When he plunges into a chasm, he is saved by some mysterious power, which then sends him back into the world to snatch Frodo and his resilient friend Samwise from the roiling lava of Mount Doom.

Tolkien was drawn to the world of *faerie* for just this reason: Through fantasy, we find metaphors that murmur about spiritual, unseen realities. Middle-Earth is a fantasy world, rich with magic, continuing in the vein of great fairy tales from King Arthur's epic to *A Midsummer Night's Dream* to Aslan's Narnia to Harry Potter's Hogwarts. Whether Christian or otherwise, cultures throughout history have dabbled in stories of the fantastical, giving shape to their deeply rooted sense that there is more to life than the material world makes visible.

Describing his perspective, Tolkien wrote that a fairy story can express something more than tragedy. Fantasy, he said, points to a coming universal triumph of good over evil, of joy over suffering. It inspires "a catch of the breath, a beat and lifting of the heart, near to (or indeed accompanied by) tears," for through its fanciful metaphors, it gives readers "a piercing glimpse of joy, and heart's desire, that for a moment passes outside the frame, rends indeed the very web of story, and lets a gleam come through." The relevance of the fairy story to reality lies in this gleam, which is a "sudden glimpse of the underlying reality of truth."[2]

Still, the merest mention of magic can worry those who struggle to get beyond literal interpretations of art. Concerned parents have written me letters to convey their conviction that fantasy films will lure children to dabble in the occult. One who read my review of *Harry Potter and the Chamber of Secrets* was incensed at my suggestion that a story about a boy wizard could be worthwhile. She said, "If you think anything meaningful can be conveyed by pagan mythology, you've just opened Pandora's box!" She would probably be dismayed if I pointed out that she, by making a reference to a pagan myth, had conveyed something meaningful to me.

In some stories, magic represents something to be sought after and controlled. Supernatural darkness is very real, and stories that make us curious about dabbling in sorcery are certainly dangerous. But most fairy tales highlight the foolishness of bargaining with devils. "Good magic" is usually a whimsical invention of the storyteller that serves as a representation of spirit, talent or faith. Without these imaginative elements, we could never have met Pinocchio, Peter Pan, Cinderella, the King Arthur of legend, old Scrooge and Aslan, for starters.

Traditional fairy tale elements are not what trouble me about the Harry Potter tales. I am, however, distressed by J.K. Rowling's tendency to let Harry's frequent disobedience go unpunished, sometimes even rewarding him for trespassing and exercising his power to humiliate schoolyard bullies. That sends dangerous messages, whatever one's view of fairy tales.

J.R.R. Tolkien's stories, on the other hand, are filled with magic that whispers about the glory of a paradise lost, the majesty of angels, and the sovereignty of God. The "dark magic" of Middle-Earth poetically conveys the corrupting power of evil, which distorts what is natural and drives away the grace of characters such as the elves. Tolkien's vision speaks to our sense that there is a conflict of dangerous malevolence and grand benevolence playing out through history. He celebrates those humble souls who ask for help from the one trustworthy source of guidance in a darkening world.

Frodo exhibits a kind of courage and virtue most action heroes lack because he apprehends his own weakness and finds the grace to extend compassion toward his enemy. But it is more than courage that distinguishes this young hobbit—it is his admission that he will need help from something else before the story is over.

My Failing Hero

Watching George Lucas's spiritual sci-fi epic unfold on the screen and reading J.R.R. Tolkien's fantasy adventures caused me to revise my understanding of the conflict between good and evil. Frodo's humble service and Skywalker's compassionate restraint became more inspiring than heroes who solved problems with swords. I had to reconsider the identity of villains and wonder where they came from, who their parents were, what motivated them, and whether or not they could be saved by something greater than themselves.

Then another big-screen icon seized my young imagination. This fellow had a knack for failing at almost everything he did. He made it clear that the mark of a true hero is, in the end, more about what he believes and honors than what he accomplishes.

* * *

The Paramount Studios logo, a crooked, rocky peak, fades out and is replaced by a real-world equivalent—a stone pinnacle jutting into an ivory sky. We're looking at it through a gap in the trees that surround the screen. A silhouette steps into the frame, classic and unmistakable: a bullwhip slung from his belt, a leather jacket, a fedora. Hands on his hips, he regards the peak he has eclipsed. Then he continues into the jungle, followed by his watchful, nervous companions. We do not see his face. He's a mystery.

He makes his way nonchalantly through the jungle, headed into peril. The brim of his hat conceals his visage until that memorable, shocking moment when he senses a betrayal, turns, and knocks the pistol from a disloyal Spaniard's hand with a lash of his bullwhip. That rankled brow, those flaring eyes, that unshaven jaw—this is a man on a mission, fully aware of the dangers ahead *and* behind.

We watch him proceeding into secret passageways, pushing through thick curtains of spider webs. Brushing off tarantulas, ignoring Satipo's warning that no one has come out of the place alive, he expertly dodges deadly darts and traps, including the one that skewered a famous competitor.

At last, he kneels before a fabulous idol, the treasure he wants to preserve and display in a museum, where it "belongs." With the skill of a surgeon, he replaces the glistening golden god with a bag of sand. Has he thought of everything?

No, alas, he has not! Moments later, Indy is running from the most dangerous big-screen boulder since the asteroids that his intergalactic look-alike dodged in *The Empire Strikes Back* a year earlier. In an artful dive, Indiana launches himself out of the tunnel . . . and lands almost in the lap of his waiting nemesis, Rene Belloq, who, smiling wolfishly down on the dusty Indy, wastes no time in demonstrating his villainy.

Immediately, the world is divided into hero and villain. Indiana Jones is the kind of man who can cheat death. But Belloq is the sort of man who will steal the prize and the glory right out from under Indy's nose.

Jones just can't get a break. When he later enters Marion's bar, the same thing happens to him. He treads carefully, shows respect, gets jarred around, and then leaves disappointed. The prize has been snatched from his hands . . . again. Later, after his long pursuit of the Ark of the Covenant, he loses that contest as well. It is Belloq who gets to lift the holy lid on its secrets.

What makes Jones such an appealing hero if he's prone to constant failure? Well, there's the issue of a costume. Like all superheroes, he has his public disguise: the tweedy suit-and-tie of a New England archaeology professor, complete with over-sized Clark Kent glasses. Further, he has the concerns of an adventurous kid. When he's summoned by visiting authorities, Indiana reflexively asks, "Am I in trouble?" Any man who's ever been a boy has asked this question. And Indy just doesn't have time for girls. There's too much fun to be had. When Marion starts kissing him, it's his cue to promptly fall asleep (a reversal that secretly delights those boys who were annoyed that fairy tales all came down to kissing). Like the boy tells his grandfather in *The Princess Bride*, we want to get on to the good stuff.

We're also in Jones's corner because he's interesting—the toughest thing for a hero to be. Bad guys get to be outrageous, while good guys must remain dutiful. But Indy, he's Odysseus, venturing into the unknown and overcoming various threats. He's Orpheus, the troubled champion descending into the underworld to perform a rescue. He's Batman, the haunted crime-fighter who casts a shadow everyone can recognize. Yet we're also rooting for Indy because he's always being treated unfairly, always coming up short. He's the ultimate underdog. He even has a weakness: he's scared to death of snakes.

* * *

For me, the most interesting and enduring appeal of Indiana Jones is his temperamental relationship with a higher power.

At the beginning of his quest for an Old Testament relic, Indy's colleague, Marcus Brody, curator of the National Museum in Washington D.C., has a premonition that they may be about to trespass on sacred ground. Indiana laughs it off, declaring that he has faith in the pistol he's packing in his luggage. You half expect him to repeat Han Solo's lines from *Star Wars*, "Hokey religions and ancient weapons are no match for a good blaster at your side. . . . I've seen a lot of strange stuff, but I've never seen anything to make me believe . . ."

Later, drowning his woes and mourning the loss of Marion, Indy is confronted by Belloq, who boasts that the ark is "a transmitter, a radio for speaking to God." Indy sneers a smile. "You want to talk to God?" he says. "Let's go see him together. I've got nothing better to do."

Is that faith or just a smart remark? The quality of Indy's faith won't be resolved until he is pressed to the point of death. For all of his skill navigating practical threats, he has yet to encounter the great mystery that will leave him as helpless and vulnerable as a child: the power of an angry God.

In the end, Indy fails so utterly that he can only hope for the help of someone a whole lot stronger than his sidekick Sallah. And even then, he doesn't ask for it. He quietly awaits his doom.

But God is gracious. In his final failure, Jones is given a thorough education in the power of the Almighty. The best Jones can muster is a simple show of respect. He turns his eyes away from God's holy secrets. Belloq is the one who, in his vanity, defies God. When God intervenes, Belloq is engulfed in the wrath of God while Indiana Jones receives grace. While all of those seeking to apprehend God's power for their own purposes are punished for their pride, Indiana and Marion are left standing unscathed, their bonds broken. It is left to Indy to carry the Ark now, with responsibility and reverence.

Most action heroes are cocky, self-reliant fellows who soldier on against all odds and somehow come out on top without ever looking around to see if their steps might be protected or whether they might need guidance or salvation. Indiana Jones's adventures lead him to further steps of faith, where he will learn to reject the temptation of power and accept his humble place in God's service.

Indy ultimately learns that humility and faith matter more than pistols and sarcasm. The fear of God is the beginning of his wisdom. He's my kind of loser.

Heroes of All Kinds, for All Seasons

Of course, we all know Indiana Jones is not really a loser. He's making a fool of himself because of his convictions, taking a lonely stand against oppression. He's an obstacle in the path of the advancing forces of cruelty and arrogance. And something in me resonates when his prideful enemies fall. I know that this reflects the larger story that God is writing in history and in all of our particular plotlines. The Almighty's wrath consumes those who oppose Him, just as his mercy rescues the faithful.

Growing up with movies, I've come to recognize that Skywalker's sense of a higher calling, Frodo's appeals to unseen power and Indiana Jones' reverence for the sacred are all relevant to my everyday tasks. I may not be asked to jump on a horse and chase down a Nazi tank, carry a magical talisman or duel with a dark lord. But there are tests that require the mettle of a hero in situations that seem ordinary. Thus, many heroes themselves are so ordinary as to be overlooked, coming and going without any fanfare, without any recognition of their triumphs.

The movies give us a chance to focus on such thankless heroism—to recognize those acts of courage that take place in the heart rather than on a battlefield. The compassionate Sister Helen Prejean, played by Susan Sarandon in Tim Robbins' film *Dead Man Walking*, is a bold big-screen example of someone who can face the danger, condemnation and humiliation that come from answering the call of Christ. She is not merely resisting a sentence of capital punishment. She is fighting for the salvation of a soul, serving a greater Judge than the one who will determine whether the imprisoned Matthew Poncelet lives or dies.

When the American Film Institute selected its list of the Top 100 Heroes, the voters honored Atticus Finch, the principled father and champion of justice in *To Kill a Mockingbird*. An admirable choice, to be sure, but the American Film Institute list is missing one of the big screen's monumental heroes. This hero is superior to Finch when it comes to passion, conviction and eloquence in court. Further, he knows the source of that still, small voice of conscience, which enables him to surpass heroes who merely resist the bad guys. He is a man who blazes a trail for men of faith. His name is Thomas More, and he's the central character in Fred Zinneman's *A Man for All Seasons*.

As I sat down to write about More's resilient virtue, I remembered that my friend Steven Greydanus, who writes for

DecentFilms.com and *The Catholic Register*, cherishes this film. I asked him to describe what it is that sets More apart from other characters he's encountered.

> Some saints, like John the Baptist, are in your face. They are God's gadflies, "society's sore teeth," as Robert Bolt put it in the introduction to the play that inspired this film. Spurning success and acclaim in this life, they set themselves on a collision course with the world, make themselves a sign of contradiction, eagerly accepting opprobrium and even martyrdom. Blessings on them. God calls them to it, and society is never unable to use a good kick in the pants.
>
> At the same time, the older I get the more I find that I am attracted to the other sort of saint, the saint who makes himself as thoroughly at home in the world as possible while remaining unapologetically a citizen of the next. Thomas More, to me, exemplifies this sort of saint. Attractive, successful, urbane, witty, respected, he was a man who loved his work, his life, his country, his family and his God, more or less in that order, and only very reluctantly allowed himself to be deprived, one by one, of each of the first four (*not* in that order) out of fidelity to the fifth.
>
> The fact that *A Man for All Seasons* was written by a non-Christian is to me an extraordinary tribute to the winsomeness of More's Christian humanism. If even a tenth of the world's Christians were the kind

of people who might inspire a non-Christian artist to want to capture or honor or evoke their lives in some way, Christianity would conquer the world.

Even so, many of cinema's greatest heroes are not religious characters, and they make no formal profession of faith. Artists and storytellers who steer clear of engagement with spiritual questions find themselves appealing to whatever aspect of the truth inspires them. It may be justice, love or freedom. Whatever the case, they are making their way along the borders of true faith, tracing its outline, drawing audiences nearer to the source of those values.

One such character teaches young boys in a carpentry shop in Liege, Belgium. He's the broken-hearted hero of the Dardenne brothers' film *The Son,* a man mourning more than one excruciating loss in his life. Watching him carry the long beams of timber on his shoulder, viewers may be reminded of Christ carrying His cross, and it's enough to make us wonder whether or not this was included as a deliberate reference. This resonates more deeply with us when a troubled, nervous boy joins his class of students and the carpenter must shoulder an even greater burden—answering a call of love that will make him a fool in the eyes of others.

In Mike Leigh's *Secrets and Lies,* Timothy Spall plays a heavy-hearted photographer who guards secrets that keep the members of his family divided from each other. He plays the patient listener until he can tolerate their subterfuge no more, and then he explodes in a tirade of truth-telling that places him in danger of an equal and opposite reaction.

In Paul Thomas Anderson's *Magnolia*, Philip Parma is a nurse tending to a dying man. When he discerns the old codger's last wish, Parma risks humiliating himself in order to track down the man's grudge-hardened prodigal son. In the same film, Jim Kurring is an uncommonly endearing policeman. But this character is a Christian. He has a name for the source of his higher calling. Kurring strives for excellence and appeals to God for help when he stumbles. His benevolence and his brokenness come to the surface when he befriends a broken-hearted junkie and becomes exactly what she needs: a strong, guiding hand directed by a merciful heart.

*   *   *

"The world speaks of the holy in the only language it knows, which is a worldly language," says Frederick Buechner. We can hear a sense of the holy in the profoundly moving words of Dorothy, a timid and undervalued servant who serves in a great house full of miscreants and windbags in Robert Altman's upstairs/downstairs mystery, *Gosford Park*.

Upstairs, in the celebrated manor of Sir William McCordle, wealthy American guests and their aristocratic hosts all find themselves trapped in the house as a murder investigation takes place. We are introduced to so many characters that it's almost impossible to keep track of their rank, much less their relationships. Most of the people seem more inconvenienced than grieved by the murder.

The murder has doomed Anthony Meredith's business affairs. Despite the fact that there's a corpse upstairs, he is consumed by anger and despair over his ruination. He flees the scornful gaze of his family and retreats into the pantry far below the house. As if reverting to boyhood, he takes comfort in some spoonfuls of fruit preserves. He is sadly licking the spoon when one of the servants, the nervous-but-dutiful Dorothy, accidentally interrupts him.

Dorothy apologizes for disturbing him and recommends another flavor. (Other maids might have reprimanded him for getting into the pantry stock, especially considering the value of a jar of homemade jam.) Seeing that he is in no mood to take out his frustrations on her, she then inquires about his trouble. Anthony speaks the question clawing at his conscience. He asks her why some people seem to get whatever they want in life, whereas others can strive and strive and have nothing. "Is it luck?" he asks. "Are the fates of men controlled by mere chance?"

Dorothy was born for this. "I believe in love," she replies. "Not just getting it, but giving it. I think that if you're able to love someone, even if they don't know it, even if they can't love you back, then it's worth it."

Her words resonate like a depth charge. We share Anthony's astonishment. While Dorothy may be one of the lowest of the low in the house—one of the least educated and most easily intimidated—she has no ego. She is all heart. Her words, should they stir Anthony to anger, will probably get her fired. But she puts that out of her mind. Here, with this lost soul in the dark cellar, she reveals herself as belonging to a different hierarchy, a different order. She's reflecting light.

"That's a good answer," Anthony says. Overwhelmed, he rises and departs. When next we see him, he is a changed man.

Dorothy, meanwhile, returns to her duties. Her words are never recorded. She goes on with her routine, blending in with the other uniformed servants. But we in the audience recognize that she has done a great thing and that her humble testimony, unheard by the rest of the house, is likely to change the course of the story. Deep in the cellars of that great house, she has slain a monster. Her conviction flares like a lantern that illuminates everything around her.

Notes
1. J.R.R. Tolkien, in a letter to Miss J. Burn dated July 26, 1956, quoted in Humphrey Carpenter, ed., *The Letters of J.R.R. Tolkien* (Boston, MA: Houghton Mifflin Company, 1981), p. 252.
2. J.R.R. Tolkien, *The Tolkien Reader* (New York: Ballantine Books, 1966), pp. 86-88.

CHAPTER
SIX

A Personal History of Violence

Power is when we have every justification to kill, and we don't.

Whoever fights monsters should see to it that in the process he does not become a monster. And if you gaze long enough into an abyss, the abyss will gaze back into you.

FRIEDRICH NIETZSCHE

A Scene from *Unforgiven*

Just outside the town of Big Whiskey, beneath a lone tree on a hilltop, the grizzled gunslinger William Munny stares toward town in grim apprehension. Behind him, sitting hunched at the base of the tree and gripping a large bottle of booze, a boy who calls himself the Schofield Kid is shuddering under the chill of realization. They've just killed two cowboys, and they're waiting for their reward money.

The prostitutes at Skinny's whorehouse had offered a prize of one thousand dollars to anyone who would come to Big Whiskey and kill the brutes responsible for the disfigurement of Delilah, one of their own. Word of the offer had been carried from Wyoming all the way to Texas. Big Whiskey's sheriff, Little Bill Daggett, had fined the offending cowboys five ponies for the crime. But the horses were not given to Delilah—they were given to Skinny, because it was his "property" that was damaged. This satisfied Little Bill, but the prostitutes were furious. So, they decided to take steps to achieve their own idea of justice.

Munny had given up killing years before when his wife, Claudia, softened his heart and stoked the fires of his conscience. She had helped him break his dependence on the bottle. He revered her as a saint.

But Claudia had died not long before the Schofield Kid arrived looking for a partner. She wasn't there to dissuade her husband when he heard the troubling story of Delilah's rape and disfigurement.

With his farm failing, disease spoiling his livestock and his children hungry, Munny was desperate. The story of Delilah rankled his nerves and woke up his old temper. He succumbed to the Kid's goading and summoned his old partner, Ned Logan, to join him on the revenge quest.

The Kid, on the other hand, was motivated by more than conscience—he aspired to become a vigilante hero like the legendary gunslingers he had read about growing up. So he started telling lies about his own violent exploits. Eventually, he struck out to find one of those legends—Munny himself—in order to learn from a master. The cry for help from Big Whiskey seemed like a clear-cut case of injustice, the perfect opportunity for the Kid to start his own history of violent heroism.

Things did not go the way the Kid had envisioned.

Munny, Ned and the Kid moved into Big Whiskey at night and, sure enough, shots rang out. Things got ugly. Ned Logan turned to head for home, sensing that this was all a big mistake. But Munny and the Kid remained until the job was done.

The Kid is a killer at last. But now he knows the truth—killing isn't fun. It doesn't make him feel cool. In fact, it has jolted his conscience, a feeling so unfamiliar to him that he looks as though he's come down with a terrible fever. It's a rude awakening. He fumbles around, trying to convince himself that there was glory in his action. "Was that what it was like in the old days, Will?" he asks. "Everybody riding out, shootin', smoke all over the place, folks yellin', bullets whizzin' by?"

"I can't remember. I was drunk most of the time." Munny, his face like an unsmiling skull set against the dark sky, watches a rider approaching from the town. Hopefully, it's their reward money coming. Hopefully, he can put this dirty business behind him. But Munny knows the truth about killing. Things rarely play out in real life the way they do in legend.

A few moments later, Munny has the bag full of cash in his hands. But the rider delivered more than the reward. There is news. Bad news. The Sheriff has captured and killed Ned Logan and put the body on display in town as a message to all hired guns. And so it goes.

Unforgiven does not deny that violence is sometimes necessary and that righteous men must intervene with force, on occasion, in order to defend the innocent. But it stares unblinking at the gravity of such endeavors. It conveys the need for conscience and understanding, and the fact that violence—even in the hands of the just—can do grievous damage not just to the villains or bystanders but also to the heart of the avenger himself.

A Violent Dissonance

By the time *Die Hard* arrived on the big screen, I had begun to think a great deal about why I was so drawn to stories of gun-toting heroes. I was learning to consider the values that a hero represented. I knew that the thrill of the hero's victory resonated with my desire to see the humble exalted over the mighty and to see the proud fall. I wanted to see oppressors overthrown and justice accomplished.

Yet I also noticed that I walked away from seeing many of these films thoroughly impressed by the "cool"—the macho attitude and cocksure gun slinging of Indiana Jones, James Bond and *Die Hard*'s John McClane.

This created a dissonance that became distracting to me. Was it wrong for me to admire these violent men and celebrate their exploits? How could I reconcile this with Christ's call in Matthew 5:44 to love our enemies and pray for those who persecute us?

All of these hero films were about a righteous underdog confronted by an intimidating goliath. All of them involved some kind of violent clash that resulted in the hero walking away triumphant and the villain either dead or damaged. The stories were generally the same. But I began to understand what Roger Ebert meant when he said, "A movie is not about what it is about. It is about how it is about it." More and more, I was seeing the same stories, but certain versions were making me very uncomfortable. I often walked away feeling burdened rather than inspired, a bit dirty rather than relieved.

Shouldn't we feel relief when the wrongly accused is vindicated? Of course. Proverbs 24:25 tells us, "But it will go well with those who convict the guilty, and rich blessing will come upon them." But it's a little harder to stomach the verses that precede this good counsel: "Do not gloat when your enemy falls; when he stumbles, do not let your heart rejoice, or the LORD will see and disapprove and turn his wrath away from him" (vv. 17-18).

Where is our attention focused as we watch stories of righteous men striving to foil the plans of evildoers? What is it that generates the "thrill of victory"?

I saw *Unforgiven* for the first time when it opened in 1992. Like so many of my favorites, this film told a story of horrific injustice and the endeavors of a few good men to right what had gone wrong. Hollywood celebrated as Clint Eastwood returned to the territory of Dirty Harry, and the Academy went on to honor the film with awards for Best Picture, Best Director, Best Supporting Actor and Best Editing. But a good deal of the film's power came from David Webb Peoples' Golden Globe-winning screenplay, which doesn't have an ounce of fat on it. Every line is necessary. Lean, mean and meaningful, *Unforgiven* has an arresting sense of focus, expertly guiding us toward its nightmarish conclusion so that we find ourselves torn between anticipating and dreading the act of justice.

That tension seized my imagination, for it vividly portrayed the very questions that had begun to trouble me. Was it ever right for me to rejoice in stories of violent retaliation? Was I hardening my heart through exposure to violence? I saw my own romantic notions about vigilantes reflected back to me. Watching movies about vengeful heroes would never be quite the same.

Violent Catharsis and Porn for Justice Junkies

Unforgiven made moviegoing more complicated for me. Was I wrong to enjoy films in which the bad guys were vanquished in a blaze of glory? Eastwood's film suggested that it has everything to do with *how* such stories were told. I began to feel dissatisfaction with those big screen heroes who would bring down fiery justice and then saunter off with that enviable cool.

In films such as *Star Wars* and *The Matrix*, the heroes participate in a fantastical representation of good versus evil, revealing the stark differences between the "good guys" and "bad guys." While the heroes stop to note the value of mercy and compassion, they also set up the cathartic moment that assures the audience that good will overcome evil and the wicked will fall victim to the poison of their pride.

In *Star Wars*, the heroes strive to find the weakness in the enemy's defenses. Luke Skywalker is able to save whole planets full of endangered lives by blasting away at a small, unnoticed weakness on the Death Star, just as Bilbo Baggins in *The Hobbit* is able to discover a break in the glittering armor of the dragon Smaug. In *The Matrix*, Neo finds that he can overcome his fear and dodge Agent Smith's bullets by achieving a supernatural peace. In *Top Gun*, Maverick has to learn a few lessons about ego in order to achieve the kind of excellence necessary to do his job. When he and his wingmen vanquish the enemy, it's a demonstration of newfound discipline and teamwork.

In these films, we cheer not for the suffering of the villains—this is only noted in passing—but in the salvation of many endangered innocents and in the growth of our heroes in wisdom.

Other films, however, draw us into more complicated territory.

* * *

In *Braveheart,* William Wallace raises an army of persecuted Scotsmen to strive against the oppression of King Edward I. We know what the cruelty of the king they call "Longshanks" has meant to Wallace. His family was killed, his wife was murdered and his countrymen have suffered greatly. We want to see him and the Scots set free.

Many moviegoers, including several friends of mine, rate *Braveheart* as one of their favorite movies. It's easy to see why. Mel Gibson's film provides massive, memorable spectacle. We feel a visceral thrill as we witness monumental courage and the hero's willingness to put his life on the line for the sake of the suffering. Wallace is a deliverer who fulfills what Christ described when He said, "Greater love hath no man than this, that a man lay down his life for his friends" (John 15:13).

Yet I found *Braveheart* wearying and worrying. Each violent sequence was designed to out-do the one before it. While I sympathized with Wallace's plight, the film's preoccupation with long battle sequences, rage and the glory of bloodied warriors sent me out of the theater exhausted and troubled. For all of the lip service given to virtue, I felt that the plot was little more than an excuse for the filmmakers to stage battlefield chaos on a whole new level. There was very little in the way of character development—the good guys were larger than life, funny and easy to support, while villains were menacing, heartless and easy to despise. (It didn't help that the film embellished the tale of Wallace's virtue by giving him the privilege of a sexual liaison with an attractive princess, all in the name of honoring his wife's memory.) Every time we approached another battle, someone seemed to hit the pause button on the storytelling, and everything onscreen became calculated to draw us to the edge of our seats. I became bored. The film was no longer interesting to me.

Fast forward to the year 2000, when Mel Gibson would star in another film that followed the same formula—*The Patriot*. Once again, we were brought into an epic in which the main character's home is violated by a powerful enemy, and he spends two or three hours of screen time doing spectacular feats of violence in order to achieve revenge. Many were heartbroken by the tragedy and inspired by the hero's victory. And rightfully so— *The Patriot* reminds us of the cost of America's independence and the courage of those who fought to free us from oppressors. But in doing so, it also focuses our attention on one man's quest to kill his enemy. The events in the film proceed so predictably that I was again bored and exhausted by the focus on choreographed violence and left wondering when we would get to the meat of the storytelling.

In the same year, *Gladiator* arrived. "Here we go again," I said to myself. "First, a great injustice is done against a virtuous man—this time his name is Maximus. He embarks on a quest to avenge himself against the authoritative villain—and this time the bad guy's name is Commodus. It's just a matter of time before we experience the catharsis of the killing blow." It all felt mechanical to me. I could not join the crowd in cheering Maximus' revenge. As he pranced around the Coliseum and shouted, "Are you entertained?" I felt that the film had reached a moment of self-realization. While I was supposed to be caring about the grief of this poor man, I was instead sitting through long exhibitions of violence styled for excitement and other scenes designed to make me despise the villain so much that I cannot wait to see him suffer.

In the review I wrote the next day, I predicted that *Gladiator* was designed to be a crowd-pleaser. I observed that it worked so powerfully on the audience that it was bound to be an Oscar-winner. Sure enough, it won Best Picture. When it did, stories of far greater depth, humor, heart, subtlety and insight—such as *You Can Count On Me, Divided We Fall, Almost Famous, Pollock, O Brother Where Art Thou?, Requiem for a Dream, Wonder Boys* and even the thoughtful but action-packed *Crouching Tiger, Hidden Dragon*—were overlooked.

And yet, when I spoke with Ralph Winter, a Christian and a film producer working in Hollywood on such intelligent action movies as *X-Men* and *X-Men 2*, I discovered that *Gladiator* really meant something to people. "*Gladiator* is inspiring," Winter told me. "It's a wonderful journey of someone who is sort of an also-ran in the process but who aspires to greatness and asks the huge questions. It *seems* to be about 'Win the crowd and win your freedom.' But I think that movie is truly about love, and not just about choosing. Even when Commodus smothers his dad, what is it that he says? 'If you would have loved me, I would have butchered the whole world.'

He wants love as well—in a different sense than Maximus—but it *is* about love at some level."

Through Winter, I was given a humbling reminder that such familiar, formulaic stories can still strike chords in the hearts of viewers. And yet, for all of its quiet observations about love, I still wonder—has *Gladiator* served to make viewers more sensitive, more concerned with love? Or is it watched over and over again for the visceral thrill of the violence and for the charge we feel when revenge is carried out?

Some films offer us heroes who show surprising flickers of conscience, conviction and restraint against their enemies. In Sam Raimi's *Spiderman*, Peter Parker musters the strength to walk away from his enemy without killing him. This choice gives him a nobility of character. But a moment later, the audience is shown the spectacular destruction of the villain anyway. This strikes me as slightly disingenuous. While it's cathartic to see the villain fall, the rush of pleasure we receive from that sight makes us quickly forget the admirable restraint shown by the hero, who denied himself such lurid satisfaction.

It happens again in *Batman Begins,* when Batman gets the upper hand in his struggle with the villain. He has an opportunity to pull the man back from certain death and deliver him to the authorities for the proper procedure of justice. "I'm not going to kill you," Batman growls, *"but I don't have to save you."* He leaps from the train, leaving the villain to die in the customary explosion.

Similarly, *V for Vendetta* gains our sympathies by portraying the oppression of a fascist government and by championing democracy and love. But in doing so, the film also asks us to cheer for a violent uprising that endangers the lives of innocents, endorses the tactics of terrorism, and results in the destruction of government buildings without any thought to "collateral damage."

Steven Spielberg's *Munich*, on the other hand, shows evidence of deep thought about the effects of violence on those who commit it. Like William Munny in *Unforgiven*, Avner becomes a battle-scarred Mossad agent, prone to nightmares after completing covert assassination assignments. And yet Avner's cause seems just—he serves Israel's retaliation for terrorist attacks. The film sends us away contemplating how easy it is to be drawn into moral compromise and how heavy the necessary burden of military violence can be.

There are other films in which the audience is invited to question the ethics of "an eye for an eye." *The Widow of St. Pierre, Mean Creek, In the Bedroom, The Limey, Blade Runner, Dead Man Walking, A History of Violence, Caché* and *Rob Roy* have become some of the most controversial and yet convicting works of recent years. Come to think of it, you'd be hard-pressed to find a more vigorous exploration of the theme than in Shakespeare's *Hamlet*, and there are plenty of film versions from which to choose.

But as films such as *Die Hard, Braveheart, Gladiator* and Peter Jackson's *The Lord of the Rings* films have raised the bar higher and higher on the intensity of big screen violence, it seems that each year brings more and more movies that, in their ambition to provide even bigger spectacles, abandon thoughtful storytelling. They avoid acknowledging moral complexities and matters of conscience. They're designed to shock, repulse and dazzle us with portrayals of cruel and unusual punishment.

There is something within each of us that wants to see our enemies suffer, and these films pour fuel on that fire without cultivating any conscience or appreciation of mercy alongside it.

How daring it was of Clint Eastwood to film Americans bravely fighting the Battle of Iwo Jima in *Flags of Our Fathers*. And what a demonstration of conscience it was for him to then tell the story again in *Letters from Iwo Jima*, considering the perspective of the Japanese. A Christlike perspective is concerned with more than justice. To love one's enemy is to consider and care about what happens to him.

*   *   *

The more I pay attention to the way in which some films play to an audience's bloodlust, the more I see how this kind of lurid entertainment reflects the strategies of pornographers. In both pursuits, the filmmakers exaggerate certain elements in order to appeal to unhealthy appetites. Both tend to cultivate hungers that increase with each occasion. It's designed to become addicting.

The hero of Tony Scott's *Man on Fire* is a former counterterrorism agent sent to Mexico City as a bodyguard for a young girl named Pita. We're told that kidnappings occur every 60 seconds in this area and that 70 percent of the victims are never rescued. This gives the film a feeling of relevance and importance, but it really boils down to a case of Big Gunslinging American Comes to Town to Settle the Score.

Right away, we sense that this bodyguard is something special. He's a struggling alcoholic with a feeble grasp on hope.

"Do you see God in the work that you do?" inquires a nun from Pita's school. "Not anymore," Creasy replies. The film looks likely to become a spiritual journey.

There's more. Creasy's initials are J.C. His hands are scarred. For Pita, he's security and a refuge. While he holds a pistol in one hand, he has a Bible in the other. Sometimes, he looks heavenward, as if searching for affirmation. Ultimately, he'll pay the ransom in order to save the captive.

And yet, *this* is the kind of Christ figure who prefers to fire a missile launcher first and ask questions later. Restraint? That's for wimps. As Creasy aims his grenade launcher out the window, targeting an oncoming car, the elderly residents of the apartment he's invaded ask him, "Doesn't the Scripture say we should forgive?" He replies, "Forgiveness is between them and God. It's my job to arrange the meeting." Cue the explosions.

Sometimes, Creasy is not content to just eliminate the enemy. This all-American hero ties them up and tortures them first. He performs these torments in a cold and calculating way, as if curious to try out new and cruel techniques on each victim. Viewers around me laughed and clapped as a villain's fingers were sliced off one by one. They cheered as he pinned explosives to his enemies. We watched as Creasy sauntered away, a picture of cool set against a backdrop of flames. This contemporary Christ figure destroys all in his path without flinching for those poor sinners and without a moment's thought to the other lives that will absorb the consequences of his wrath. As the confrontations escalate, he eventually berates a bad guy in front of a statue of Jesus on the cross, until the exchange ends in a truly unholy fashion. Creasy talks a villain into committing suicide.

With films like *Top Gun, True Romance, Enemy of the State* and *Domino*, Tony Scott has proven himself to be a powerful entertainer. He crafts films so overcrowded with sensation that they steer viewers clear of opportunities to reflect on what's happening. His editing style hypnotizes, dazzles and distracts. For many, it's a thrill in the same way that a jarring carnival ride is exhilarating.

There's nothing necessarily wrong with a roller coaster. But as I've learned more about the ways in which big screen spectacle coaxes us into different frames of mind, I've become frustrated with sensory assaults. I feel I'm being baited, in sequence after sequence, to anticipate—and eventually enjoy—an obscene display.

It's almost insulting when, in the final minutes of *Man on Fire*, Scott gives his hero a brave choice that signifies some kind of change of heart. Do we really believe that audiences will walk away admiring this man's selfless humility? After all of this "entertainment," it's hard to take seriously any conclusion that affirms Christlikeness. Imagine justifying a porn flick because the lead actress finds Jesus at the end of it. If there's such a thing as a double-minded film, *Man on Fire* is it.

A line in the trailer for *Man on Fire* betrayed that the film was being marketed to appeal to revenge fantasies. A character played by Christopher Walken says, "Creasy's art is death. He's about to paint his masterpiece." A few weeks later, the movie opened at the top of the box office.

* * *

As American forces moved into Afghanistan and Iraq for post-9/11 endeavors, it was hard to ignore the increase in the number of American movies that indulged in revenge fantasies.

First, there was *Kill Bill*, then *The Punisher* and *Walking Tall*. While some of these films were typically cathartic and cartoonish entertainment, *Man on Fire* was characterized by a certain solemn sense of importance. Viewers took it seriously—they seemed eager to cheer for any American who went out to blow up the foreign bad guys, whether or not that hero used honorable or legal procedures.

In an article posted at Blackfilm.com, Denzel Washington showed no misgivings about *Man on Fire*'s portrayal of cruel vigilante judgment. "Look at the wicked stuff they did," he says. "They deserved it."[1] In another interview, Washington noted that there seemed to be something pent up in people, particularly Americans, but he did not show any evidence of perceiving a connection between the cheers and national attitudes of anger and vengefulness.

Pondering the film's reception as a post-9/11 revenge fantasy, Tony Scott thought back to the genesis of the project and said, "I didn't think of it then that way, but the reaction to it now is making me reconsider."

Betrayed by Legends

If W.W. Beauchamp, the gunslingers' biographer in *Unforgiven*, were a screenwriter today, he might have written *Man on Fire*.

When we meet Beauchamp, he is accompanying a would-be assassin, English Bob, by train into the town of Big Whiskey. Beauchamp is so enraptured with the glory of these vigilantes that it's likely his writings have influenced the Schofield Kid's romantic notions about trigger-happy heroes.

We watch as English Bob talks big, describing his own legendary exploits with such drama that the imagination reels. Saucer-eyed, Beauchamp scribbles them down in his journal, raw material for a book he intends to publish as *The Duke of Death*.

"The *Duck* of Death," laughs Little Bill, the Big Whiskey sheriff, after he has beaten English Bob half to death and then locked him up in a holding cell. Shaken, Beauchamp can only sit and listen as the sheriff debunks tales of English Bob one by one, revealing to the writer what a wretch, a coward and a drunkard Bob really is. In doing so, of course, Little Bill begins to set himself up as the true champion of Western justice. You can hear him shift from belittling Bob to the beginnings of his own campaign to be seen as a hero. "I do not like assassins," he dramatically intones, "or men of low character." He says it boldly, but slowly, so Beauchamp can write it all down.

We have seen Little Bill's low character, however, and we know the truth. In their zeal to become the deliverer of God's judgment, men sometimes forget that they themselves depend on God's grace and can end up becoming too much like the monsters they abhor. So long as they have good PR men at their side, though, they can do damage control and make themselves the stuff of thrilling rumors. They can strike awe into the hearts of folks like the Schofield Kid.

And so it is that, long after the hollow shell of English Bob has been exported from Big Whiskey, Little Bill goes on to teach other assassins the hard lessons that he thinks they deserve. The Kid, having learned the hard way what killing is really about, sobs quietly on the hilltop, gulping down whiskey to silence his dismay.

"It's a hell of a thing, killin' a man," Munny states flatly. "Takin' away all he's got, and all he's ever gonna have."

"Yeah." The kid takes another swig of the bottle and searches for a rationalization to appease his conscience. In his mind's eye, he can see the face of the man he killed. "Well," says the kid. "I guess he had it comin'."

"We all have it comin' kid," says Munny.

Note

1. Todd Gilchrist, "Man on Fire: An Interview with Denzel Washington," Black film.com, April 2004. http://www.blackfilm.com/20040416/features/denzel.shtml (accessed November 2006).

CHAPTER SEVEN

The Least of These

I mortally and strongly defend the right of the artist to select a negative aspect of the world to portray, and as the world gets more materialistic there will be more to select from. Of course, you are only enabled to see what is black by having light to see it by. . . . Furthermore, the light you see by may be altogether outside of the work itself.

FLANNERY O'CONNOR, FROM A LETTER TO BETTY HESTER, 1956

You never know someone until you step inside their skin and walk around a little.

ATTICUS FINCH IN *TO KILL A MOCKINGBIRD*

A Scene from *The Motorcycle Diaries*

Ernesto has gone down to the river.

The doctors and nurses, dancing and celebrating Ernesto's birthday, forget for a moment to look for the guest of honor. He has stolen away into the evening. He is on the boat dock, staring across the quiet, flowing Amazon River. His gaze is so intent that it might just burn away the foggy veil. He stands at attention as though summoned by a clarion call.

He's experienced so much. The journey. Encounters with needy people along the road. A letter—the kind that breaks a lover's heart. Hunger. Asthma attacks. The comfort of strangers. A motorcycle breakdown. So many miles and faces. So much fear and injustice. And it has all been leading to this.

Behind him, up the slope, the shelter glows. The celebrants inside are intoxicated not only by the music, but by Ernesto's farewell speech as well. Tomorrow he will leave the mission to find his future as a doctor. So before he slipped away from the dancing, he raised a glass—to thank the people who taught him so much about tending to the sick and to thank his traveling companion Alberto Granado, a 29-year-old biochemist. He then challenged them all to work together for a better future. It was his own personal "I Have a Dream" speech, offering them a vision of a day when the people who live and work the land will be free from abuse and governmental neglect. He believes that someday their country will not be divided by civil strife, but united with common national pride.

When Ernesto first set out from home, he was just a boy on a journey, rocketing into the unknown on Alberto's motorcycle. Now he's emerging from the chrysalis of his experience, a leader of passion and conviction.

Before him, the Amazon River rushes past, indifferent.

The river divides the homes of the compassionate caretakers from the camp of the 600 lepers they serve. Unlike the staff and nuns of the mission, Ernesto believes that walls are to be climbed, barriers are to be crossed, and divisions are to be denied. On his arrival in the colony, he refuses the protective gloves the nuns instruct him to wear. Instead, he holds the hands of the dying, talks with them in the dim light and the hush, and plays soccer with those who can run. He becomes the lepers' friend. And now, here, he's responding to the tug, the gravity of that need beyond the river. He is thinking of those who are forbidden from attending the celebration.

Alberto finds him there on the dock. "What's wrong?" he asks with the trepidation of someone accustomed to Ernesto's impulsive compassion. Earlier in their journey, Alberto challenged Ernesto to swim out into a lake, and the wet and the cold had brought on an asthma attack so intense that Ernesto barely survived. Thus, this sight of his friend toeing the edge of the water is cause for grave concern.

"Where is the boat?" Ernesto asks absently. Alberto does not know. He wants Ernesto to come back inside to the party.

Only the wide Amazon, its strong currents fraught with lurking predators, lies in the way. No one crosses it after dark. And no one ever swims. Ernesto takes off his jacket.

Missionary Horror Films

Reading the summary of *Born into Brothels,* I thought back to the Sunday evening churches of my childhood. Seated next to my parents on red-cushioned pews, I filled the time by scribbling cartoons in the margins of the church bulletin, less than interested in hearing the second sermon of the day.

But during those occasional services when missionaries came to visit, I put away the cartoon. A testimony from missionaries usually included a slideshow. I remember looking at the images from exotic, faraway lands such as New Guinea, Haiti, the Dominican Republic or Calcutta as they flickered with devastation and despair.

The missionaries had come from the field—which, in the slideshow, looked more like a wilderness—in order to impress on us the need for funding and humanitarian aid. Photographs were their most powerfully persuasive tools. Figures in the pictures did not even look human—such deformed, malnourished children. And then there were the skeletal adults hooked up to IVs, flesh as frail as cellophane wrapping their bones, protruding bellies shiny and spherical.

I wondered if R-rated movies were as scary as this. Even now, I flinch at such images of decay. So it was with a professional journalist's burden of responsibility that I dragged myself off to see *Born into Brothels*, a film focusing on the poverty-stricken city of Calcutta.

Did I really *need* to watch another movie about such suffering? Feeling the pressure of a busy work week, I was inclined to avoid it. I already knew a few things about the troubles of abuse, drugs, crime and prostitution there. I knew that the girls, if they survive a traumatic childhood, can look forward to following in their mothers' footsteps and sleeping with lustful, drunken, drug-wrecked men for a living. Most of the boys end up drowning the memories of their childhoods in alcohol and drugs, and they perpetuate the prostitution with the girls they once played with as children. I doubted that there was much more I needed to know.

Couldn't I just donate the price of the ticket to the cause, skip the movie, and go see something more enjoyable instead?

Zana's Crossing

There must have been a moment when photographer Zana Briski, the director of the Oscar-winning documentary *Born into Brothels*, walked down to her own personal Amazon River and faced the darkness. Behind her was a bill-paying job as a photographer with *The Baltimore Sun*. But she could feel something pulling her forward toward fathomless need.

In an *LA Weekly* article by Andrew Mann published January 20, 2005, I learned how Briski, a biology major at Cambridge, took a leap of conscience. Animal experimentation proved unconscionable to her, so she switched to something different—theology. And then, on New Year's Day 1995, in a similar spasm of conscience, she quit her newspaper job.

Briski said, "*The Sun* would have me shoot some woman who just finished a quilt. Or somebody's cow. . . . It was awful. And meanwhile, there were gang wars going on down the block. But they didn't want to know about that."

The next day, Briski was airborne, India-bound. She testifies that the decision to go to that nation was a choice to live in the world rather than to retreat. Her new plan was to live with the prostitutes in the red-light district of Calcutta—women ranging in age from young teens to grandmothers, standing elbow to elbow in "the line," advertising themselves to the appetites of the weak-willed men who hunch under the weight of various addictions. She would photograph them, document their daily realities for the world and try to help them.

She must have felt some of what Christ felt before entering a city—that premonition of immeasurable pain and the knowledge that her words and endeavors would only mean something to those with eyes to see and ears to hear. She jumped in anyway.

India had never been her dream destination. The crowds and the chaos made it the last place on earth she wanted to go. "But I couldn't do anything else," she said. "The alternative would have been death."[1]

The prospect could have overwhelmed her. But Briski worked hard to find a way into that chaos and squalor, finally convincing a brothel owner to give her a room. We can be grateful for her efforts and for what happened next. The result was a film called *Born into Brothels* that revealed the treasure of vibrant lives swept under the world's carpet.

If we allow that still, small voice to coach our decisions, we never know where it will take us. Like Briski, we can't know how it will turn out before we do it. Faith is the assurance of things hoped for, the conviction of things not seen. It's going to be risky. It's going to be scary. What transpires may not bear any resemblance to what we imagined. But we must remember that the voice that's calling us hasn't told us everything. This isn't about our vision. It's about something bigger—and better.

Art-making is like that. If the artist sits down to work knowing full well what the message will be, she may be confining the work, which has a life of its own. In an interview with *Mars Hill Review*, the poet Scott Cairns said, "I think writers with actual intentions generally end up saying things they already thought they knew, and I'm not much interested in reducing my vocation as a poet to something like propagandist. I write poems to find things out, not to communicate some previously ossified conclusion."[2]

Briski's endeavors led her to a conclusion she could not have anticipated. Once she arrived among these needy women, she realized that she would have to deal with the children, who were everywhere. And, as children will, they became curious about her and the camera she carried. They wanted to take pictures too, just like "Auntie Zana." She suddenly caught a glimpse of a whole new idea. In an inspired gesture, Briski handed out point-and-shoot cameras to the children and sent them running amok through the whorehouses, alleys and streets.

When she sent her initial footage to her former boyfriend, photographer Ross Kaufman, he too made the leap. And an ambitious project began in earnest.

Surprised by Joy in the Brothels

Three years later, having seen *Born into Brothels* four times, I find myself sitting on a panel in front of an audience as the lights come up. They've just seen the film. I see a lot of tissues being drawn from pockets and purses. But I see a lot of smiles as well.

"Dreams of Our Childhood"—that's the theme for this year's University Presbyterian Church film festival. Jennie Spohr, who's so excited that you might mistake the event for her birthday party, chose the theme, selecting six films that would give us a child's-eye view of the world.

The Sixth Sense put us in the childlike perspectives of heroes who could see more, or at least differently, than the rest of us. *Big Fish* reminded us of the value of seeing our lives through a lens of imagination, as grand stories of romance and comedy. The children in *To Kill a Mockingbird* learned about courage and virtue as their father took an unpopular stand in a courtroom. All these made sense.

But *Born into Brothels*? It seemed an unlikely choice—not the kind of film to draw a crowd.

And yet, it *did* draw a small crowd. And when the time came for questions from the audience, several viewers raised their hands. A microphone was passed to a man who sat blinking in bewilderment. "I came here expecting to see *The Sixth Sense*," he said. (To be fair, there had been a mix-up in the schedule posted online—this hadn't been a subversive way of drawing an audience.) "I had decided not to bother with *Born into Brothels*. It was a sunny day, and I felt the subject was too depressing, too heavy, for me to spend my afternoon on. But when the film started I was so surprised by the joyfulness. I didn't expect that. I didn't expect to see so much joy."

Joy. It's everywhere in *Born into Brothels*, leaping out at you giddily like neon lights in dark tavern windows.

Jennie knew, as I and so many others have discovered, that Zana Briski's documentary is bursting with joyful surprises and unforgettable characters. She knew that the darkness of the context only makes the lights flare out all the brighter, making this a veritable Fourth of July extravaganza.

Disease? Check. Addiction? Check. The men in this film are meandering wraiths. Their eyes, clouded, unseeing, distorted, remind me of those essence-drained pod people in *The Dark Crystal*, or worse—the rage-infected zombies of Danny Boyle's *28 Days Later*.

Sexual abuse? Everywhere. But the women sell themselves because they have no options.

Neglected children? On every corner, climbing on the rooftops, scurrying up and down the stairs of the brothel. There will not be any hero who can save them with a bullwhip and a gun.

But no, *Born into Brothels* doesn't seek to guilt-trip anybody into saving the world. Instead, it introduces us to several imaginative children, and they give us total access to their secret worlds. From the housetops to the waste-stained corners, we watch them chase down the men who left without paying, sit on dirt floors and scrub pots, and scream as hot-tempered mothers drag them down the corridors and refuse them opportunities to escape.

As I watch those images go by, I'm reminded of the effect of the beautiful, sad music on that stubborn, wounded camel that I wrote about earlier. Even sinful behavior, seen through the lens of a child, can tune the delicate instruments of our hearts so that we see things the way they should be. By giving us beauty with the ugliness, joy with the pain, laughter with the groans, these revelations give us a vision more complete and more affecting than any slideshow of poverty and pain half a world away.

That was Briski's stroke of genius: Don't just show us the children. Show us what the children see . . . and how they see it.

I can't remember ever seeing a congregation respond like this to a slideshow about suffering children. Sure, occasionally God uses an image of suffering to call out someone in the pews, to encourage them to sign up for the next trip. And that invitation is usually spelled out in the film. Christians know better than anybody how to get a message out. It's easy to react to abrupt jolts of horror by tossing coins into an offering plate or getting in line to sign up for a mailing list.

But *Born into Brothels* isn't a message movie. It picks us up out of our daily details, plants us in a specific dark alley, and leads us to a specific address. It leaves us there to get our bearings and asks us to pay attention so that we can distinguish one child from the next. Before long, we shift from marveling at Briski's bravery to feeling instead that we would travel to meet these children if we could.

That hopeful vision is contagious. At the end, we want to know more. Where are these children today? Is the Kids-with-Cameras project still going on? Can we help?

While a solemn documentarian might have focused on Calcutta's dark alleys like a surgeon exposing tumors in a dying body, Briski doesn't feel the need to make the camera linger on spectacles of suffering. She expands the frame, capturing their laughter, expletive-punctuated tantrums, embraces, beatings, sweat of hard work and exhilaration of a trip to the beach. And when they take the kids on a trip to the zoo, Briski and Kaufman don't need to comment on the sight of animals trapped behind bars. The metaphors speak for themselves.

Kenneth Turan of *The Los Angeles Times* says that *Born into Brothels* "will reorder the worldview of whoever sees it" and declares that it "demands to be experienced not just because of the good it does but because of how unexpectedly good, even buoyant, it makes you feel."[3]

A Scene from *The Five Obstructions*

"I'd like to put your ethics to the test," filmmaker Lars von Trier tells his former instructor, Jorgen Leth, in his documentary *The Five Obstructions*.

Von Trier lays down a challenge for his beloved filmmaking mentor. He asks Leth to remake one of his earlier short films, a philosophical piece called *The Perfect Human*. In fact, Von Trier asks him to remake the film five times, using five completely different styles. But Von Trier gets to set the constraints on each version. That's the condition of the challenge.

Von Trier playfully suggests that he wants to cause his teacher to fail. He endeavors to place almost impossible constraints on the project. But as *The Five Obstructions* proves again and again, artists can flourish when given restraints. Leth's seemingly impossible tasks reveal the strength of his formidable artistic vision. Each time he remakes the film, it's more impressive. Leth is invigorated, and Von Trier diabolically plots another impossible task.

One of Von Trier's challenges does put Leth's ethics to the test, to be sure. He tells Leth, "I'd like to send you to the most miserable place on Earth. It's up to you to define the most miserable place. . . . I want you to go close to a few really harrowing things. Dramas from real life that you refrain from filming. . . . And when you come back, you have to tell the story."

Leth accepts the challenge. He will remake his film, which includes a scene of a wealthy man in a tuxedo eating a gourmet meal. He will film this scene on Falkland Road, in Bombay. Leth describes this Bombay neighborhood as "a horror beyond compare. The kind of thing you run away from screaming." He keeps valium on hand, in case the situation becomes too "enervating."

Wearing a tuxedo, Leth seats himself at a table with a white tablecloth and an elegant place setting. He opens a bottle of

Chablis. To all the world, he looks like a rich man dining alone in a fine restaurant.

But behind him, a screen—slightly transparent—is stretched, creating a wall between him and his environment. When you begin to observe the shapes, colors and movement beyond the screen, your stomach may turn against you. Leth is eating this exquisite meal in the midst of the poverty and desperation of Bombay's red-light district. Fish, rice, onions, lemon and a green sauce. He's in the middle of the street, and the suffering residents of the neighborhood are watching him through the screen.

"The wine looks splendid in the glass," says the detached narrator, while Leth sips it and savors it. Behind him, stage right, young children marvel at the sight.

"How does the perfect human eat?" the narrator muses.

An ethical test indeed. Arguably an example of inhumane filmmaking. And yet, it is worth considering the effect of such imagery on an audience. How do we respond to such indulgent behavior when people in great need are seen in the frame? Is this more or less moral than adventure films made in desperate regions where the camera stays trained on its glamorous stars and hides from us the impact of their visit?

The scene haunts me. I think of it when I notice something I've purchased was made in a poverty-stricken country. I feel the presence through the screen. Is it more moral to proceed with our habits, turning a blind eye to the impact on the impoverished? My initial response has been completely revised—*The Five Obstructions* is a profound, honest and challenging piece of filmmaking.

Leth describes the experience, admitting that he was "cold-blooded" to agree to such an activity. He also admits that in the days following the experiment, he was haunted by nightmares and felt as though he had made a Faustian bargain . . . selling something of his soul in order to prove his lack of boundaries.

Matthew's House

"Why does your teacher sit at a table and eat with such people?"

The Pharisee's question probably caused an uncomfortable silence. That would be the desired effect. Standing there in the doorway of Matthew the tax collector's home, he wanted to remind everyone about the obvious order of things: A righteous man should keep his distance from those commonly regarded as immoral. A righteous man should spend his time in the Temple, not at a table with cheaters and swindlers.

What kind of troublemaker went around touching lepers and blind people, shaking hands with thieves and scoundrels, dining with manipulators and those who routinely break the law?

Jesus replied directly, "It is not the healthy who need a doctor, but the sick. But go and learn what this means: 'I desire mercy, not sacrifice.' For I have not come to call the righteous, but sinners" (Matt. 9:12-14).

So, what's it going to be? Jesus implied. Are we going to say that we are not sinners? Are we going to separate ourselves from these people and stay on the other side of the river? Or are we going to admit that we too are sinners, erase these false boundaries, and join Him at the table with other criminals?

The Pharisees could not stand the thought of crossing the river. They could not bear the idea that they, too, were unclean and crooked. They had to keep up appearances, so they departed, furious at having failed to separate Christ from His true mission.

This Nazarene, if His claims were true, had all sorts of good reasons to stay on the other side of the great divide between heaven and earth. While He was in essence God, He did not regard His heavenly privilege as something to be grasped.

It was not enough for Him to send a donation to the needy. He did not appease His conscience by saying a token prayer for the lost. He didn't create a congregation out of His disciples and start Wednesday night casual gatherings and all manner of programs to attract target audiences, hoping the needy would come to join Him of their own volition. He did not decide to help them by lashing out with violence against their oppressors, leading a ragtag band of warriors in face paint. And He did not set conditions for the needy, saying that He would walk away if they spoke profanity, behaved inappropriately or had the wrong sexual orientation.

No, as a good shepherd, He went out to find them and loved the sick, the weak, the appalling, the offensive, the reckless, the foul-mouthed, the addicted.

He allowed the Pharisees to express their reservations and then made His choice. The truth was plain to see for those willing to see it.

Branded, Condemned, Overlooked

In 2005 when *Born into Brothels* played in selected theaters around the United States, Americans had the chance to see a true hero story that had been inspiring audiences around the world. Of course, that doesn't mean Americans *did* see the film. It didn't have a massive marketing campaign or superstars. Without television commercials or fast-food tie-ins, it came and went quietly from the art house theaters.

Zana Briski didn't use revolvers, grenades or bullwhips. No, we don't get to see her foil the plans of a child molester or drag a gang lord away in chains. There's no moment when the persecuted children hurry out into the bright daylight of freedom, putting their dark days behind them. But the film did show us *real* slaves and a *real* slave-saving hero. It did give us a model for how to embed ourselves in the world as God's agents.

Viewers may assume that the movie will teach them about the need to rescue Calcutta's poor, trapped, miserable children. But they're likely to discover by the end of the film that the opposite has also occurred—the children have actually delivered the audience from a false and crippling perspective.

At the UPC screening of *Born into Brothels*, the woman seated next to me on the discussion panel was Jacquelline Cobb Fuller, a representative of the International Justice Mission who has worked to help the women and children trapped in the conditions portrayed in the film. Fuller praised Zana Briski for the courage it took to create such a project and also for her artistry. Having seen these nightmares up close, she was grateful for *Born into Brothels* and told the audience that we need more movies like it.

I can remember the celebration of Christian media voices across the country when *The Passion of the Christ* ruled the box office. They heralded the beginning of a new era when meaningful films reflecting the call of Christ would come to the big screen. Such exhilaration strikes me as strange when I consider that *Born into Brothels* was celebrated worldwide and won an Oscar, yet the religious press remained almost silent on the film. I have not heard of any congregations gathering to discuss *Born into Brothels* or its revelatory call to action. Even today, I'm hard-pressed to find the film reviewed or even mentioned in Christian publications or in the archives of Christian film-review websites. However, many of those same publications regularly cover forgettable comedies and empty action flicks, even offering interviews and heavy coverage to forgettable releases like the shoddy remake of *Around the World in 80 Days* or the sequel to *Garfield: The Movie.*

Why was the Christian media almost silent when Terry George's *Hotel Rwanda*, another tale of inspiring Christlike courage and sacrifice, reached the big screen? Perhaps it is because we're uncomfortable with the present-day relevance of films like this—movies that remind us of our responsibility as the Body of Christ.

The Motorcycle Diaries, meanwhile, was condemned by the few Christian press outlets that reviewed it—not because of anything wrong with the film, but because Ernesto grew up to become Che Guevara. One reviewer called the film one of the "most unbearable" movies of 2004 because of its glorification of a "political terrorist."

But *The Motorcycle Diaries* does not glorify the violent endeavors of Che Guevara. The revolution, its character and its consequences are still far off at the end of the film. In fact, the filmmakers go out of their way to raise the question about the wisdom of Guevara's later exploits. In its closing moments, Ernesto asks, "Was our view too narrow, too biased, too hasty? Were our conclusions too rigid?"

It's tragic to think of how young Ernesto became instrumental in making Cuba a communist state. The intimate concerns of a tenderhearted doctor would be replaced by the violence of a rifle-wielding revolutionary. As Roger Ebert wrote, "[Che Guevara] was a right-winger disguised as a communist. He said he loved the people but he did not love their freedom of speech, their freedom to dissent or their civil liberties. Cuba has turned out more or less as he would have wanted it to."[4] A friend of mine compared this story to the mythic transformation of Anakin Skywalker into Darth Vader.

Communist propaganda clearly plays no part in *The Motorcycle Diaries*. It is the story of youthful idealism, of how a young man's conscience awakens to the needs of the world around him. What remains is the idea that we can help heal the world if we, like Christ, humble ourselves to serve. We are reminded that even compassion can go wrong when it is compromised.

The Motorcycle Diaries is just one of hundreds of worthwhile films that have been unnecessarily and unfortunately condemned by Christian film critics. But there is another reason we overlook vital artistic vision. Sometimes we just aren't paying attention.

Intimate knowledge of those who are different from ourselves is essential if we are to cultivate the kind of care and love that we see in the story of Ernesto or in the work done by Zana Briski. Like Christ, these people got involved, conversed, touched, and asked questions. They visited the orphans and the widows. They ministered to these "little ones."

If we open ourselves to art that introduces us to perspectives and experiences of people around the world, we begin to close the distance. We draw closer to understanding our neighbors. Following Briski and Ernesto into their river, we may surface in a different place, baptized by beauty and changed by truth.

Notes

1. Andrew Mann, "People, Chaos, Everything," *LA Weekly*, January 20, 2005. http://www.laweekly.com/film+tv/film/people-chaos-everything/1050/ (accessed November 2006).
2. Brent Short, "Interview: Poet Scott Cairns," *Mars Hill Review*, Fall 1996, issue 6, pp. 140-143.
3. Kenneth Turan, "Movie Review: 'Born into Brothels,'" *Los Angeles Times*, January 28, 2005.
4. Robert Ebert, *The Motorcycle Diaries* movie review, *Chicago Sun-Times*, October 1, 2004. http://rogerebert.suntimes.com/apps/pbcs.dll/article?AID=/20041001/REVIEWS/40920008/1023 (accessed November 2006).

PART THREE

Fools and Jokers

CHAPTER
EIGHT

Suffering Fools Gladly

The fool doth think he is wise, but the wise man
doth know himself to be a fool.

<small>TOUCHSTONE IN WILLIAM SHAKESPEARE'S *AS YOU LIKE IT*</small>

I'm the janitor of God . . .

<small>PARRY IN *THE FISHER KING*</small>

Parry the Knight

Truth can explode in a split-second, knock you off balance, strike you speechless and leave you searching for comfort. One man, Saul, fell to the ground, and stood back up a whole new person. The experience transformed him, and his subsequent adventures seemed like foolishness to those who did not share his new perspective.

Most of us only catch occasional glimmers of the glory beyond human apprehension. We glance over our shoulders with a strange sense that someone might be following us. Or we glance skyward during a time of trouble in hopes that someone up there is watching. But if we stop and think seriously about how our lives would change if we could apprehend the movement of angels and see the things that God has kept from our senses, we're likely to say, "No, thank you. I have enough trouble coping with what I *can* perceive." In Scripture, when someone is exposed to more truth than he or she ordinarily beholds, that person either falls on his or her face in shame, walks around glowing for a while, or starts writing things like the book of Revelation.

Once in a while, when a person suffers a trauma or becomes dramatically inspired, it knocks that person's sanity sideways. He or she gets banged up pretty badly but emerges raving about the encounter. Like Roy Neary in *Close Encounters of the Third Kind*, that person is not fit for family conversation anymore. But he or she does, indeed, have something to show us.

As I look back on the films that have moved me most, I find that many of them are not about heroes at all. The characters that have meant the most to me have often been downright foolish. In fact, some of them seem to be out of their minds. These characters serve a similar purpose—they inspire us, they reveal things to us, they expose our lack and our need. But they do so through aberrant behavior, making us uncomfortable, demanding that we attempt to understand the way they see the world.

If I am confronted with bizarre behavior on the street or on the bus, I am likely to cross at the nearest crosswalk or get up and move closer to the bus driver. But in the safety of my theater seat, I sometimes find that these characters reveal a great deal not only through their ranting but also by the way they provoke people around them to all manner of revealing behavior.

* * *

Shock-radio D.J. Jack Lucas stands beneath the Manhattan Bridge, with cement blocks strapped to his feet. He's looking down at the rushing river, ready to give up for good. Taking one last swig of whiskey in order to numb his shame, Jack makes plans to ensure that he will never come to his senses again. He's going to complete his fall from fame and fortune.

What has brought Jack to this point? The arrogant words he spoke in a live broadcast. In fact, it would be his final show. In a rant about the hedonism of wealthy New York yuppies, Jack inadvertently inspired a sociopath to go on a killing spree at a popular restaurant. Since the gunman then killed himself, Jack himself has become public enemy number one.

So here he stands, ready to punish himself in a permanent way. But no, God has other plans. Before Jack knows it, he's dragged back from the brink and down into the life of a homeless man named Parry, who fancies himself to be a knight of the Round Table.

Parry's quite a case. When he's not talking to the "little people," who apparently float around invisibly, giving him career counsel, he's talking about the cosmic struggle in which he's playing a part.

"You seem to be some kind of vigilante," Jack muses.

"That happens along the way, of course," says Parry, dropping to one knee and brandishing a makeshift sword. "I'm a knight. On a special quest."

Jack blinks, uncomprehending. Then Parry's rapture is broken, his mad smile quivering slightly. He adds, with a hint of fear and desperation, *"And I need help."*

Parry explains that he has been charged with a sacred quest—to find the Holy Grail. Parry knows his stuff. He was once a professor of medieval literature. He understands that the Grail is a symbol of God's divine grace. The only thing standing between him and the solace he desires is fear, manifested in the form of the Red Knight.

As Parry drags Jack along New York streets in pursuit of the fiery devil he sees in his mind, Jack tries to get to the root of the vagrant's madness. When he does, his own sins find him out. Parry's beautiful wife was gunned down at the restaurant. Parry's fractured mind is the result of Jack's broadcast bile. Collapsing into the comfort of his girlfriend, Anne, Jack cries, "I wish there was some way I could just pay the fine and go home."

Jack will slowly come to understand that redemption isn't about karma or paying a fine. It'll take more than a favor to make things right with Parry. Jack will have to step into Parry's perspective of the world. In attempting to heal the man, he'll learn to speak that imaginative language and catch a glimpse of things that will address his own longings as well. The rantings of this unhygienic, holy fool will lead him along a path to peace.

A Grand Tradition of Foolishness

In 1992, on the one-hundredth anniversary of J.R.R. Tolkien's birth, I sat in the office of a literature professor at Seattle Pacific University and asked for his perspective on Tolkien's contributions to literature and imagination. He thought for a moment, making a tent with his fingers, as professors so often do to signify deep thought. The first thing he said caught me off guard.

"His wife must have been an extraordinary person. It would have required incredible patience to live with a madman like that."

I bristled. Tolkien was such a hero of mine that the word "madman" sounded at first like an insult. But my professor went on to explain that artists who have such momentous vision often find themselves consumed by it, losing touch with the world around them to some degree. Tolkien, he said, had become a fool in the eyes of his peers and must have been a difficult person to befriend.

It's likely that Tolkien's ability to slip out the back door of the real world was learned as a survival mechanism after the trauma of losing his parents at a young age. Later, during World War I, Tolkien lost two of his closest friends in the Battle of Sommes. And when he went back to visit his childhood home, he found that industrialization had polluted its natural glory and torn it apart. His fantasy stories became a form of escape.

When others questioned the wisdom of such escape, Tolkien responded, "Why should a man be scorned if, finding himself in prison, he tries to get out and go home?" For him, escape was not denial, nor was it madness. It was an escape into a simpler world of ordinary things in which the escapist could gain perspective and open himself to insights that can be crowded out by the chaos of the modern, manmade world.

Grief and trauma are frequently seen as the provocation to acts of creative genius. Unable to find relief from his immediate pain, an artist may concoct an alternate reality where he can find his way through the crisis indirectly. By imagining the experiences of characters in trials of their own, he can find his way to the healing that he needs.

Just like Parry. And by entering into Parry's conflict, Jack might find a way to his own salvation.

*　*　*

The more I thought about Tolkien's escapism, the more I began to understand my own inclinations. I had not suffered any traumatic loss or grief. Not yet. But I did perceive the world as having gone horribly wrong. That seemed obvious to me from an early age, confirmed by my lifelong exposure to the biblical stories of sin, consequences and the longing for a paradise we have lost.

How many times had I heard a pastor exhort the congregation that faith in Christ would make us seem like fools to the rest of the world? "God chose the foolish things of the world to shame the wise; God chose the weak things of the world to shame the strong. He chose the lowly things of this world and the despised things—and the things that are not—to nullify the things that are," wrote the apostle Paul in 1 Corinthians 1:27-28. When we live with the assurance of things hoped for, the conviction of things not seen, we live with one foot planted in an unseen world.

Perhaps that is why, as I grew up with the movies, my interests shifted from the courage of heroes to the bizarre behavior of fools who possessed a vision that confounded their friends and neighbors. Eric Liddell refused to run for Olympic gold on the Sabbath. Others called him an idiot. But he was a sane person. Others who inspired me were not so stable. Their understanding of greater things made them living contradictions, so that their misbehavior seemed to grow right alongside their understanding of perfection.

Mozart made me uncomfortable from the moment he appeared in Milos Forman's *Amadeus*, crawling around under the skirts of a giggling young woman and making crass jokes. It's easy to sympathize with the grand court composer Salieri, who works so hard to compose something beautiful and then watches as God blesses this bawdy rabble-rouser with a hundred times more talent than a lifetime of study could deliver. So Salieri turns against God. "From now on we are enemies, You and I. Because You choose for Your instrument a boastful, lustful, smutty, infantile boy and give me only the ability to recognize the incarnation."

Meanwhile, Mozart scampers about, a cackling fool, romancing the women that Salieri, with all of his sophistication, cannot seduce. Then, without confession, without even a blink, the little hedonist steps into the grand auditorium to perform for the king with unprecedented virtuosity. "God was singing through this little man to all the world," Salieri laments, "making my defeat more bitter with every passing bar."

Salieri unwittingly demonstrates for us the purpose of holy fools. God employs them to reveal that He showers grace on everyone so that none of us may boast. Holy fools humble us, and remind us of our depravity by speaking thoughts we would contain and doing things that embarrass us. Further, they remind us of glory and how far we fall short.

*   *   *

The Fisher King's Parry is not so much a hero as he is a participant in a grand literary tradition.

Any conversation about the history of "holy fools" will take us back to Shakespeare's plays—to Falstaff, Hamlet and King Lear's fool, who tempts the king's wrath with his constant, brash truth-telling. Lear loved the fool, because that ranting buffoon served as a voice of conscience, keeping him from losing his grip on wisdom. But in the end, Lear's willingness to be swayed by the deceit of others took the fool, and much more, away from him. As a result, he crumbled, taking on the fool's perspective. Somehow, this madman's presence was linked to the preservation of all that was beautiful and honorable in the king's world.

Of course, holy fools were not an invention of Shakespeare. They have been the agents of revelation in mythology for ages. Even certain saints qualify. Paul and his fellow apostles were fools for the sake of Christ. Saint Francis of Assisi caused a few memorable scenes with glory on his mind. These individuals weren't blind fools like Parry; they knew what they were doing. But they were inspired to acts of outrageous humility, illustrating the kind of faith that the rest of us lack.

Holy fools figure prominently in Russian literature, notably in the novels of Fyodor Dostoyevsky. Fools such as the deformed Lucynell Carter of "The Life You Save May Be Your Own" play essential roles in the shocking stories of Flannery O'Connor.

Today, they continue to show up on the big screen. In two of cinema's greatest treasures, Akira Kurosawa's *Ikiru* and Robert Bresson's *Au Hasard Balthazar*, seemingly-foolish characters highlight the wickedness of everyone around them. (Interestingly, both films are believed to have been inspired by Dostoyevsky's *The Idiot*.) In *One Flew Over the Cuckoo's Nest*, *Finding Neverland* and *Nurse Betty*, these characters stir up trouble for the strict, the proud, the uptight and the overly rational. Some of these characters are deliberate clowns. Mel Gibson and Kenneth Branagh perform wonderfully manipulative insanity in film versions of *Hamlet*.

Parry himself lives in the imagination of director Terry Gilliam, who is preoccupied with these half-mad characters. They appear not only in *The Fisher King* and *The Adventures of Baron Munchausen* but also in the dark, strange, sci-fi thrillers *Twelve Monkeys*, *The Brothers Grimm* and *Tideland*.

The memorable documentary *Lost in La Mancha* reveals Gilliam's personal obsession with the greatest ranting madman in all of literature: Don Quixote. Gilliam's interest in the character shows the director to be a sort of real-world holy fool himself—his artistic endeavors often frustrate his more practical collaborators. There are glimmers of genius in all of his work, but when he has the resources to follow his vision, we're treated to some of the big screen's most memorable and meaningful visions.

Chumps for Gump

I have heard people complain that they were put off by *The Fisher King's* Parry because of his foul mouth and bawdy behavior. It is true that most of us would step slowly away if we encountered him on the street.

The archetype of the fool is often cleaned up in popular entertainment, sentimentalized so that we can laugh in his company without being profoundly challenged by the implications of his behavior. He's endearing and, perhaps, able to nudge us with a little wisdom here and there. But we want him to keep his feet on the ground.

We love *Forrest Gump*'s title character. Gump is adorable in the way he can recite one of Mama's platitudes for every occasion. Furthermore, he ends up quite successful. There's no suggestion that he might actually need special guidance or care to help him manage in a life of arrested development. Nor is there any evidence that he apprehends or points to any greater spiritual reality. Rather, Gump possesses the common sense that those around him seem to lack. In its lighter moments, I appreciate the film's whimsy, but at times it feels as though it's leaning into self-importance, suggesting that things are really very simple when, in fact, some things are too complex to be addressed with Gumpish (Gumpian? Is there an adjectival form of "Gump"?) maxims.

Similarly, in *Radio*, a small-town football coach learns important lessons—"winning isn't everything," and so on—from his experiences with a mentally disabled young man who exhibits unparalleled passion for the sport. Radio's childlike preoccupation is endearing. It's easy to see that the young man's dedication to the local team is motivated, in part, by his need to belong to some kind of family. But when psychologists come along offering some professional care to help the young man with his disability, they are quickly defined as villains. And when the school principal questions the wisdom of allowing Radio to be perceived as a sort of unofficial "mascot," the coach is outraged at the suggestion.

The filmmakers seem desperate to escape any suggestion that Radio might benefit from any help. We like him the way he is—cute and cuddly and capable of reminding us of the simple things. This strikes me as a rather self-interested perspective. Radio may be gentle and perceptive in his own way, but wouldn't it be in his best interest if we considered the possibility of help that goes beyond warm, friendly moral support?

I'm much more challenged by the example of *Rain Man*, in which Raymond is a complicated character whose positive effect on those around him rings truer because he is allowed to be difficult and flawed.

In *The Fisher King*, Parry's grasp of a greater, redeeming truth feels authentic to me because Parry himself is abrasive, alarming, fractured and more fully human. Knee-deep in denial, he fails to grasp the simple demands of basic hygiene and propriety. He seems to have no pride, no sense of self. He speaks his mind without hesitation, obscenities and all. Meeting Jack's girlfriend, Parry immediately makes sexual advances without understanding that he is out of line. His ideas about how God is communicating to him involve elaborate visions that occur during "particularly satisfying bowel movements."

But to me, Parry's recklessness is key to his revelatory capacities. As is the case with many of art's greatest lunatics, the wisdom that comes from his visions is accompanied by an exaggeration of his human failings. Caught up in his second sight, he becomes rather oblivious to the effects of his behavior on others. Some of the great fools, as Hamlet proves to be, behave in this manic fashion more deliberately and strategically in order to unsettle those around them and lure wrongdoers into exposing their devices. Whether or not they know what they're doing, these characters flaunt their flaws, reminding us of our own even as they point us toward a perfection we cannot reach.

Because of his lack of self-knowledge, Parry is able to grasp realities that we miss in our agendas and busyness. But he is in need of healing. He represents the other end of the pendulum swing of human nature. Behaving as an exaggerated opposite of Jack Lucas, he draws Jack closer and closer toward the center, where they can both regain stability.

My attraction to the revelations these characters provide probably has its roots in Scripture, where God often chose to lead us through fools who were clearly short of perfection. When they pursued their calling, those around them could only stare and shake their heads, uncomprehending. Noah built an ark, the prophet Hosea married a prostitute, poor suffering Job refused to curse God, and John the Baptist ate bugs in the wilderness. They all experienced doubt. They all had things to learn. Yet their unconventional behavior drew attention to their vision, which conveys essential truth.

But if there is one holy fool in the history of cinema who best exemplifies the term—one that continues to challenge, discomfort and inspire me so that I seek his presence frequently—it is Johannes, the strange and difficult man who claims to be Jesus even though he's living on a farm in the West Jutland territory, the same corner of the world where Babette served her feast.

Johannes the Prophet

"A corpse in the front living room!" Thus sayeth Johannes in Carl Dreyer's 1955 classic, *Ordet*.

This wandering, deranged prophet has become my favorite holy fool. He is at once a man whose mind has come unhinged and a visionary capable of seeing the truths that his family fails to comprehend. He is frightening and endearing. He is lost and found. He leads the way, and yet he too is in dire need of healing.

Johannes is the second of farmer Morten Borgen's three sons. He's a tall man with a thin beard and wide, gentle eyes that stare fixedly as if into another world. He moves stiffly and somewhat mechanically, like a quizzical bird. Shuffling from room to room, he insists that he is Christ the Lord.

When the spirit moves, Johannes speaks in the language of biblical prophecy, words that will sound familiar to churchgoers. "Woe unto you hypocrites . . . for you lack faith," he declares. "Verily, I say unto you, judgment is at hand." Yet Johannes delivers his pronouncements in a high-pitched moan, which accentuates the strangeness of his prophetic utterance. Listening to him, I realize how desensitized I have become to such language, having heard it recited in countless sermons.

Weary of his son's doom-saying prophecies about corpses and judgment, farmer Borgen sighs, exhausted. Enduring Johannes' madness is a burden from minute to minute, especially when the men must rise early to retrieve him from his sermonizing on a nearby hilltop. It's unsettling, even annoying—the new local pastor says, "It's appalling"—the way Johannes delivers his monologues and disrupts conversations, seemingly oblivious to all around.

We learn that Johannes has not always been this way. Old Morten is a man of passionate and particular Christian convictions, and he had hoped to raise Johannes up to become a prophet who would convert the surrounding community to these beliefs. So he assigned Johannes to strict religious studies. Apparently, it proved too intense.

Observing the fool's deranged behavior, the pastor inquires, "Was it love?"

"No," Mikkel, the oldest son, sighs. "It was Søren Kierke-gaard."

That may be the funniest line in Carl Dreyer's catalog. Enjoy it. Things take a troubling turn soon after, when death does, at last, pay a visit to the Borgen farm.

*　　*　　*

Set in the 1920's, Dreyer's *Ordet* is a strange, unsettling film that demands we pay attention to its every aspect: the movement of the actors in each scene; the way the camera slowly turns to gradually reveal a room; the rhythm of editing; the timing of the sounds of farm animals outside the house; the fractions of chambers caught in the light, and those corners veiled by shadow; the silences.

Ordet originated as a stage play written by Kaj Munk, a Lutheran minister who was killed by the Nazis in 1944. But Dreyer incorporates powerful elements that could only take place in cinema. His genius becomes evident only through patient observation. But if we pay close attention to any given scene, we discover that there is purpose in the most incidental detail.

Those who appreciate the virtues of *Babette's Feast* will find that *Ordet* has similar delights, being set in the same West Jutland territory and reuniting some of the same cast members. The similarities don't stop there. *Ordet* is one of those rare spiritual works that can reverently uphold Christian faith even as it critiques and reprimands the faithful for their blindness, cruelty and hypocrisy.

As Mr. Demkowicz always told us, "Things mean things." Each time I watch *Ordet*, I see the significance of something new.

I'm not the only one. Darren Hughes, who blogs about film at LongPauses, writes:

> I grew up in the church, so the parables and teachings of Christ are barely distinguishable in my social/cultural memory from any number of myths, parables, fairy tales and stories. They all seem to occupy the same part of my brain, formed sometime during childhood, where they continue to shape the ethics and morals (and something like faith) that determine my behavior. Christ isn't really *real* to me, or my life would be radically different. I imagine that is probably true of many Christians.
>
> But something happens to me during the last 20 minutes of *Ordet*. . . and I experience an overwhelming gratitude, a peculiar emotion that I don't recall ever feeling in any traditionally religious context. I mean real *gratitude*, mixed with shame and joy and awe and any number of other emotions and desires that I so seldom feel for things not of this world. I guess, in a word, *that is* transcendence, and I'm so grateful for this film for giving me that. It's like a gift.

* * *

If Johannes had been sculpted by most other filmmakers, it's very likely that he would have been portrayed as an appealing fool, a smug prophet, even a hero. But Dreyer makes sure that the character's "otherness" causes us to share the Borgen family's discomfort. Johannes' presence is abrasive and sometimes almost odd to the point of absurdity. He is, without a doubt, out of his mind. But there is the possibility that in losing his own mind, he has made room for someone else's to speak through him.

When Johannes' family suffers a devastating loss, this holy fool realizes that his visions are wasted on them, and he suddenly departs. It is then that the family turns from merely tolerating him to earnestly seeking him. Their own language seems suddenly insufficient, and the thought of the house being emptied of the fool's subversive speeches is too much to bear.

But in the end, Johannes too needs to be saved from his imbalance. He is clearly related to *The Fisher King*'s Parry in this way but also to Max Klein, Jeff Bridges' character in Peter Weir's *Fearless*, who becomes a holy fool through a traumatizing plane crash. Johannes, Parry and Max all gain a new kind of perspective that makes them aliens to their families, and they must be brought "down to earth" when their vision has served its purpose.

Foolish Moviegoing

I don't have personal experience in being a holy fool—okay, not that I'm aware of. But I can say that I feel sympathy with these characters. As I strive to follow Christ in my own clumsy way, I find myself challenged to follow an example that does not make sense to society at large.

Discernment will drive you to different, unpopular paths. Seeking excellence in a healthy diet, my wife and I find ourselves buying unusual groceries and ordering unconventional items on the menu. Many popular film critics merely affirm the choices moviegoers already make, and their recommendations keep us focused on what big Hollywood studios deliver to the shopping-mall cineplex. But the preferences of the most experienced and insightful film critics often differ significantly from the opinions of the masses that turn mediocre movies into blockbusters.

In an article published in *USA Today* in January 2003, a "cultural crusader" criticized other film critics for including obscure film titles in their year-end top 10 lists. He wondered why more awards weren't being handed to commercial crowd-pleasers such as *Signs* and *My Big Fat Greek Wedding*. He was discouraged that critics' organizations were celebrating arthouse films like *The Pianist, Far from Heaven* and films from overseas that were not box office hits. "Endorsing such movies not only enhances a critic's conviction that he serves some important purpose," he wrote, "but also strengthens his sense of superiority, suggesting that the reviewer possesses knowledge, refinement and sophistication that set him apart from ordinary movie goers."[1]

These words have dangerous implications. The writer suggests that it is arrogant for a critic, who applies himself to viewing hundreds of movies every year from all around the world, to behave as if he has knowledge different from ordinary movie goers. Personally, even as a movie critic, I have no trouble believing that other critics who study film more intensely than I do develop some refinement that I lack. That is, in fact, why I pay attention to their opinions.

Further, the writer implies that crowd-pleasing films are just as rewarding as the works that film scholars tell us are the most accomplished. In that case, we do not need critics. We should just follow the crowds. But I learned otherwise at an early age. By reading reviews, revisiting films, and pursuing discussion, I learned that there were rich rewards in works of art that I couldn't fully comprehend without study and experience.

If we apply this writer's critique to any other field, the problem becomes clear. If food critics focused primarily on what's available in shopping-mall food courts, we would receive very little guidance regarding healthier and rewarding choices. Just because the masses eat fast food doesn't mean that food critics are exhibiting arrogance when they write about higher quality cuisine. It means that there are millions of people who would do well to reflect on their diets. If a critic says that he prefers an incredible Thai restaurant on the edge of town, he may be trying to sound important, but I doubt it.

This isn't just about moviegoing—it's about the choices we make all day long. When we apply ourselves to look more closely, we see more, learn what is possible and move beyond elementary fare. Our choices begin to seem like foolishness to others, just as the preferences of discerning adults often seem ridiculous to children. But we can't let that stop us. The more we learn to find greater sources of truth and beauty, the more we will be transformed.

Jack Lucas, for all of his popularity and pride, couldn't find the perspective he needed without wandering so far from the beaten path that he became a sort of fool himself.

Note
1. Michael Medved, "Film Critics Often Frown as Movie Fans Delight," *USA Today*, January 15, 2003.

Laughing at My Reflection

[Humanity] has unquestionably one really effective weapon—laughter.
. . . Against the assault of laughter nothing can stand.

MARK TWAIN

The opposite of "funny" is not "serious." The opposite
of "funny" is "not funny."

G. K. CHESTERTON

A Scene from Brian Dannelly's *Saved!*

Hilary Faye is the crown jewel in a Christian singing group at Eagle Mountain Christian High School.

This young woman is so artificially virtuous, so plastically pleasing to the eye, that she's bound to succeed in her dream of becoming a Christian pop star someday. She walks the hallways of Eagle Mountain with the pomp and severity of a cruel queen among underlings, devoting herself to convincing everyone that she is the most righteous Christian on the block. So zealous is she about protecting her purity that she spends her spare time at the Emmanuel Shooting Range—slogan: "an eye for an eye"—blasting away at cardboard cutout assailants who represent potential rapists.

So when Pastor Skip, the school principal, calls Hilary Faye and her backup singers aside to ask them for a favor, the girls are more than ready to respond. Together, the Christian Jewels are not just a band—they're a gang.

"Listen, I'm concerned about Mary," says Skip, referring to the one Jewel who's missing from the scene. "Something's going on." The girls agree. Mary's been acting strangely lately. They're convinced that she is being lured into some secret sin.

"Well, she's part of your posse," says Skip, employing any lingo he can in order to sound hip, "and I think that you could help her. I'm gonna need you to be a warrior out there on the front lines for Jesus."

"You mean, like, *shoot* her!" says one of the Jewels.

No, says Skip, that's not quite what he has in mind. But the girls resolve to intervene with force anyway. So when Mary is dragged kicking and screaming from the sidewalk and into Hilary Faye's van—license plate, "JC GRL"—you know it's not for a prayer meeting. No, the Christian Jewels have come to perform an exorcism.

Mary tries to break free, but Hilary, dressed in a powder-blue track suit, is holding a Bible and shouting, "In the name of Jesus Christ, I command you, leave the body of this servant of God!" Desperate, Mary dives out of the van and hits the ground running. The Jewels come after her.

"We have got to get rid of the evil in you!" Hilary Faye declares as the Jewels follow her. One of them is holding a large, framed picture of Jesus. Together, they unleash the heavy-duty vocabulary of Christian condemnation: "backsliding," "flames of hell," "magnet for sin." Hilary Faye raises a hand to the sky and says to Mary, "Jesus *loves* you."

Mary argues that Hilary Faye doesn't know the meaning of the word and turns to walk away. Infuriated, the self-righteous Hilary turns her Bible into a projectile. Throwing it hard at Mary's back, she screams, "I am filled with Christ's love!"

The Laugh of Love

That is a painful scene for many reasons. We see the arrogance of the pious high school students and sense the betrayal Mary feels when her friends behave judgmentally. And yet, the audience is laughing.

So am I. I'm feeling severe discomfort, but I'm laughing anyway.

Having attended a Christian high school, I am familiar with such acts of hypocrisy, judgment and arrogance among teenagers. I have seen Christians, young and old, behave this way. And I've participated in similarly disgraceful exchanges.

Some in the audience may be laughing because they find Christians to be ridiculous. But I suspect that most of them, even those who have never been religious, relate to this scene in some way. Many of us are laughing because we see and reject the errors on display and because we are admitting our own culpability in such folly, without despairing from the shame of it. The laughter is a release: *I've been there, I recognize that, I acknowledge the folly of human behavior, and I know there's a better way.*

*   *   *

If we didn't sin, stumble and make mistakes, we wouldn't have comedy. Bloopers. Practical jokes. Parody. Satire. Slapstick. In each of these, something has been jarred from its appropriate place, baited or shoved into error.

But just as there are many kinds of comedy, there are many kinds of laughter. When bullies laugh to condemn and to ridicule, such mean-spirited laughter serves to make them feel superior. But the laughter of recognition is different—it allows us to nod at familiar errors and misbehavior, acknowledging that this is a distortion and that we can see the distance between this display and what is right.

Distortions are disturbing, sometimes terrifying. When we suffer the changes of adolescence, we don't think it's funny at all. But in a comedy, we laugh in pained recognition at the awkward antics of high schoolers as they suffer from hormones, peer pressure and trends. We understand the horror they're going through. We've been there. We know there's hope for them. Laughter cushions the pain and acts as an expression of hope and sympathy.

That is the great gift of laughter in all of its forms. It is a mark of recognition that rejects despair. Laughter allows us to approach indirectly, with a healthy distance and perspective, things that are too dismaying to approach head-on. And the laughter of joy comes from the delight we feel in recognizing that nothing is ever so bad as to be beyond hope.

Charlie Chaplin gets caught in the gears of a machine, and the audience roars at the exaggerated predicament—even though it would be excruciating and frightful to *be* a human being stuck in a machine. We all fear being pulled into something where we have no control, whether it's a literal machine or some dehumanizing, bureaucratic process. That spectacle works on so many levels.

I love watching Wile E. Coyote's outlandish Road Runner traps backfire on him because real-world endeavors have backfired on me rather painfully a time or two (or twenty). I've seen the collapse of vain ambitions. I recognize that they were sometimes rather misguided to begin with.

When Derek's boneheaded buddies get into a playful fight, spraying each other with gasoline at the service station in *Zoolander*, we laugh in dismay when someone on the edge of the scene lights a cigarette. Of course, a real-world explosion brought on by foolishness would be no laughing matter at all.

Blooper programs show us actors flubbing their lines and losing their composure, and we laugh to see glorified talents exposed as fallible. We laugh because we can see what *should* have happened. There was a *right* way to do that scene. But we laugh, at last, because we can relate to embarrassment, and we know that such mistakes are not tragedies. Life goes on, and these stumbles will not have permanent significance.

In one of my favorite *Saturday Night Live* routines, the teleprompters malfunction during a news program and the anchorman, anchorwoman, weatherman and sports reporter are left stammering nonsense. Their professionalism and good humor quickly devolve into terror and panic. It doesn't stop there. They descend into irrational, barbaric behavior. Blood sprays across the news desk. The sketch is funny not because reporters are barbarians, of course. Most are quite talented at improvising during technical difficulties. It is funny because it highlights the illusion that newscasters are actually reporting these things based on their own knowledge and eloquence. It reminds us that this is scripted and that broadcast is a performance. Much of the comedy in Will Ferrell's *Anchorman: The Legend of Ron Burgundy* is drawn from the same well.

In darker comedies like *Dr. Strangelove* and *Barton Fink*, outrageous characterizations draw attention to troubling realities. George C. Scott, as *Dr. Strangelove*'s war-making general, argues with other military strategists: "Gentlemen, we can't fight here! This is the War Room!"

I shake my head as Barton Fink, having written a brilliant play about social issues, is brought to Hollywood to compose a formulaic, crowd-pleasing movie about wrestling. Sometimes, we recognize what we see onscreen as absurd, but the discomfort comes from realizing that these things happen. There's nothing implausible about them.

Great comedy writing is a rare and wonderful gift. The Coen brothers, in their beloved comedy *O Brother Where Art Thou*, paid tribute to the whip-smart writing in comedies such as Preston Sturges' *Sullivan's Travels*. Whit Stillman (*Metropolitan, The Last Days of Disco*), Hal Hartley (*The Unbelievable Truth*), Wes Anderson (*The Royal Tenenbaums, The Life Aquatic with Steve Zissou*), Charlie Kaufman (*Eternal Sunshine of the Spotless Mind, Being John Malkovich*) and Jim Jarmusch (*Down by Law, Broken Flowers*) write dry, sophisticated comedy of differing flavors.

Woody Allen's screenplays have given us a whole library of brilliantly funny moments, exploring the folly of lust, romance, infidelity and the lighter side of philosophy. In *Love and Death*,

Sonia declares, "Judgment of any system, or a prior relationship or phenomenon, exists in an irrational or metaphysical or at least epistemological contradiction to an abstract empirical concept such as being, or to be or to occur in the thing itself or of the thing itself." And Boris replies, "Yes, I've said that many times."

Allen also carries on the tradition of great physical comedy pioneered by Buster Keaton and Charlie Chaplin. Whether we're watching the frantic flight of a time-traveler from futuristic police in *Sleeper,* or the way a strange chameleonic man in *Zelig* transforms to look and behave like Jewish rabbis while conversing with them, or the desperate attempt of guitarist Emmet Ray to keep his balance on a crescent-moon stage prop while it raises him up off the platform in *Sweet and Lowdown,* Allen shows he can choreograph memorably hilarious spectacles with the best comedians on film. In every case, we laugh either because of the distortion of something proper or with dismay that it reflects the way real life can easily tip off balance.

I've heard many people tell me that I shouldn't laugh at Quentin Tarantino's *Pulp Fiction* because violence isn't funny. But it's not the violence that gets me laughing. The various criminals and gangsters in Tarantino's trigger-happy world are laughably egotistical, buffoonish with their excessive bad language, and blind to their own grossly inappropriate behavior. As Vincent Vega purchases heroin from a dealer, he complains about the kid who scratched his car door with a key. The dealer declares that such hoodlums should get "No trial, no jury, straight to execution." Vega agrees, "It's against the rules." And then he completes the drug purchase. Irony doesn't get any thicker than that.

Even so, we must not laugh in mere contempt but with the realization that we, too, sometimes contradict ourselves. We too respond to accidents with childish complaints and brash shows of ego. We too sometimes take things into our own hands and suffer disastrous consequences.

* * *

Healthy laughter can occur in the middle of trouble—as comic relief or as an expression of defiance. When Jackie Chan is cornered and the villains grin in triumph, we laugh because he may be stuck for the moment, but we know what's going to happen later. We laugh because we know that all is right, or will be right, with the world—even though Tom Hanks and Shelley Long are watching their house fall apart in *The Money Pit* and even though two old women are poisoning the visitors in their home in *Arsenic and Old Lace*.

But sometimes the laughter comes *after* the moment of tension and dismay, when hopes are fulfilled unexpectedly. We learn this kind of laughter as early as infancy, playing peek-a-boo with our parents. "Where's Mama?" The child's brow wrinkles in worry. She doesn't see her mother. Then, boom! The blanket falls, or the hands open, and . . . . "There she is!" The child erupts in peals of glee.

When Darth Vader's warship closes in on Luke Skywalker and all seems lost, we laugh when Han Solo arrives out of nowhere to save the day—not only because our fears have been blown away but also because this moment represents the correction of a distortion. Han Solo has finally acted out of selflessness and responsibility. The distance between wrong and right has been exposed, and we laugh in favor of rightness.

Those who deny the existence of absolutes must have a difficult time explaining away the universality of comedy. Comedy confirms that something has gone very "wrong." In doing so, it also affirms that "right" does exist.

When we watch *Monty Python's Flying Circus* and see John Cleese on his way to work for the Ministry of Silly Walks, his feet meandering in all directions and carrying him on a circuitous route to the office, we laugh at the silliness of it all. We know there is a "normal" way to walk.

Similarly, when Hilary Faye throws the Bible at Mary in *Saved!* we laugh because we can see the presumptions and condescension in her behavior. We know there is a better way for her to behave.

The healthiest laughter is that which recognizes our shared fallibility. We are human, made from dust and prone to error. I like to believe that God laughs with affection when I stumble, much the way parents laugh if their child stumbles while learning to walk. Can I be so patient, so forgiving, so willing to laugh at the stumbles of others, mirroring that grace? I hope so, because I hope others will be so gracious with me.

Of course, sometimes comedy dares to address subjects we hold dear, and in our pride and defensiveness, we take offense. Perhaps that is why some of the Christians in the audience at *Saved!* are not laughing at all.

Is *Saved!* Funny?

When *Saved!* opened in theaters, I braced myself for the weekly survey of Christian film reviews, ready to sort through a predictable array of outrage. Among religious-press film writers, there are some who seem to believe that any joke made at the expense of Christians is actually an attack on God Himself.

But let's face it—quite a few lampoons of churchgoers have been right on target in their portrayals of folly. It would serve us well to step back and learn a thing or two from those who are outside looking in. I always get a good laugh out of that moment in Woody Allen's *Hannah and Her Sisters* when a cynical artist, played by Max Von Sydow, sits shaking his head in dismay at the television while a greedy televangelist misleads his audience. The artist remarks, "If Jesus came back and saw what was being done in His name, He'd never stop throwing up."

If we're humble enough to recognize our flaws, satire can be a powerful and instructive experience. Republicans are sometimes uncomfortable when Republican agendas are spoofed. Some Democrats can't take a joke about their party. African Americans, Hispanics, Native Americans or white folks like me have all felt a bit hot under the collar when someone has called us out in a stand-up comedy routine.

Having grown up in a Christian community, I can remember feeling incensed when Christians were mocked on television. But that began to change the more I looked around and saw people behaving badly in God's name. It changed all the more as I began to realize my own capacity for hypocrisy.

Eventually, I began to wonder why Christians overlook the comedy prevalent in Scripture. Christ's disciples were a laughable crew, kicking up sand along the road and arguing about who would get to sit closest to Jesus in heaven. How could these men—who spent their days and nights in Jesus' company—be so oblivious to their own arrogance? It's funny, not just because they're foolish, but also because I still worry at times about where I stand in the pecking order with other Christians. I recognize myself in that mirror.

A satire like *Saved!* is like a funhouse mirror. It exaggerates our flaws just enough to draw attention to them.

And yet there was a wave of outrage when *Saved!* reached theaters. You could find Christians ranting about it on all kinds of websites. They didn't think it was funny to see a parody of their culture and their lingo.

Granted, it's one thing to see our flaws reflected in Scripture and quite another to sit in a crowded theater watching them projected onto a big screen. It's hard to laugh at the darts of comedy when they're flying straight at you. It takes humility to accept such a public critique.

Molière, a master of comedies for the stage, addressed this difficult subject, saying, "As the purpose of comedy is to correct the vices of men, I see no reason why anyone should be exempt." A few Christian film reviewers seemed to agree, taking a more thoughtful approach to Dannelly's film. They noted that his barbs were not wounding Jesus Himself but were snagging the self-righteousness of pharisaical evangelicals. The jokes were targeting people who seize and manipulate the parlance and particulars of Christianity for their own glory.

David DiCerto of the *Catholic News Service* noted the movie's "mocking tone and unflattering wall-to-wall stereotyping of fundamentalists." But he added, "Turning the critical cheek, *Saved!* does seem sincere in trying to remind viewers that religion can be twisted into something divisive rather than unifying and can be used as an excuse for intolerance."[1] DiCerto was also pleased to see the central character—young, unwed, pregnant Mary—behaving responsibly and choosing to keep her baby.

In my Film Forum column, I set one Christian writer's dismayed review alongside that of author Greg Wright. It looked as if the two were in a heated debate. "Christians are depicted as notorious gossips," complained one. In contrast, Wright said, "As a former church elder, I can vouch for the veracity of this charge." The first reviewer complained about seeing a pastor carry on an extramarital affair. Wright wrote, "I can provide firsthand accounts of plenty of church-wrecking affairs by pastors. I mean, really, this is no secret, is it?" Then the first reviewer lamented about seeing Christians portrayed as "liars, adulterers and hypocrites." Wright remarked that Christians are definitely not exempt from such charges, expressing surprise that churchgoing film buffs would be surprised by these portrayals.

I agree with Wright—Christians like me are a fair target for criticism.

Nevertheless, I take issue with Dannelly's film for other reasons. Dannelly is correct in recognizing the tendency for hypocrisy and judgment in Christian culture. But the solution his movie recommends falls far short of wisdom. If he had stuck to cultural satire, as Monty Python did so memorably in *Life of Brian,* the film could have been brilliant. As it is, Dannelly surrenders the satire and becomes moralistic in the end. He concludes with a vague, wishy-washy lesson about tolerance, basically asserting that Jesus teaches that we should be happy to let everybody do his or her own thing. Even a quick scan of the Gospels will show us that Christ cared about more than just tolerance—He had a fair bit to say about right and wrong and the narrow path to salvation.

Still, *Saved!* has reflected some embarrassing and important truths about Christian culture that have provoked healthy soul-searching in people. Beyond that, it's a meaningful comedy about much more common human experiences: the problem of peer pressure, the pitfalls of legalism and the painful challenges of adolescence. Human troubles, not just Christian troubles.

A Comedy That Hits Close to Home

Unlike Dannelly, I *enjoyed* 12 rewarding years in a small private Christian school. But while I cherish those memories of friendships, growth and wise teaching, I also witnessed many things that resemble what we see in this movie. I even participated in them.

During my senior year, the student council planned a pageant. But, being Christians, we knew better than to vote on physical attributes. Thank goodness! We weren't that superficial. Instead, we were directed to vote on the merits of a girl's Christian example. Which young woman was of the most admirable character? This soured my stomach even then. How could I know which girl was the most virtuous? Wasn't this a bit like determining who was greatest in the kingdom of heaven? In a school where we had been taught that people look at the outward appearance but God looks at the heart (see 1 Sam. 16:7), how could I be so audacious as to vote on goodness?

Yet there I am in the photo of the royal court, a tux-clad date for one of the princesses, participating against my better judgment and feeling guilty about the whole thing.

Yes, we were just kids. But we were also young adults on the threshold of becoming leaders in our own churches. Looking around, I wonder how much has changed. If we cannot recognize Brian Dannelly's parody as speaking powerfully about our weaknesses, how will we avoid the consequences of self-righteousness demonstrated in the film?

* * *

It didn't stop in high school. I continue to catch myself in moments when judgment flares up and singes the edges of my writing. I do not want to fall victim to the arrogance and condescension that colors so many of the Christian movie reviews I have read.

In February 2002, I read a review of Marc Forster's film *Monster's Ball* in which the Christian reviewer went beyond condemning the movie. He also lashed out at a popular mainstream critic for recommending the film. Incensed, this Christian media personality publicly claimed that the mainstream critic only liked the film because he "was obviously attracted to the steamy sex scenes" and that he "apparently didn't mind ogling the naked breasts of Halle Berry . . ."

These accusations were clearly unfounded. The accused critic had, in fact, published quite a different opinion. Rather than praise the film's unnecessarily explicit footage, he called Forster's preoccupation with Berry's shapeliness "the film's only flaw." So, what prompted such an inappropriate and presumptuous attack from the Christian reviewer? It's hard to say.

I wish I could say that the angry reviewer stopped there. But no, he went on venting his grievances against the mainstream critic, saying "it should be noted" that this apparently depraved critic "got to see similar sightings of a voluptuous nude black woman in *Beloved*." So? A lot of people saw *Beloved*. Why even bother to bring it up? And why is the accuser so upset about another film critic seeing movies that include "nude black women"? Is that *particularly* scandalous, somehow? Is he implying that this is somehow worse than Caucasian nakedness?

This confounding, venomous attack still astonishes me for all kinds of reasons. Why use a review to attack another critic? And why is this critic so preoccupied with presuming another critic's thoughts and motives?

Similarly, when Jack Valenti, head of the Motion Picture Association of America, resigned in 2004, another prominent Christian film critic published an article blaming Valenti for corrupting America and the world, stating, "I hate to see what happens when you face the judgment of God."

When public representatives of Christian communities use the platforms God has given them to say such rash and judgmental things, it is no wonder that other people call us out. Christ Himself had a few choice words for the pompous and pious.

* * *

Of course, I'm only scratching the surface here. And I can't point fingers as if I'm innocent—I've published plenty of things that I have regretted, and I can only hope that if I do so again, my friends will not hesitate to coax me to reconsider. I would like very much to avoid being the subject of someone else's satire, but I cannot claim immunity from the sharp needles of comedians. I share in the faults of a Christian culture that has shown its own fallibility in a way that deserves a few pointed jabs.

Christ Himself did not hold back from employing comedy to make a point. His metaphors were often laughably extreme. When He spoke of the blind leading the blind, it's easy to imagine a few chuckles. He also said this: "How can you say to your brother, 'Let me take the speck out of your eye,' when all the time there is a plank in your own eye?" (Matt. 7:4). Painful, true . . . and funny. His exhortation that anyone who lusts should resolve the situation by gouging out his eyes is a fantastic exaggeration that makes a profound point even as it causes us to cringe. I don't know many Christians who miss the humor in it. (And I've never met a man who has gouged out his own eyes for lust.)

It's healthy to laugh at ourselves when error has been exposed. In fact, by behaving in humility, knowing all too well our weakness and our need, we preempt the derisive laughter of those standing apart and judging us. When we acknowledge our faults, the humility subverts most attacks from outside.

The laughter of love frees us from pomposity and fear and takes the sting out of mockery.

Can We Laugh at Anything, Then?

Does that mean anything goes? Of course not.

When it comes to human affairs, well . . . everything we do is fair game for comedy, because everything we do is flawed, and most of it is foolish. Anything we touch is loaded with comic potential. This keeps us humble and accountable in all things.

That is why we love it when men and women of status can laugh at themselves. When Donald Trump participates in comedy at his own expense, he becomes a more endearing figure. At the White House Press Correspondents' Dinner in 2006, George W. Bush stood alongside a brilliant impersonator named Steve Bridges and participated in a hilarious routine that let us eavesdrop on the president's unspoken thoughts. The audience roared in appreciation.

However, when comedian Stephen Colbert took the stage with a scathing satire, the audience was often silent in discomfort, offended or alarmed at the way he drew attention to their flaws. Jabbing the lack of press coverage on serious issues, he pretended to praise the reporters: "Over the last five years you people were so good—over tax cuts, WMD intelligence, the effect of global warming. We Americans didn't want to know, and you had the courtesy not to try to find out. Those were good times, as far as we knew." Satire allowed Colbert to question the reporters' behavior in a way that a lecture or mere gags would not.

Political humor lends itself to cruel caricatures. David Mamet's *Wag the Dog* is a sharp-edged satire about the ways in which the government can manipulate public opinion. Tim Robbins' "mockumentary" about political campaigns, *Bob Roberts,* made fun of the way that politicians fool the public with show-biz savvy. Robert Altman's *The Player* is a fantastic satire about superficiality and corruption in Hollywood. Both allow us to laugh in painful acknowledgment of fault.

But I almost walked out of Michael Moore's *Fahrenheit 9/11* on opening day. I thought the movie contained a mix of creative direction, some revealing information, sharp-edged wit and some rather manipulative arguments. But it was the *audience* that troubled me.

Many of the Seattleites packing the theater cheered for Moore as if he was leading a revolution. Their hatred for President Bush and his administration was so intense that the people booed whenever his face appeared or his name was mentioned. When cabinet members or Republican congressmen were caught in embarrassing moments, the viewers laughed in derision, shouting obscene names at the screen. I do not believe many of these viewers were thinking through Moore's arguments. That kind of mad, cackling, sanctimonious laughter does not help anything. It unites people in wrath without providing them with any constructive tools for change.

In the same way, religious humor can be healthy or destructive, although both varieties tend to make believers uncomfortable. When Terry Gilliam's Monty Python cartoons portray a big-bearded, grouchy God in the clouds, we laugh because we have seen such insufficient representations of God before. We're laughing at our own feeble illustrations of someone too mysterious and powerful to be illustrated. In short, we're laughing at ourselves.

But try to make a joke at the expense of God Himself and we'll be hard-pressed to come up with anything funny. It just doesn't work. That's because there's nothing wrong with God. There's nothing out of place. Those who try to make fun of God end up exposing their own limited views of Him. They're usually driven by pride, cruelty, anger and outrage, which ultimately turn the jokes back against the jokers, revealing them to be arrogant and misguided. Likewise, any attempts to degrade Christ through humor reveal the lack of proper reverence and respect in the joker.

When comedy steers our attention downward in a condescending manner, giving us pleasure at the belittlement of others, that's not healthy either. If a joke is intended as slander or harm to a person, the fault lies with the comedian. For example, due to recent headlines about priests caught in sexual crimes, comedy has taken a harsh turn. Comics have lampooned the priesthood so viciously that they've gone beyond merely exposing error—they're also exposing their own gross prejudice against religion and an eagerness to defame all priests as deviants. This does dishonor to the majority of priests who are innocent of such crimes.

Charles Schulz noted the distinction between comedy and cruelty in a four-panel "Peanuts" comic. Charlie Brown looks on as Lucy draws a picture. "I've decided to go into political cartooning," she declares. "I'm going to ridicule everything!" Charlie Brown responds, "I understand, Lucy . . . By the use of ridicule, you hope to point up our faults in government and thus improve our way of life." "No," says Lucy. "I just want to ridicule everything!"

Employed properly, humor and satire are restorative, not weapons of personal attack. If they remind us of our tendency toward misbehavior and ignorance, we should take our punches with grace and allow for the acknowledgment that we fall short of the glory of God.

The House Without Humor

When I wrote a positive review of *Saved!* on my website, I received e-mail from readers who told me I should appreciate Christian defensiveness. They said I should respect believers' desires to defend the Church against its enemies.

I cherish the Church. It is the Body of Christ at work in the world. Any misguided attacks on the faithful grieve me. But the key word here is "misguided." If we're critiqued for our flaws, we should listen and be willing to laugh at our mistakes.

"Humor is not a mood but a way of looking at the world," wrote Ludwig Wittgenstein. "So if it is correct to say that humor was stamped out in Nazi Germany, that does not mean that people were not in good spirits, or anything of that sort, but something much deeper and more important." In other words, communities that object to any jokes made at their own expense are exhibiting pride and arrogance. If we cannot see the humor in our own failings, we have too high an opinion of ourselves.

It was Terry Gilliam's testimony that awakened me to the gravity of this situation. Gilliam knows a great deal about clowning in religious territory. In fact, he has some background in the Church.

In the book of interviews titled *Gilliam on Gilliam*, the film-maker reminisces about his youthful zeal for the Bible. He led a church youth group. His pastor's sons were his best friends. He almost became a Presbyterian missionary. "But, in the end," Gilliam says, "I couldn't stand the fact that nobody felt able to laugh at God. Hold on a minute, I said, what kind of God is this that can't take my feeble jokes? It was the sanctimoniousness and, ultimately, the narrow-mindedness of the people who were protecting this deity that I never thought needed any protection. Their God was a much smaller God than I was thinking of—less powerful—and he needed them to protect him."[2]

Feeling forced to choose between comedy and the Church—a choice no one should have to make—Gilliam became a comedian.

Yet he has consistently affirmed the truth of the things he once more formally professed. Whether or not he would still call himself a believer, Gilliam's sharp wit has persistently mocked the behavior of the proud, the fearful and the power-greedy. His art relentlessly encourages us to hear a higher call and to have faith in things unseen.

In spite of those who fret that the Almighty might be easily offended, I don't have trouble believing that Gilliam's boisterous sense of humor has given God more than a few good laughs. And I am concerned about the perspective that humorless religiosity reveals. If it shakes our faith to hear jokes about Christians' behavior, perhaps we need to reconsider why we need Christ in the first place.

Notes
1. David DiCerto, *Saved!* film review, *Catholic News Service*, www.catholicnews.com, May 2004.
2. Ian Christie, ed., *Gilliam on Gilliam* (London, U.K.: Faber and Faber, 1999), p. 9.

PART FOUR

Art of Darkness

CHAPTER
TEN

One Is the Loneliest Number

In any real city, you walk. . . . You brush past people, people bump into you. In L.A., nobody touches you. . . . I think we miss that touch so much, that we crash into each other, just so we can feel something.

GRAHAM IN *CRASH*

I'll send an S.O.S. to the world . . . I hope that someone gets my message in a bottle . . .

THE POLICE, "MESSAGE IN A BOTTLE"

The Faucet Problem

During the last quarter of my senior year in high school, I invited a friend out to coffee in hopes of encouraging him through a difficult time. Thinking that I could help out with a listening ear, I wasn't prepared for what I learned. He slid a thick folder of poems across the table, like an informant delivering classified information to a nosy journalist, fixed me with a solemn stare and said, "I haven't shown these to anyone before."

The poems were like war photographs. The words were bloodied with rage, burdened with fear and tear-stained. He watched me as I read them, and I squirmed in discomfort. While the poems left little doubt about what crimes had been committed in his home, his metaphors depicted types of damage that no incriminating photos could reveal. Reading his poems, I felt helpless and angry. How could someone so young and vulnerable go home to such disrespect and mistreatment?

But I'll admit . . . I wasn't disturbed only by the implications of trouble. I was also disturbed that someone would actually commit such words to paper. I was not accustomed to being taken on tours of personal haunted houses. Should I even be reading things that contained such obscenity? If any of these poems had been handed to the wrong classmate or teacher, the author would have been suspended.

I approached a counselor and described my worries. The counselor asked if I believed the writer would hurt himself, and I said no. If anything, he seemed more likely to target something, or somebody, else. I didn't think he was that far down the road yet. Without revealing the writer's identity, I asked if honoring his privacy and confidence might be dangerous. The counselor's response surprised me. "Keep the poems to yourself for now. It's too early to tell if the writer is spiraling downward. It might be the other way around. This could be his first step toward escape."

"What do you mean?"

"He's trusting you with these feelings. To go and turn him in to some authority figure would only throw fuel on the fire of his anger and sense of betrayal."

"But the language is so . . . foul."

"Have you ever had a faucet in the basement go unused for a long time? When you finally turn it on after a long winter, it shakes and chokes and makes strange noises. Then, suddenly, it spews all of this dark, cruddy water into the sink. Art can be like that. When it starts, it can be ugly. Undisciplined. Explosive. Sometimes that means that the pipes are corroded and spoiled. But sometimes it's just a buildup of dirt and dust and sludge that will, eventually, work its way out. If it's shoved out, that could mean that clean, pure water is on the way. You just have to be watchful, letting it run for a while."

"But what if it doesn't? What if more and more of the ugly stuff keeps coming out?"

"The time may come when you need to do more than just listen and go to someone with experience in broken plumbing. But let's give it a little time to see if your friend can make progress now that he's worked this much out on paper."

*　*　*

Many of the movies that are written off by hasty reviewers as foul and dark and depressing have reminded me of those sad, angry poems. It is true that a lot of contemporary art is reactive, focusing energies on ridiculing or bashing whatever religion or political party or individual has betrayed the artist. Much of that work seems merely spiteful.

But some of it—though it may be discomforting, shocking, even sickening—is also helpful in revealing what we need to know about the problem. These expressions can be constructive in making us sensitive toward others. They may even catch the conscience of the person who has contributed to the problem in the first place. Once the work is out there, it may prompt responses in others that give the artist the comfort of knowing that he or she is not alone.

Sometimes the artist is not expressing his own experience at all. Sometimes he or she might be taking us on a compassionate journey into the experience of someone who has been wronged. For me, such works remind me of my own hard-heartedness . . . how all of my talk about healing and caring is meaningless if I cannot exercise care in attending to someone else's lament.

Hell's Cab Driver

Travis Bickle has parked his taxi outside of the diner and gone inside to sit and listen to the chatter of the other night cabbies.

Greasy, weary, hunched over the table, he listens to the drivers talk trash while he looks around the restaurant at the various pimps and crooks in their flashy suits. He seems entranced by their mirrored sunglasses, their proud posture. When another cabbie asks him a question, he doesn't hear it. He is numb from driving through the darkness, from following the orders of his tough customers.

Absent-mindedly, he drops a tablet into his water. It begins to fizz and dissolve. He becomes absorbed in watching the water's turbulent surface. Behind him on the wall, a poster, all red, white and blue, promises great things from a political candidate. What is it about the disintegration of that submerged tablet, that rush of hissing air, that has captured Bickle's attention?

* * *

You hear it all too often on the news—a madman goes on a shooting spree. No one saw it coming. Reporters investigate where he came from. They ask his neighbors, who shake their heads and shrug, incredulous. "He didn't seem like the kind of person who could do something like this." The questions remain unanswered. Maybe drugs played a part in his murderous rage. Maybe he had been depressed lately.

But these are not answers. Yes, they're contributing factors in the man's depravity, but how does a person end up so numb, so desperate to make a mark on the world?

In *Taxi Driver*, Martin Scorsese takes us into Travis Bickle's head, giving us a close-up of an alienated, lonely man whose attempts to connect with other human beings fail him at every turn. That look in his eyes, that blankness in his expression . . . it's frightening. It frightens Bickle too, because he can feel himself losing his balance and slipping toward insanity.

Bickle is an insomniac, but we're not sure why. Perhaps it has something to do with his past in the Marines. It's 1973. Did he see action in Vietnam? Is he haunted by violent memories?

Bickle is not an unpleasant character—not yet. He's hardworking. He has a sharp sense of humor. When he sees something he wants, he is bold enough to step right up and ask for it.

His moral compass, as imprecise as it is, tells him that things should be better than they are. He's repulsed by New York's sleazy nightlife. "All of the animals come out at night," he muses, watching the prostitutes, gamblers and crooks lurking on the dark streets. Then, trying his hand at a little poetic expression, he says, "Someday the rain will come and wash all of the scum off the streets." As he drives his gleaming cab through a sprinkler, water streams across the windshield and blurs our vision of the colorful lights.

But we also see a troubling void in Bickle that makes him vulnerable to the cultural obsession with cool. Feeling weak and threatened, he wants to make an impression. The varieties of recreation available to him in this ugly part of town are sordid and corrupting. In his neighborhood, going to the movies means paying for cheap porn flicks. Bickle doesn't seem like a pervert. He watches porn because it keeps him awake, and probably because it shows him distortions of something he really needs: intimacy.

On his paycheck, Bickle isn't likely to make a new start. And he doesn't seem to think much about his options. The darkness of his past seems to confine him to this wilderness, as if it is the only territory he understands. Whether he likes it or not, he's a part of the nightlife that fills him with such contempt.

*   *   *

Eventually, Bickle places his hopes on winning the heart of a pretty blonde woman named Betsy (what an all-American name!) who musters enough kindness to chat with him. That friendly gleam is like a lighthouse beacon to a lost boat, and he begins to invest in impressing her.

While most viewers will feel some sympathy for Bickle, it's easy to see that his bold attempts are bound to go wrong. His eagerness betrays his desperation, and his attempts are obvious and awkward. Betsy is working on a political campaign, promoting an idealistic and optimistic view of America's future. She's focused on what's ahead and what rises to the top. She believes the hype she's hawking. She falls for the candidate's self-promotion and recoils at the kind of man whose flaws are visible for all to see.

What can a man as limited as Bickle offer a woman like Betsy? What meaningful part can he play in the candidate's vision for a better future?

Back at the office, Betsy jokingly challenges her coworker Tom to try to light a match while pretending that he is missing one hand and several fingers on the other. It feels like a humorous tangent, included in the film to lighten the oppressive mood. But in a film by Martin Scorsese, nothing is incidental. We think again about Bickle's limitations. Can a guy with so few opportunities and so much baggage, lacking money and social skills, strike a spark in the darkness?

Films about sociopathic killers usually focus on comfortable, happy citizens threatened by an unstable and dangerous man. But Scorsese's perspective is more compassionate. He considers the forces that contribute to making this lonely man. Looking at the world through Bickle's damaged gaze, he makes some sense out of the cab driver's dangerous choices.

Bickle's world is forbidding and loveless. His downward spiral seems as natural as the path of a stray leaf floating on a cold wind, slowly descending to the ground until it is sucked into the gutter. Bickle is watchful. As you observe him, you realize that he is paying close attention. His behavior is learned, and the film seems to say that his sociopathic deeds follow a natural path based on his surroundings.

I'm grateful for the experience of *Taxi Driver*, as disturbing as it is. It reminds me of what others are experiencing outside of my daily routine. For many of these individuals, a kind word, a conversation, or a gift could come as a bright and guiding light in a time of crisis.

* * *

Filmmaker Scott Derrickson, director of *The Exorcism of Emily Rose*, is watchful as well. He finds surpassing excellence in *Taxi Driver*— the kind of artistry that teaches other artists what is possible.

"I dissected *Taxi Driver*," he tells me, "and then read about it, and read criticism about it. I started to realize that the cinematic language itself was stating what the film was about. The shots had meaning. Overhead shots in that film—Scorsese described them as being 'a sacramental perspective,' God looking down on this lonely man. Right down to the way color is used in that film [and] the lonely aggressiveness of the score. Every cinematic element!"

Derrickson admires the way the film gave people a uniquely subjective view of New York City by planting them in the perspective of a man who sees the untelevised sections of the town. "When I think about that film, I think about Travis Bickle, but I think equally about the society of buildings, and streets, and people, and cars, and activity that can leave a person like that completely alone and completely cut off from any real human contact. [I think about how these things] can facilitate an alienation that can lead to that kind of mental illness and to that kind of violence."

Derrickson contrasts two key moments in the film that reveal the power of Scorsese's visual strategy. First, he mentions the film's violent climax, when Bickle lashes out at his targets. "There's all this explosive slow-motion violence, where blood is spraying the walls, and a guy gets his finger shot off. It's all very graphic. And most of it's shot at high speed. The camera slows down, forcing you to take a real hard look at this. That's inspired by Sam Peckinpah's films.

"But it's so interesting that earlier in the film, when Bickle's on the phone and he's getting rejected by Betsy . . . the camera literally just drifts off him and looks down this lonely hallway. That's an echo of Michelangelo Antonioni's style—the camera lands on this visual space of emptiness. I think the point was that *that* moment was the harshest thing in the film, not the gun going off and not the blood flying, but that moment of pure rejection, where the only hope that this person had for human contact was being severed. And it's like the camera says, 'I can't even watch this,' and it just moves on."

Derrickson is thrilled with the discovery that cinema can be so expressive and artistic without being obvious. "You have to interact with it to get all of that. When I started to realize that kind of stuff was in there, it really opened up the potential that movies have."

Two Lonely Men, Two Cries for Help

Travis, weighed down by disappointment, sickened by the perversity of the men who ride in his cab, stops by the diner again. His friend, a driver known as The Wizard, who talks like he knows everything, is just leaving. Travis decides to consult with the wise man. They step outside.

Wiz, whose hair has receded to a half-circle that gives him a monkish look, is the equivalent of an oracle in Travis's world.

He's the guy who has seen it all. Maybe he'll be able to give Travis some guidance.

"Things got you down?"

Travis nods. "I just want to go out and really, really do something." He's laughing uncomfortably, finding his own thoughts absurd.

Wiz doesn't understand.

"I just wanna go out . . . and really . . . I got some bad ideas in my head."

The best Wiz can offer Travis is just what he doesn't need to hear: "You get a job, and you become that job." Then Wiz tells him to numb himself to the misery. Get laid. Get drunk.

Travis thinks that's the worst advice he's ever heard. Wiz leaves him standing there, alone, misunderstood, and assured that there is no way out of his despair. The music plays dark, dissonant, descending notes.

Does our job define us? Are we what we *do*?

If so, then Travis has every reason to feel hopeless and humiliated. He's sinking, disintegrating. He has no release. No direction. No way to find fulfillment. Looking around at others with their busy lives, their confidence and their causes . . . it's embarrassing. If he doesn't find a ray of light soon, a cause to take up or something to live for, he's afraid of what he might do.

* * *

Fast forward 25 years to Paul Thomas Anderson's *Punch-Drunk Love*.

It's an Adam Sandler comedy, right? Not really. *Punch-Drunk Love* is a complex film that revises past classics while breaking new ground. It may seem unlikely at first, but several clues suggest the film is Anderson's answer to the bleak and despairing story of Travis Bickle.

Barry has grown up with loud, overbearing, manipulative, insensitive sisters. Seven of them. Barry has always been told what to do. Any original thought has either been rejected, mocked or completely disregarded. He's been mothered to the point of persecution.

Even as an adult, he's still a jittery, insecure child. When he raises the loud metal garage door behind the warehouse where he's trying to start his own business, the world outside is fiercely bright. He emerges as awkwardly as a penguin, waddling out into this industrial ghost town, squinting and twitchy.

Anderson employs musician Jon Brion to surround Barry with a soundtrack that behaves like another character—one who is armed with sharp objects, rattles and noisemakers. The music comes to manifest the sparking nervous system that keeps Barry jumping at the slightest provocation.

Invited to a family dinner, Barry's grown sisters, who have families of their own now, once again disregard him and treat him as a joke. Barry is so busy dodging their aggressive interrogation and cruel jokes that he can't contribute anything to the conversation. Standing there in his blue suit—the one thing he has truly chosen and made his own—he's little more than a target. As they gather round the table, Barry can't take it anymore. He needs an outlet for his rage. So he smashes the panels of the dining room's sliding glass door—one, two, three.

Later, Barry has a conversation with the smartest man he knows, his own "wizard," a brother-in-law named Walter, who happens to be a doctor. Surely Walter can help.

"I don't . . . like myself sometimes," Barry confesses. "Can you help me?"

"Barry, I'm a dentist. What kind of help do you think I can give you?"

Barry asks for a recommendation to a specialist.

"Like a psychiatrist?"

"I just don't have anybody else I can talk to about things. And I understand it's confidential with a doctor."

Now we're getting to the root of Barry's lifelong problem. If he admits weakness, there's blood in the water, and the sisters will start snapping. He's never had someone trustworthy. He's never been able to confide in anyone. If he's going to see a psychiatrist, he can't bear the idea of his sisters knowing about it. They spoil everything. And it's just a matter of time before this quiet, private trust in Walter is betrayed.

Like Travis Bickle, Barry needs a friend. And so much more.

But in Paul Thomas Anderson's world, there's always hope for losers like us.

When Barry discovers an odd, unwanted musical instrument—a harmonium—sitting on the side of the street, he grabs it and carries it back to his office. He doesn't really understand why he's drawn to this dusty antique. He doesn't even know how to play. It's as though he can relate to this rejected, broken, unclassifiable instrument. As he begins to carefully repair its wounds, pressing the keys to release its feeble cries, he may be taking his first steps toward healing.

And Barry needs a lot of repair.

Travis Bickle's vocation helped us understand his state of mind. He wasn't just a cab driver. He was the chauffeur to the scum of the earth, driving back and forth but getting nowhere, trying to keep his car and his conscience clean. Barry, on the other hand, is a toilet plunger salesman. That, in its own way, is revealing. He's doing his best to be a businessman. But his heart and head are so clogged with repressed rage that it's all he can do to keep from exploding.

Something's gotta give.

Dial-Up Redemption

Punch-Drunk Love opens with a shot of Barry Egan hunched in a corner on the telephone with a vast empty wall filling most of the screen. That blank space conveys something to us about Barry's experience. There's a great emptiness in his life.

But the telephone is also significant. It shows us that Barry is a disconnected, alienated soul who is uncomfortable with personal contact. On the telephone, he has some control over the situation.

Barry spends a lot of time on the telephone in this movie, and in each conversation he's seeking some kind of relief, relationship or redemption. But he's bound for disappointment, because it's almost as difficult to achieve intimacy over a phone line as it is to find love by talking to a toaster. Worse, everything he tries is a transaction.

In one call, he inquires about an error printed in an advertisement for Healthy Choice food products. Healthy Choice is offering customers a chance to earn frequent flyer miles with every Healthy Choice product they purchase. Barry has discovered that there are some very inexpensive Healthy Choice products.

If he buys a pack of pudding cups, each cup qualifies as a separate item. Basically, if he buys a ton of pudding, he'll make a fortune in air travel.

But Barry's not the kind of person to take advantage of people. So he calls up Healthy Choice, hoping to alert the company to its mistake. As in most of Barry's relationships, the person on the other end of the line isn't really listening. Once again, he's made to feel like a fool.

Walking away wounded and angry, Barry decides to go ahead and take the company up on their offer. He starts buying Healthy Choice products with coupons, earning all kinds of mileage for pocket change. His intention: someday, he'll *redeem* those credits.

In a journey like this, any form of the word "redemption" is loaded.

* * *

One lonely night, after finding rejection everywhere else, Barry's eyes wander from a newspaper ad for Healthy Choice to another promise of reward—an advertisement for a phone sex line.

Again, he's crouching near the wall with the phone in his hand. Even in the safety of his apartment, he's afraid he'll be discovered and condemned. The woman on the phone sounds friendly, albeit aggressive with her sexy talk. Barry's not interested in talking about sex. He just wants a conversation, even if he has to pay for it. Since in-person conversations so often end in disaster, it must be comforting to have the option of hanging up if things take a wrong turn.

Yes, she's talking dirty, and that can be as unsettling to moviegoers as it is to Barry. And I know some moviegoers who reached this scene and then walked away from the film, disgusted with Barry's behavior and with the crass language used by the woman on the telephone.

But let's think about this—what's really happening here? Is Barry a pervert? Or is his desire for intimacy leading him to choose poorly?

Whatever the answer, Barry's going to pay for his choice. He's about to meet the devil on the other end of this deal.

*　　*　　*

Every week as I peruse Seattle newspapers, I see numbers for phone sex, escort services and sexual escapes of all kinds. In the same section of the paper, I see advertisements for pills and services that help prevent pregnancy. It's easy to purchase vitamin supplements that promise to change your life and to sign up for exercise programs that promise quick results with minimal effort.

They're after us like paparazzi to celebrities—salespeople eager to sell us redemption at a reasonable price. In seeking satisfaction along these misguided paths, we ensure that we, as a culture, remain dissatisfied. Pursuing happiness, we try to steer clear of anything difficult or inconvenient, convinced that there are shorcuts to joy. As a result, we end up unhappy, disconnected, weak and lonely.

When we add to this the proliferation of personal technology, we end up with a world of people buying ways to seal themselves off from each other. Half of the commuters on my bus riding home from the office are wearing headphones. Are they all music fans, or are some of them making it clear that they're not interested in talking to strangers? With cell phones attached to their faces, they can talk to anybody they want at any time, without ever needing to relate to the stranger sitting next to them. Caller I.D. lets us screen our calls so that we can shield ourselves from unwanted encounters. Thanks to iPod and Zune, we can tune in to our favorite things wherever and whenever we want, making entertainment an increasingly solo experience instead of the community event it once was.

We may think we're saving ourselves trouble. But we were designed for intimacy. If that need goes unfulfilled, it begins to manifest itself in other ways. Our hunger for contact mutates into unhealthy habits. We try to appease that hunger by force— by making purchases and engaging with others in terms of a contract. That way, we get what we want without becoming vulnerable and without any lasting commitment or accountability. We've been taught to think that we can purchase something to scratch every itch. But dollars and cents can't sate this desire.

During my visit to the God Room for interviews with the cast of the exorcism-adventure film *Constantine*, a journalist asked Rachel Weisz if she thought her character's alienation from society was something the audience could understand. She responded with conviction:

> The breakdown of the relationship between man and God, and the breakdown of nuclear families . . . society is moving more and more toward very alienated individuals. Individuals are on computers all day, and [they're]

not interacting with other human beings, not being part
of a church, not being part of a community. They're
[interacting] less and less. People are alone and alienated.
Playing computer games—for me, that's a very alienating
thing to do. Anything where you're not in relation to
family, friends, community, God . . . that's alienating.

I thought of Travis Bickle and Barry Egan.

* * *

In *Taxi Driver*, Travis Bickle's understanding of intimacy comes
from pornography. Consequently, when he goes out with a
beautiful woman and experiences further rejection, he ends up
lonely and bitter.

Punch-Drunk Love's Barry Egan is similarly drawn to cheap,
artificial forms of intimacy, since they're the only sort available
to him. That is, until Lena walks into his life. Barry is saved
from disintegration by the kind attentions of a woman who
seems to sympathize with him. There's something unlikely
about her. What kind of woman would want to bother with a
wreck like Barry?

But there she is, living, breathing, beautiful . . . and lonely.
Most important, she'll accept his occasional breakdowns, his
bursts of violent language and his temper tantrums. And she'll
keep on loving him.

Knowing that someone cares about him and values him,
warts and all, Barry begins to find the confidence that he needs
to stand up and defend himself against his oppressors. When
he starts to talk back, watch out! If you turn on that faucet,

you're not going to like what comes pouring out.

When I watched Barry first blow his top on the phone with one of his harassing sisters, I immediately remembered those wrathful poems, those outpourings of pain and dismay that had been entrusted to me in high school. If I had encountered Barry while he was roaring into the telephone, I would have flinched and moved past him, disgusted. It would never have occurred to me that this was the beginning of his liberation.

When Barry finally confronts his enemy, the weapon he holds in his hand is not a gun—it's a phone receiver, torn loose. He has broken the cord. He is born . . . again . . . into the world of the living, with the confidence to engage the challenges and meet his enemies face to face. He won't be hiding anymore. In fact, he'll discover that his enemy is really just a coward like him, sitting in a warehouse, connecting to the world by telephone. The enemy has used his own concealment, his own anonymity, to wreak havoc on the lives of others. Barry has found him and barged into his cave.

There he stands, the daylight blazing behind him, an avenging angel silhouetted in the doorway. But he's not quick on the trigger. Barry's willing to extend his enemies a pardon. In the end, through the influence of grace, Barry's future is so much brighter than Bickle's.

He might even learn to play that harmonium.

Bringing Order Out of Chaos

Creative expression, like Barry's harmonium playing, Wolfgang Amadeus Mozart's symphonies or my lonely friend's poetry, can become more than just a reaction.

The steps of art-making can become a path out of pain and confusion because art requires us to make some kind of sense out of chaos. It's a way of releasing pain by forcing it into a form and a language. It can allow us to find names for our demons and expel them once and for all.

In *Pollock,* Ed Harris plays a great artist who, on the verge of despair, fills vast canvases with seemingly chaotic color. To some, it appears to be madness. But as we watch Jackson Pollock struggle, misunderstood, through painful relationships with family and friends, we begin to see how essential his expressions of emotion on the canvas have become. They give him release, but he also comes to sense layer upon layer of revelation there. In expressing his feelings, he finds purpose. It's an intense and profound film about the process of creating.

In *Lost in Translation,* one of the most beautiful films about loneliness I've ever seen, two lost souls stranded in Tokyo, an aging American actor named Bob and a young photographer's wife named Charlotte, find each other and commiserate. Their melancholy relationship finds occasions of joy—especially one night when they crash a karaoke party and sing songs to each other that express their own desires. *"More than this,"* sings Bob. *"There has got to be more than this."*

The more Bob and Charlotte express themselves to each other, the more we can see the possibility of romance growing. But as they honestly confide in one another, they also discover a clearer understanding of themselves and what is lacking in their marriages. In their growing intimacy, Bob comes to care about Charlotte in a way that she doesn't understand. He does stumble into a foolish sexual affair, yes, but not with Charlotte.

Taking Bob's foolish one night stand as a rejection, Charlotte gets angry and jealous. Yet we can see that his decision has revealed his desire to protect her from behavior as empty as his own. While *Lost in Translation* lacks any truly happy ending, there are glimmers of hope in what they learn from each other as they turn back to their troubled marriages.

In *The Station Agent,* a man named Peter runs away from his disappointing life and moves into an old abandoned train ticket station. The trains go by, but he stays put, solitary and sad.

Despite his best efforts, Peter cannot avoid entanglement in the lives of those around him. When he tries to walk a lonely road, he's run off that road by a crazy driver. When an affable espresso-cart worker sets up shop beside the station, Peter can't succeed in frustrating the man's friendly inquiries.

Eventually, through his neighbors' intervention and encouragement, Peter will learn to engage these moving trains rather than merely observe them. Like Damiel in *Wings of Desire,* he'll have to take the plunge and seize life in all of its risk, pain and glory. His creative outlet: train-chasing. He'll learn to take a video camera and document the exhilaration of riding alongside a train, just as others have pulled up alongside his simple life and are cheering him on.

* * *

When you start to look around at the movies that are making strong impressions, you begin to realize the prevalence of these issues. We are a fractured society, painfully oblivious to how disconnected we've become.

Curious about this parade of films exploring similar questions, I asked an online community of cinephiles what films sprang to mind when I said the word "loneliness." I also posted this question on my blog.

The tidal wave of responses caught me by surprise: *Last Life in the Universe. Fight Club. What Time Is It There? To Kill a Mockingbird. Grand Canyon. Local Hero. Italian for Beginners. Dogville. Naked. The Truman Show. Junebug. Crash. Edward Scissorhands. The Breakfast Club. Time Out. In the Mood for Love. The Remains of the Day. The Straight Story. The Elephant Man. Henry Fool. Down by Law. Three Colors: Blue. Three Colors: Red. The Double Life of Veronique. What's Eating Gilbert Grape. Buffalo '66. Pieces of April. The Aviator. About Schmidt. Collateral. Crazy/Beautiful. Eternal Sunshine of the Spotless Mind. Finding Forester. Flawless. Heavy. The Hours. Kolya. Life as a House. Shall We Dance? Smoke Signals. Ulee's Gold. You Can Count on Me. 2046. Chungking Express. Reconstruction. Donnie Darko. The World. With a Friend Like Harry. The Machinist. Garden State. Adaptation. Barton Fink. The Last Picture Show. Magnolia. Rushmore. Broken Flowers. Morvern Callar. Harold and Maude. Thirteen Conversations About One Thing. Ghost World. About a Boy. Castaway.*

Even as I sit writing this chapter, more titles are arriving. *Babel. Stranger Than Fiction. Three Times. Half Nelson. Tideland. Little Miss Sunshine.*

Film is such a collaborative medium for artists, and yet the stories of loneliness keep coming. Perhaps that's why so many lonely, misunderstood people become artists. Unable to express themselves meaningfully in conversation, struggling to understand or describe their plight, they are drawn to the meaning that they find in the process of art-making. They discover that others can relate to that expression. A community may begin to grow.

I can't think of any film that addresses contemporary alienation more thoroughly than *Code Unknown*, a masterpiece made by Austrian filmmaker Michael Haneke in 2001.

Confounded by an Unknown Code

Code Unknown begins with a vulnerable girl standing against a wall, flinching as if she anticipates being struck.

This image caught me off-guard. I remember immediately sitting up straight, bracing myself for something horrible. Who is she? What kind of danger is she in?

But then the camera shows us the faces of other children in close-up. They seem puzzled. They're looking at this girl just as we are, trying to interpret her expression.

We have joined a game of charades. But it's not just any game. These are deaf children, trying to learn how to communicate nuanced emotions to each other. One by one, they make their guesses. "Afraid?" "Captive?" For each guess, the girl shakes her head. No. No. No one gets what she's trying to say.

With this powerful scene, Haneke sets the stage for a bewildering whirlwind of a movie filled with characters of different ages, races, religions, backgrounds and income levels who pass through the same Paris square in the movie's second scene. In 27 scenes, most of them filmed in single shots, we are drawn into intense exchanges between strangers and close friends who do not understand each other.

* * *

In the second scene, Haneke moves his camera up and down a Paris street, challenging us to decide which pedestrians we should consider. Whereas most filmmakers quickly zoom in so that we know who the story is about and disregard everyone else, Haneke lets us see the merchants, the people on their way to work, a begging woman, the police . . . everyone. It's a dynamic, busy scene—a crossroads for the whole world.

Among the bustling array, a moping young man named Jean runs into his brother's wife, Anne, who is surprised to see him. She asks why he isn't back at the farm with his father. The boy insists that he won't be going back there. He's not interested in taking over the family business, no matter what his father says. Jean wants to see his brother Georges in hopes of finding sympathy. But Georges is out of town. Anne explains that there's not room in their apartment for three, but she buys Jean a pastry—probably to appease her conscience. She's an actress on her way to work, and he's an inconvenience.

When they part ways, Jean walks past the despondent panhandler on the corner, crumples up the pastry bag, and tosses it into her lap as deliberately as if she were a trash receptacle.

This spurs another onlooker—Amadou, a principled young African man—to intervene. He grabs Jean and confronts him for his insulting behavior. When Jean refuses to acknowledge or apologize for his offense, they come to blows. The beggar, a refugee from Romania named Maria, tries to slip away as the struggle draws the attention of the police.

Things go from bad to worse. The police automatically assume that Amadou is the real problem here. When the owner of the corner shop steps out to complain about the panhandling, the officers end up questioning both Amadou and Maria. They seem disinterested in Jean, especially when Anne returns to defend him. Everyone wants to blame the man with the dark skin and reprimand the immigrant woman.

Everyone is wrong.

* * *

It is hard to trace the fault lines splintering this scene. These encounters are fractured by economic, generational, political, moral, racial and language conflicts. Individualism and diversity, two words celebrated in contemporary European culture, have created societies of isolated people whose frames of reference are so incongruous that their hope of connection is slim.

To explore *Code Unknown* and organize its content under thematic categories seems a rather damaging endeavor—the film is so rich with insight on so many levels. Haneke himself said, "I think that, by reducing it to its most obvious ideas (the Babylonian confusion of languages,[1] the incapacity to communicate, the coldness of the consumer society, xenophobia, etc.), we cannot avoid a mere string of clichés. That is always what happens when you try to isolate 'themes.'"

But that doesn't mean we won't benefit from taking careful note of the range of themes evident in the film. The subject that interests me most, at least during my recent viewings, has been Haneke's aggressive inquiry into how we can truly know each other.

When are we acting, and when aren't we? What does it take to truly communicate something? How much information do we need in order to be certain of each other? How can people from different cultures understand one another? What about different sexes? Different generations? If we can't connect, why are we so obsessed with trying?

In that turbulent scene of civil unrest, each character thinks he or she has a handle on someone else—and so do I. By the end of the ordeal, I'm furious at those fumbling, presumptuous authorities. I'm impressed with Amadou's conviction. But a few scenes later, I'm rattled by how little I understood these people. Amadou turns out to be a complicated person. So does Jean, when we learn the source of his frustration. Maria is a puzzle. And Anne's life is a real mess. As the film progresses, we come to realize just how much each character's form of expression is a "performance."

*　*　*

Code Unknown could be, for some viewers, nothing more than a 118-minute downer. But the watchful may find glimmers of hope. And perhaps we can find understanding by noting what is absent from these confused lives.

After all of the words thrown back and forth, what remains with me are the haunting images of people going silent and clinging to each other in sad desperation—Maria standing in a storm of dust clouds, embracing her husband who has come to welcome her home; Anne and Georges crying and holding each other in the middle of a supermarket. (And again, *Babel* proves a poignant companion piece, offering similar moments of silent communion between lonely characters.)

One character, who appears only briefly, stands out as an exception. Anne is taking the Métro home. At the back of the car, some disgruntled young Arab men are making loud, rude comments to the actress. Frustrated with a society that marginalizes their culture, the men see Anne as a symbol of the proud and dis-respectful. So they make her a target. Watching this scene now, I am even more unsettled because of events that have happened since the film's release. The bitterness poisoning these young Arabs is growing in France and the surrounding nations, setting off riots that are a shocking wake-up call to those of us who have been ignorant of the cultural shift happening in Europe. (The chaos that may lie ahead can be glimpsed in the terrifying artistry of Alfonzo Cuaron's *Children of Men* and Haneke's own speculative fiction *Time of the Wolf.*) So there's a frightening authenticity when one of these men turns violent toward Anne.

But lo, someone intervenes. At great risk to himself, with no personal connection to the actress, a world-weary commuter calmly folds his eyeglasses and stands up to face whatever con-sequences may come for his compassion. It's a small moment of selfless virtue that stands out from all other actions in *Code Unknown*. He demonstrates a kind of care that transcends lan-guage and cultural barriers. Although the film moves on, leav-ing him behind, I cannot get him out of my head. Once again, a courageous gesture exposes what is lacking in all that has come before. And an anonymous stranger seizes a moment to demonstrate true heroism.

These moments of visceral need, expressed in gesture and touch, seem much more eloquent than all of the characters' spo-ken attempts to untangle relational knots.

*   *   *

Haneke's aesthetic suggests, perhaps inadvertently, another hope-ful possibility.

The camera roams left to right, searching for some sign of real communication and relief. Watching the film with an audience at the Flickerings film festival in 2003, I heard my friend Stef gasp during one of the concluding scenes when the camera suddenly turned and moved vertically, allowing one character a glance skyward. Stef pointed out that even though the character was only looking up at a high window, the aesthetic effect of the moment drew our attention to the fact that no one was looking beyond the human plane for help. Whether Haneke intended this or not, the effect is intriguing.

As Haneke's sad stories accumulate, the constant emphasis on the difference between reality and art suggests he's questioning the power of cinema itself. Perhaps we, like the deaf children, are unlikely to discover what he's really trying to convey with his "charade."

Those children who were so unable to speak to each other at the beginning eventually join forces for a public percussion concert. Unable to hear what they are playing, they are still united in a breathtakingly precise rhythm, pounding out patterns for the whole world to hear.

The sound is overwhelming. At first, I took it to represent a sort of S.O.S., sent out into the universe by the human race. But then I noticed that the children were smiling.

* * *

Haneke seems to suggest that through the shared experience of creative expression, we might be able to find an intimacy that we cannot otherwise share. By admitting and expressing our shared sufferings and flaws, we find union with our fellow, fallen human beings.

Interviewing Alejandro González Iñárritu, the director of *Babel*, for ChristianityTodayMovies.com, I asked him what all of *Babel's* portraits of loneliness reveal to him. He answered, "I started out making a film about what really *separates* us. But during the process I was transformed—and my films are extensions of myself. I ended up doing a film about what *unites* us.... These many characters never get together on screen; they're not completely connected. But what connects them is not happiness but pain, and the process that they go through to . . . break down walls and connect to the ones they need and love."

I know that it meant a great deal to my lonely friend when I pondered his alarming poems. It gave him confidence. He went on to pursue poetic expressions of his pain, eventually connecting with audiences as a singer and songwriter. I often wonder if he found release in doing so and if he eventually found pleasure in moving into new artistic territory rather than going around and around on the same troubling track, stuck on refrains about darkness.

When we open up that faucet, we don't know if the water will run clean. But if a heart opens to reveal ugliness and corruption and we respond by recoiling and turning away, we also turn away from the possibility of redemption. No matter what emotions Travis Bickle or Barry Egan elicit in us, we cannot deny that we share some measure of their longing for intimacy. To deny that sends a strong message—that we are too proud to love and too blind to see our own needs.

Note

1. I suspect Haneke was referring to the Tower of Babel, not to Babylon. This idea became the basis for Alejandro González Iñárritu's film *Babel*, a film worth discussing in contrast with *Code Unknown*.

CHAPTER ELEVEN

Making Darkness Visible

I think of horror films as art, as films of confrontation. Films that make you confront aspects of your own life that are difficult to face.

DAVID CRONENBERG

There are two equal and opposite errors into which our race can fall about the devils. One is to disbelieve in their existence. The other is to believe, and to feel an excessive and unhealthy interest in them.

C. S. LEWIS IN THE PREFACE TO *THE SCREWTAPE LETTERS*

The Ugliest Billboard

During my morning commute, the car passes a billboard that I've learned to ignore. On the left panel of the picture, a cigarette rests against an ash tray. On the right, there is a photograph of a human lung festering with sores, black and encrusted as a chimney.

Who wants to see *that* during the drive to work? I'm thinking about the day ahead, sipping my coffee, catching up on the world with the news on KUOW's NPR news broadcast, when suddenly—*black lung!*

I don't even remember what the print at the bottom says. Don't need to. The pictures say it all.

This "public service" billboard doesn't do much for me. I've always trusted those studies about the damage done by smoking. I don't need to touch the hot stove to see if I'll be burned. But I'm sure that the billboard makes a difference for some people, especially kids. That nauseating image of rotten tissue is enough to make a few of them say, "No way! Not in *my* chest cavity!"

Films may provide a similar service. Michael Mann's *The Insider*, one of my favorite thrillers, showed us more than just the horror of nicotine addiction. It exposed a corporation's capacity for facilitating human evil and protecting the criminals. But this is no recent revelation. From dramas such as *Erin Brockovich* to documentaries as straightforward as *The Corporation* and as entertaining as *Roger and Me*, big screen artists have been warning us about corporate wickedness for decades.

In fact, one of the greatest horror films ever made gives us the very same warning—although it took me years to realize it. Like the black-lung billboard, it's a glimpse of horror that serves a purpose. And I'm glad it's out there.

A Horror in the Chest

In 1979, Ridley Scott's *Alien* gave moviegoers a whole new kind of nightmare. He frightened us with a villain who attacks from the inside and wreaks havoc in the ribcage.

It's not easy to forget the violence of the alien that attacks the vulnerable, bewildered crew of the starship Nostromo. But the more I watch the film, the more I realize that there are suspicious similarities between the vicious creature and the corporation that sent the Nostromo's vulnerable passengers into the monster's lair.

In the film's pivotal scene, Officer Ripley confronts her colleague: a curious, analytical fellow named Ash. Ash is intent upon preserving the deadly creature they have brought aboard their ship. The alien has already caused the death of officer Kane, one of Ripley's colleagues, by implanting an egg in Kane's chest cavity, where it developed and eventually hatched. And yet Ash seems strangely obsessed with keeping the creature alive.

Suspicious, Ripley demands that he explain why he strayed from proper quarantine procedure in allowing the creature to get aboard the ship. A struggle ensues. (It's the only time we've ever seen Sigourney Weaver fight Ian Holm, and it's quite a spectacle.) But Ash is no match for the mighty Ripley. He's finally forced to admit that a company with a secret agenda has sent the Nostromo's crew into dangerous territory. The crew was meant to bring back an alien life form. At any cost.

Betrayed and furious, Ripley lashes out at the company and how it has devalued the lives of the crew. Ash can only reply that all other priorities were "rescinded."

She has no time for tears. The alien is still loose, scuttling around the ship, looking for another victim. Desperate, Ripley presses the point. "How do we kill it, Ash?"

Ash, who seems to be enjoying this, says that the alien is impossible to kill. "You still don't understand what you're dealing with, do you? *Perfect organism.* Its structural perfection is matched only by its hostility."

How can this scientist consider such a creature to be perfect? "I admire its purity," Ash explains. "A survivor . . . unclouded by conscience, remorse or delusions of morality."

* * *

And so, the crew turns to scouring the ship, searching for this "perfect organism." This allegedly ideal being uses human bodies as nesting material, after which the spawn emerges, killing its host, heading out to hunt for a new biological nest. If cut, the alien bleeds acid that can burn a hole in the hull of a spaceship. That makes killing it a risky proposition, at the very least.

If we subscribe to a purely evolutionary perspective—that is, if life really is all about survival of the fittest—then humankind is in deep trouble. Conscience, morality, love . . . these things often lead us to selfless choices rather than self-preservation, and they do not make us better able to fight soulless monsters. In terms of strength and survival, the game belongs to the heartless eating machine.

Alien poses an important question to us: Do we accept Ash's definition of the perfect organism? Is this savage survivor, which serves only itself and its offspring, an example of purity?

Clearly, the crew of the Nostromo differs from its enemy. Business has led some of them to live according to the bottom line—a paycheck—but Ripley exemplifies conscience and care for her coworkers. And in James Cameron's extraordinary sequel, *Aliens*, Ripley risks her life again and again in order to save a vulnerable child from the alien's jaws. We admire her. On some level we know that she is more perfect, even if the alien is stronger.

The corporation has more in common with the predatory alien than Ripley. It is, as Ash puts it, "unclouded by conscience, remorse or delusions of morality." The corporation is a machine, and in its most basic model its primary purpose is to produce a profit. When the people steering the corporation determine to make a buck at all costs, they endanger the lives of conscientious human beings.

Thankfully, not everyone shares this way of thinking. There are a few brave souls in business today who believe that business is first and foremost about *service*. Profit is an important piece, but they value conscience more highly than cash. There are some in the business community who laugh at this philosophy. But as more and more corrupt corporate executives make headlines for their disgraceful behavior, discontent with present-day priorities is bound to increase. Anyone who has ever been laid off knows how it feels when a company treats its employees as expendable. We want to believe in our employers, our families, our churches and our nation as well. These are human organizations, all of them, vulnerable to perversion due to the appetites of those with influence.

The horror we feel in films like *Alien*, *The Thing*, *Slither*, *28 Days Later* and *The Shining* is really about our fear that the entities on whom we depend will suddenly morph into something dangerous. These types of films exploit our notion that our own human resources are not enough to save us. God does not intervene in the world they portray, nor are there many signs of hope. Most suggest that the world is just as the former reverend in *Signs* declares that it is: "There is no one looking out for us. We are all alone."

In some of these films, there is a greater horror than death. As we see in *Star Wars, Episode Three: Revenge of the Sith,* the dark side strives to turn us into a slave, a zombie, a vehicle, an instrument of its terrible will.

I suspect that these films resonate not merely because they're outrageous but also because we know they are illustrations of the truth. Evil does exist as a force outside of us, seeking to lure us into error. That leaves us to determine if we are ultimately helpless, or if there might be a power greater than evil seeking to help us escape the monsters.

A Healthy Dose of Horror

I know plenty of people who recoil from the horror section of the video store, and I don't blame them. Most of those movies simply provide that visceral charge of seeing human beings stabbed, dismembered or eaten.

In that sense, horror movies can themselves become the tools of a real-world horror—the exploitation of fear for profit. Almost every month, moviegoers are introduced to another cheap fright fest in which teenagers become the prey for a serial killer or are carried off to be tortured by sadists, or something to that effect. Checking the paper today, I count four new releases of that sort on the big screen.

Yet there are some meaningful films in this genre—stories that comment on the horrors of contemporary culture. If we stop to consider *why* the monsters scare us, what it was that made them or what the creature's victims have in common, we might be surprised at the insight we can gain. We may begin to understand the nature of the menace and learn to recognize monsters growing within our own chests.

Like Virgil guiding the dismayed Dante down into the circles of hell to witness the suffering there, conscientious artists are sometimes moved to take us on a tour of nightmares. This can be an act of social responsibility . . . even love. If we love each other, we sometimes have to tell each other the painful, ugly truth about sins we've ignored or overlooked and the consequences of our behavior.

Flannery O'Connor's short stories about sin cause readers to recoil in dismay when they see the characters expose their pride, greed and hatred. If the portrayal of sin itself isn't enough—and it *was* enough to frighten and convict Hamlet's wicked uncle— then the sight of souls in hellish torments can shake us up and even provoke nightmares. But "the fear of the Lord is the beginning of knowledge" (Prov. 1:7), and sometimes we remember the gravity of a situation by glimpsing the wrath of God poured out on those who oppose Him. We shouldn't *remain* afraid. That's why the Scriptures say fear is the *beginning* of knowledge.

As we grow up, most of us come to appreciate the rewards of good behavior, and we no longer need the threat of punishment for wrongdoing. But as a child, I needed to learn from my parents that disobedience would lead to punishment. They were wise to dissuade me so that I would not continue in rebellion and stumble into the natural consequences of misbehavior, which would be far worse.

For many, the movies affirm wisdom by dramatizing the consequences of foolishness. But if the portrayal of evil causes us to lean forward in anticipation rather than driving us back from the brink in dismay, something—whether in the art or the audience or both—has gone terribly wrong.

An acquaintance of mine once staggered deliriously out of a hyper-violent film, grinning. When I asked him why the movie made him so happy, he replied, "During the torture scenes, I don't know . . . I've just never felt more *alive*." I was tempted to ask him if he realized that he was participating in the torturer's pleasure. The adrenaline rush of fear can become as powerful as any drug—addictive, enslaving and destructive. Cheap horror films titillate our curiosity about evil and leave us wanting to see darker and darker things, desensitizing us to the suffering of others. Artful, meaningful horror films expose the evil so that we run screaming in the other direction.

In an interview I conducted with Sam Phillips about her music, I observed that she, unlike most Christian artists, took time in her concerts to musically and lyrically take her listeners to some dark and disturbing places. She replied, "It's getting less and less likely that people really write *about* the darkness. There are a lot of [merely] sensational writers, artists and musicians. But to be *really honest* about it, that's humiliating and embarrassing and leaves you vulnerable. Nobody really wants to do that. Everybody wants to look cool. And to try to fight that is important for me."

Real horror does not make the darkness look "cool." Darren Aronofsky's *Requiem for a Dream* is a horrifying film about the damage that drugs (prescription or otherwise) can do to us. Some have condemned the film for such explicit portrayals of drug abuse, but it serves the fundamental purpose of horror. By showing us distorted behavior and self-destructive people, Aronofsky gives us a greater appreciation for responsibility and wholeness and a deeper awareness of our limitations and need. If I walk away from *Requiem* wanting to experiment with drugs, I wasn't paying attention.

When Flannery O'Connor offers writers wisdom on their craft, she's often speaking truth about art-making as a whole. She says that a discerning artist will "take great pains to control every excess, everything that does not contribute to this central meaning and design. He cannot indulge in sentimentality, in propagandizing or in pornography and create a work of art, for all these things are excesses. They call attention to themselves and distract from the work as a whole."[1]

When a filmmaker shifts from serving the audience to merely shocking them with sensation, audacity and excess, he or she has become a threat—a pornographer appealing to misguided appetites. But such monstrous behavior only succeeds if victims make themselves vulnerable by wandering mindlessly into dangerous territory.

Spiritual Horror

Horror movies sometimes scare us with something darker than the familiar progression from sin to consequences. Just as art can encourage our faith in a supreme benevolence and reveal the grander designs of our lives, so it can pull back the veil on more troubling realities. There is more at work in our world than mere human misbehavior.

The horror artist walks a dangerous path when approaching this subject. The success of *The X-Files* wasn't a fluke. We're fascinated by the paranormal. Even responsible portrayals of spiritual darkness will draw those with an unhealthy curiosity about supernatural evil. Like foolish children coaxed into danger, they head out into the forest at night with flashlights, thrilled at the possibility of glimpsing some menace.

The menace is real, and so are its claws. And if we tempt it, something wicked this way will come.

The apostle Paul was not famous for encouraging paranoia. He was all business. In Ephesians 6:12, he exhorts us to beware: "For our struggle is not against flesh and blood, but against the rulers, against the authorities, against the powers of this dark world and against the spiritual forces of evil in the heavenly realms." In 1 Peter 5:8, Peter, who watched Jesus casting demons out of the possessed—and who cast out a few himself—agrees: "Be self-controlled and alert. Your enemy the devil prowls around like a roaring lion looking for someone to devour."

Strong statements like these can make us fearful, provoking us to withdraw from the world in the name of self-preservation. But Peter then exhorts us to action: "Resist him, standing firm in the faith, because you know that your brothers throughout the world are undergoing the same kind of sufferings. And the God of all grace, who called you to his eternal glory in Christ, after you have suffered a little while, will himself restore you and make you strong, firm and steadfast" (2 Pet. 5:9-10).

Reverend Graham in *Signs* learns the hard way that when our worst fears cross the threshold, faith is paramount. And true faith leads to action, not merely to retreat. Scripture does not discount the fact that we may suffer under persecution from spiritual darkness. But to counteract fear, Paul reminds us in Romans 8:38-39 that "neither death nor life, neither angels nor demons, neither the present nor the future, nor any powers, neither height nor depth, nor anything else in all creation, will be able to separate us from the love of God that is in Christ Jesus our Lord."

Scott Derrickson Descends into Darkness

I need no convincing. I've had encounters with real evil. And while it's tempting to hope for such an encounter if only to see proof of spiritual realities, seeking such experiences is folly.

For many, even the suggestion of evil forces is troubling, not just because it makes us worry if something goes bump in the night, but because it implies that we are living in a world where there are powers beyond our comprehension and control. To acknowledge this is to admit that we need help, for we do not have the authority or the wisdom on our own to defeat such influences.

Filmmaker Scott Derrickson has done enough research on evil spirits to know the importance of believing in the one true source of help. It's the only comfort we have when we recognize the forces up against us in this world.

When Derrickson wrote and directed *The Exorcism of Emily Rose,* he put the subject of demon possession right out on the table for everyone to engage. The film avoids gratuitous gore and the kind of shocks that provide the backbone of most horror films. Sure, the flashbacks to Emily's attacks are horrifying, especially because Derrickson eschews digital effects in favor of a powerfully creepy performance. Playing Emily, Jennifer Carpenter twists herself into alarming contortions.

But Derrickson is clearly interested in raising serious questions and examining the spiritual journeys of those caught up in the case. He's not interested in indulging the viewer's curiosity about destruction.

Audience members are likely to come away from the film discussing and debating the merits of the Catholic Church's teachings on the devil instead of chatting about their favorite thrills. That should please Derrickson, whose goal was to confront audiences with a vision of darkness that might nudge them toward rewarding discussion—perhaps even to the light. He says that horror movies have the potential to force us to reckon with our experience of evil in the world and in ourselves.

When I interviewed Derrickson for Seattle Pacific University's *Response* magazine, he explained his appreciation for the genre. "There's evil in nature. We're not in control. I think [horror is] the genre of non-denial, and that's fundamentally what attracts me to it. *Emily Rose* is a movie that takes some of the darkest aspects of spirituality and portrays them in a realistic way. And the value of that is that I don't think you can watch the film without asking yourself if you believe that these things are real. . . . It's valuable for the culture as a whole to be asking itself those questions. Because once you're in that arena, you can't ask yourself if you believe in the devil without ultimately asking yourself what you believe about God. To dissect evil is ultimately to define good."

Derrickson knows that some moviegoers, drawn simply to delight in darkness, can become oversaturated with sensationalistic scary movies. "I don't think it's healthy for people to watch nothing but films like this. But I think that a dose of it in the artistic and entertainment diet is a really good thing."

But doesn't the Bible say we shouldn't have anything to do with evil? Derrickson quotes Ephesians 5:11: "Have nothing to do with the fruitless deeds of darkness, but rather expose them." He responds, "In my Christian training, I was taught to 'have nothing to do with fruitless deeds of darkness.' But I never really understood or was given much illumination [about the] idea of *exposing* them. I think the reason for that is that the act of exposing darkness involves some discomfort." He laughs. "Christians don't like to be made uncomfortable. *I* don't. I'm not saying that as a judgment."

Isn't there a thin line between exposing darkness and sensationalizing it?

"I think that the story itself has to dictate to what level a filmmaker ought to go . . . in the portrayal of evil and the portrayal of graphic material. When I made *Hellraiser: Inferno*, I went as far in that film as I would ever go as a filmmaker in terms of the graphic nature. It's a very grotesque movie. I don't like that kind of stuff, graphic violence, personally. But I was making a movie about hell. One of my ambitions [with] that movie was to create a portrayal of hell that had some personal significance for me.

"When Jesus told the story of the rich man and Lazarus and used what I believe were the metaphors of flames and fire, He was trying to create a frightening, horrible, fear-inspiring place for listeners of that story. But those images of flames and the Lake of Fire, and even the devil as we see him with his red underwear and his pitchfork . . . those things have little actual resonance now, because they've been so used up in pop culture and have become almost cartoonish." Derrickson strives, therefore, to put the horror back into subjects that should be horrifying.

"In making *Emily Rose*, I felt like *The Exorcist* had . . . taken that same approach that I was just describing, of trying to create the most vulgar and nauseating and wretched experience that a filmmaker could possibly put the audience through. William Friedkin did that so effectively, I knew that trying to top that would be a disaster." He laughs at the idea. "Trying to go farther in that direction would either be so nauseating as to make the film unwatchable, or it would more likely just become laughable."

In order to portray Emily's exorcism effectively, Derrickson researched documented cases of possession and exorcism and deliverance. "I've seen a lot of videotapes of actual possessions and exorcisms. I think that what actually happens is much less graphic [than *The Exorcist*], but equally frightening. I had to get rid of this exploitative vulgarity and grotesqueness, and focus, rather, on what is equally frightening, which is the sort of alien inhumanity of possessed people. Whether you believe in possession or not . . . you can't witness a person who is going through this whole process of possession and exorcism and not find it profoundly disturbing, even if you think it's mental illness."

So Derrickson determined to avoid focusing on gore and grossness, preferring instead to make the audience afraid of the psychological aspects of possession and frightening them with what they don't see . . . which is always scarier. "I think the result is quite effective. The movie is very, very scary, without resorting to those more exploitative elements and without resorting to makeup and CGI effects in any kind of obvious way."

Beyond *The Exorcist,* Derrickson was inspired by a work of literature: Dante's *L'Inferno.* He describes it as a work of moral and theological instruction wrapped up in "an incredibly frightening tale."

"[*L'Inferno*] is one of one of the great works of art in history," he says. "[It's] a genre piece. It's a horror story. And, yet, it's so creatively ambitious and so morally instructive. In the case of *Emily Rose,* I didn't want to make a morally instructive movie, and I didn't want to make a movie that was bent on providing religious answers for the audience, because I am so resistant to that kind of propaganda myself. But I felt that this was the opportunity to help provoke the audience into asking the right spiritual questions. I don't think you can watch this film and not ask yourself very deeply what you believe about the existence of the spiritual realm."

* * *

Derrickson credits another Italian, Dario Argento, for having taught him an essential ingredient of effective horror: *beauty.*

"It's something that very few horror directors have embraced. Horror films tend to be dark, gothic or even ugly or uninspiring. [Argento] saw that terror and beauty have an interesting relationship when they're combined. It's a very rich experience to watch his films—even though they are, in my opinion, very average horror stories—because he's giving you . . . astonishing aesthetics in the process of telling you these scary tales."

This resonates with Derrickson because of his passion for the gospel, which he calls "the ultimate merging of beauty and terror."

"It's a vision out of a horror film," he explains. "A man . . . nailed to a plank . . . At the same time, it is transformed by its meaning—and by its artistic representations through history— to become something profoundly beautiful. The great potential of the horror genre is [in] that combination of aesthetic richness and meaningful subject matter . . . and spiritual significance. All these things combine with dark tales that scare us, that shake us to our core, that make us realize that we're not sovereign in the world and that there are malevolent forces inside of us and outside of us."

Of course, even when juxtaposed with beauty, horrors— whether explicitly demonic or distortions of nature and behavior—may draw viewers seeking mere spectacle or sensation. Those with an appetite for devastation will take it where they can get it, even pulling it from places where it serves as a meaningful part of a whole. Even in the context of the gospel, horror may cause others to choke and draw away.

But that is no grounds for moviegoers to disregard these works. As we are reminded in Hebrews 5:14, "solid food is for the mature, who by constant use have trained themselves to distinguish good from evil." Mature discernment of this kind is ultimately the answer to the "perfect" monsters that we may face, or worse, become.

Note
1. Flannery O'Connor, *Mystery and Manners* (New York: Farrar, Straus and Giroux, 1969), n.p.

Judgments of the Heart

You know that Shakespearean admonition "To thine own self be true"? It's premised on the idea that "thine own self" is something pretty good, being true to which is commendable. But what if thine own self is not so good? What if it's pretty bad?

DES IN *THE LAST DAYS OF DISCO*

Sometimes the dark side overcomes what Lincoln called "the better angels of our nature."

CAPT. LT. GEN. R. CORMAN IN *APOCALYPSE NOW REDUX*

Men of Unsound Methods

Deep in the jungles of Cambodia, a legendary American soldier named Colonel Kurtz has abandoned his conscience and responsibilities, setting himself up as a god-like tribal lord.

Find and assassinate him—that's the order given to Captain Willard at the beginning of Frances Ford Coppola's *Apocalypse Now*. Willard, an American soldier whose sanity is already shaken from the carnage he has survived in Vietnam combat, is to travel up the Nang River through Vietnam into Cambodia to eliminate this renegade threat. Willard's superiors read Kurtz's impressive military history, right to the incongruous conclusion, where he deteriorates into a madman.

"His methods became . . . unsound," mutters the commander, looking halfway to crazy himself.

At first, Willard cannot comprehend how such a perfect soldier could disgrace his record. But the farther he travels into this hellish battleground, the more he realizes how the rationalizations and compromises necessary for survival in this hell could cause a man to lose his moral compass along the way. As young and bewildered soldiers abandon all moral restraint and then die meaningless deaths all around him, Willard feels as if his own spirit is suffocating. The farther he drifts down that river, the more he seems as lost as the man he has been sent to kill.

Meanwhile, Kurtz lurks in the shadows for most of the film. You half expect to feel impact tremors from his footsteps, like those we felt when the T-Rex approached in *Jurassic Park*.

But when he emerges, his words reveal a frightening coherence. As he recounts the horrors of war, the barbaric acts of his enemies, we can trace the fracture lines back to the moment when a bullet struck his conscience and he gave in to the allure of power. Looking on the bodies of children slaughtered by the enemy, Kurtz moved from revulsion to admiration for the "genius" of his enemies' methods. "The will to do that," he murmurs, awed by the memory. "Perfect, genuine, complete, crystalline, pure. And then I realized they were stronger than we." The possibility of demonstrating such willpower seduces him.

Director Francis Ford Coppola, as devoted to filming this project as Willard is devoted to his murderous quest, crossed the threshold into a sort of madness making *Apocalypse Now*, a story of ego, ambition and chaos recorded in the excellent documentary *Hearts of Darkness: A Filmmaker's Apocalypse.*

But regardless of the chaos he set in motion, Coppola's accomplishment is profound. Inspired by Joseph Conrad's novel *Heart of Darkness,* he allows us to peer into the bottomless pit of human depravity. I can think of no more fitting portrayal of hell in the history of movies than the moment when Colonel Kurtz, who has landed in hell and called it heaven, gets a glimpse into the darkness of his own soul and gasps, *"The horror, the horror."*

"Follow Your Heart"

Clearly, the heart is the problem.

This is as true in stories of romance as it is in tales of depravity. As Coppola examined the depravity of Kurtz, so James Cameron explored romantic love in the monumental blockbuster *Titanic.* Both *Apocalypse Now* and *Titanic* show ambitious human endeavors that lead to catastrophic failure. Yet the lessons that Cameron hopes to convey are quite different from Coppola's.

Young Jack is not cruel and power-mad like Kurtz, but he does answer only to himself, determined that his willpower will surpass the strength of those he perceives to be oppressors. His youthful rebellion is winsome and attractive—even admirable, given his circumstances.

It's easy to see why Rose is attracted to him. Until now, she has just been playing along with the establishment, preparing to marry a man who is a caricature—a self-absorbed, controlling, rich fiancé, intent on a trophy wife. When Jack, a penniless free spirit, comes onto the scene, the contrast is obvious. The youthful Rose cannot help seeing him as her loving savior.

Their circumstances quickly draw them together, united as much by their wish for independence as by their blossoming romance. The intensity of their feelings, heightened by the social forces that press on them, proves irresistible. They give themselves to one another as completely as they know how. Ultimately, Jack sacrifices himself to save Rose.

I have heard Christians defend *Titanic* as a "Christ story." Jack broke a zillion hearts when he gave his life so that Rose could live. It was, unarguably, a noble deed. But that sacrifice does not change the fact that Jack's "love" was tainted by more than a little bit of youthful self-indulgence and egoism. He has proclaimed himself "king of the world," pledging allegiance to adolescent independence and little else. Jack and Rose know what they want to be free from, but a mature understanding of love is still lacking.

Tradition, family and church are all swept aside by the urgency of their idealized love. "They've got you trapped, Rose," Jack tells her, "and you're gonna die if you don't break free." We don't have time to wonder where this might have gone had Jack lived. But in following their hearts, their celebration of love is running the risk of being little more than a celebration of self.

Rose shows us a series of photographs that portray her life after *Titanic*. It is a sequence of personal dreams realized, from piloting an airplane to horseback riding. Thanks to Jack, she has followed her heart and blazed her own trails. We can't be unsympathetic to this, and yet . . .

There is some virtue in questioning the limits that others set for us. But Cameron does not differentiate between mindless conformity and mature love. Religious press columnist Terry Mattingly, in his March 1998 commentary on the film, summed the movie up as "a triumphant story of how one upper-crust girl found salvation—body and soul—through sweaty sex, modern art, self-esteem lingo and social rebellion. *Titanic* is a passion play celebrating the moral values of the 1960s as sacraments."[1]

What's the lesson of *Titanic*? Mattingly quotes Cameron as saying, "I think I discovered the truth of its lesson—which is, all you have is today." The film's climactic vision of Rose slipping into a sort of resurrected *Titanic* where she is reunited with Jack (not in heaven) is a merely sentimental indulgence of the crowd's desire to see the two happy in death, united by romantic love.

* * *

"Follow your heart." That may be the most prevalent theme in American moviemaking. An individual's will, rather than wisdom, must win the day, overcoming all obstacles and odds. It's the American Way: the pursuit of happiness at all costs.

But happiness is very different from joy. Happiness is about feeling good, and so it is based on circumstances. Something that makes us happy today may not make us so happy tomorrow when a better model becomes available. Someone who makes us happy today may make us miserable tomorrow when familiarity shows all the flaws.

That's the idea powering the story of Michel Gondry's film *Eternal Sunshine of the Spotless Mind*. After Joel and Clementine fall madly in love, they quickly grow weary of each other's company and forget what originally inspired them. Eventually they separate, going so far as to have their memories of each other deleted. Once they become oblivious to all that they have shared, they happen upon each other and begin the process all over again. They are seeking happiness, and in their constant abandonment of commitment, their redundant surrender to self-centeredness, they guarantee that they will never know joy.

Joy grows from true love, and true love is patient, kind and selfless. It is a response to grace, which continues to bless even when we do not deserve blessing. *Eternal Sunshine of the Spotless Mind*, written by Charlie Kaufman, is a rare and powerful American film that directly contradicts most shallow, sentimental romances. Kaufman shows us that true love is a road into difficult territory, but that true satisfaction and fulfillment come when we are faithful and true in spite of the ebb and flow of our fickle feelings. We tune our wavering heart to pursue something greater than our own flawed impulses. We make a commitment to a cause so binding that our feelings cannot be a factor in changing our minds.

As the wise Professor Dumbledore says in *Harry Potter and the Goblet of Fire*, "Dark and difficult times lie ahead, Harry. Now is the time that we must choose between what is right, and what is easy."

* * *

In *Dead Poets Society*, Professor Keating tears up a poetry textbook by J. Evans Pritchard, a scholar he abhors. Pritchard, the professor tells his students, fails to understand the passion, the mystery and the power of poetry.

"Excrement!" Keating shouts, flinging torn pages into the air in a defiant frenzy. "That's what I think of Mr. J. Evans Pritchard!" But then Keating turns around, heralds Walt Whitman as the wisest artist of all, and prescribes a philosophy popularly known as *carpe diem:* "Seize the day."

Keating laments the loss of young boys to war; boys who were once "full of hormones," as if the great tragedy of their death lies in the fact that they will never experience sex. *"Seize the day, boys,"* he murmurs in the students' ears, his voice hypnotic. *"Make your lives extraordinary."*

Once again, the hero is defined by his rejection of conformity, with the assumption that freewill and natural goodness are enough to make us extraordinary. Professor Keating is fond of reciting Robert Frost's poem about those two roads that diverge in a wood: "And I, I took the one less traveled by, and that has made all the difference." Keating does not seem aware that the poem may be as much about regret as about triumph. Keating challenges his students to discover and walk in their own particular stride. As the boys pursue their differing ideals, hurrying off on bold quests to impress their dream girls or express themselves with reckless audacity, one of them decides that life isn't worth living if he can't act as he wants. So he chooses suicide. In affirming only a freedom *from,* Keating has provided no understanding of what such freedom may be *for.*

Even Tom Shadyac's light comedy, *Bruce Almighty*, provides a clearer illustration of this. When Bruce's definition of love is self-referential—seizing the freedom to do what pleases him— he is not capable of finding or receiving love. Some freedoms are only accessible through the denial of ego, along the humbling path of service. Freedom to follow one's baser appetites is not freedom at all, but slavery.

My initial, intuitive discomfort with *Dead Poets Society* took on greater definition during my college years. I watched in grief as some of my friends drifted into real dangers. Seizing the day, they indulged in whatever they pleased. Believing that they were following their hearts, they opened themselves to folly. Some lost meaningful relationships; others tarnished their integrity. If "follow your heart" is the American way, we may be wise to ask where the heart leads.

* * *

When I interviewed writer/director Joss Whedon, I asked him about a character named Shepherd Book, one of the motley crew on the starship Serenity in Whedon's television series *Firefly*.

Book is a preacher, a sort of Christian counselor to these space voyagers. In the film *Serenity*, which serves as a conclusion to the *Firefly* series, Book advises our hero, the roguish starship captain Malcolm Reynolds, to abandon his willful, reckless ways and commit himself to a higher cause.

I asked Whedon if he finds integrity in Book's specifically Christian worldview. Whedon responded that, with regard to spirituality in *Serenity*, he had "one definitive statement to make." He wanted to show that "the power of *belief*, the power of something greater than yourself, doesn't necessarily have to mean *religion*."

He explained that the word "belief" pops up in the film frequently because he wanted to emphasize the value of faith. He went on to define "belief" as "a simple act of subsuming yourself to the idea of something that is great." Yet Whedon determined that it doesn't really matter what we choose to believe. "Believing that there is something worth structuring your life around that will direct your moral decisions and sometimes [help] you make harder decisions—*that* is important. What that belief *is* . . . is not."

In other words, we choose our own religion. It doesn't matter which one.

It's such a popular idea, and such a dangerous one: *Just believe.* How many films have offered up that sentiment as the solution to everything? At the conclusion of the family film *The Polar Express,* the conductor tells the young boy, "The thing about trains . . . it doesn't matter where they're going. What matters is deciding to get on." That advice is just as good as a doctor saying, "It doesn't matter which drugs you take, so long as you take some."

It is a good thing when artists acknowledge that there is a higher truth than one's own. But how we define that higher truth—that makes all the difference.

Youthful passion is beautiful, poignant, humorous and delightful. Without passion, little of value can result. But alas, *mere* passion is not enough to sustain a life of joy, wisdom and maturity. We must have passion *for* something . . . and it must be the right something.

Films like *Titanic* never stop to reflect on this. Great films like *Apocalypse Now* show that our hearts may not always be trustworthy. The heart is a source of passion, but it can be passionately wrong as well as passionately right.

Losing Love to Find Romance

In the song "A Man and a Woman," Bono sings, "I could never take a chance of losing love to find romance."

There are quite a few American films that demonstrate what happens when people *do* take that chance. Films that stop to question the *carpe diem* philosophy stand out in stark contrast to the typical, misleading happy endings offered by Hollywood. Ang Lee's *Sense and Sensibility* demonstrated the director's respect for the virtue of Jane Austen's characters. The Dashwood sisters—Marianne and Elinor—knew the value of decency, respect, restraint and humility. And Lee found in Colonel Brandon, played with such grace by Alan Rickman, a hero of honor, tradition and selfless love.

So it came as no surprise that Lee's view of the amorality of the early '70s in his next movie, *The Ice Storm*, was a bleak and despairing one. Few films have more effectively portrayed how parents' actions affect their children, how irresponsibility begets irresponsibility, and how a lie is not isolated but may be the beginning of destruction. *The Ice Storm* demonstrates that a loving, devoted family gives order in the chaos of a downward-spiraling culture. Our culture loves to celebrate the free and independent spirits who bind themselves to nothing. But when the storm arrives, bonds of love, commitment, faith and tradition can make all the difference.

Lee's film, like the Rick Moody novel on which it is based, is a bit heavy-handed with the metaphors. But in a culture that embraces "seize the day," perhaps a heavy hand is just the thing to slap us awake.

In *Closer*, four lovelorn individuals risk what relationships they have in order to pursue lustful impulses. Out of a compulsive need to feed their egos with manipulation, deception and control, they violate each others' trust. Yet they respond in fury and dismay when someone else abuses theirs.

Mike Nichols' adaptation of *Closer*, which began as a successful Broadway play, puts these self-absorbed New Yorkers under the microscope, zooming in closer and closer, showing us appetites that are never satisfied. It's not really about love at all. It's about a desire to control others in order to cover up our weakness and our need. The lust for power is a cancer, and as we feed the disease, we spoil any chances we have of knowing the joys of true love.

It is interesting that *Closer* arrived while Bill Condon's film *Kinsey* was still in theatres. *Kinsey* celebrates the scientist who told 1960s America to stop thinking about sex in a restrictive moral framework and to enjoy it in any way they pleased. After all, we're all animals, he asserted, and sex is animal behavior. Many celebrated the film as liberating. Kinsey certainly encouraged people to defy cultural standards and determine right and wrong by their own desires. But did he really set them free or instead give them permission to enslave themselves to their fractured and destructive wills?

The Ice Storm and *Closer* reject Kinsey's assertions about our animal nature. They suggest that when people *behave* like animals, adhering only to their base desires and self-centered impulses instead of to conscience, they end up empty and despairing, which bears little resemblance to growth and betterment.

This underrated process of maturing is the central focus of Todd Field's masterful drama *Little Children*. In it, we meet a frustrated husband and father named Brad, who is nostalgic for the freedom of his youth, and Sarah, a woman Brad meets at the park. Sarah, too, is disillusioned with her marriage and has yet to discover that this is, in part, due to her husband's addiction to pornography.

Following their hearts, Brad and Sarah lose their grip on their responsibilities and become increasingly childish, falling into a sexual affair. When a convicted child molester named Ronnie moves into the neighborhood, they're invited to join an organized effort to drive this monster away. But we can see that the zeal for such action can grow from a person's fear and denial of their own unstable hearts. Ronnie represents what we can become when we surrender to desires. The difference between him and his neighbors is that his appetites have been exposed, while those of others remain carefully hidden.

The same theme resonates in *We Don't Live Here Anymore, The Unbearable Lightness of Being, Damage* and *Dangerous Liaisons*. These films all show that lives ruled by appetite lead us on a downward spiral to ruin. They introduce us to people who seem fascinating and beautiful. But then they draw us closer, until we can see the monster enslaving them from within.

Due to the damage that the characters inflict on one another, these are not films I readily and eagerly recommend. The characters in *Closer,* especially, are so relentless in their vulgarity that it wore on me. And the sexual liaisons of unfaithful spouses in *Little Children* are explicit, even though Field is smart enough to avoid making them glamorous. Such scenes can be seductive if a viewer disregards the consequences that follow.

So we should not underestimate these troubling morality tales, just as we should not miss the point of that anti-smoking billboard. Many movies take on the guise of a morality play in order to dazzle us with unnecessary, inappropriate imagery, which does not serve the audience. It's easy to tell stories in which selfish characters ruin each other's lives, and audiences will applaud the lurid spectacle. But the films I've referred to do not *condone* sin; they *expose* it. They are not pleasant movies, nor are they "clean." But, like it or not, they are *true*.

While visions of horrible behavior can turn us away from darkness, it's much more difficult for an artist to create an inspiring portrait of virtue. Films that do so should be celebrated and shared.

Beginning to Live

"I don't know what I've been living for all these years," says Mr. Watanabe. This comes as no surprise to viewers of *Ikiru*. Watanabe has been lost and broken from the beginning of the film.

Leaning over the bar, Watanabe may not even realize that he's given voice to his despair. But there's a stranger with a long, pale face at the end of the bar, a saki-soused novelist. Awakened momentarily from his stupor, he looks at Watanabe and asks, "Does your stomach hurt?"

"It's more than my stomach," says Mr. Watanabe, placing a hand over his heart. "It's . . . "

His face grave with concern, the stranger says, "There has to be some deeper reason for this."

"No," sighs the old man. "I'm a stupid fool. That's all." He goes on to say that he is angry with himself. He's trying to forget his painful past. So he suddenly turns to the stranger and makes a heartfelt plea. He wants to enjoy what life he has left, but he has no experience with sensual pleasure. He needs someone to show him how to enjoy a night on the town.

Like a disembodied face in the darkness, looming over Watanabe like a devil, the stranger seizes upon this plea. He hasn't seen the glowing X-ray that revealed the old man's cancer to us early in the story. But he is excited by this opportunity, this spirit of rebellion against mortality. He tells Watanabe that God wants human beings to enjoy life, to have a lust for pleasure. "Lust is considered immoral," the stranger declares, "but it isn't."

And so, happy to play Mephistopheles, the stranger ushers Watanabe out for a tour of sensory indulgence. Caught up in the pleasure-seeking crowds, they're carried along like fish in a current. Dancing. Drinking. Gambling. How much better to seize the day than to waste life in the madness of bureaucracy!

* * *

Akira Kurosawa, one of cinema's greatest directors, fills *Ikiru* with reflections so that we see this world walled in by its own image, sometimes distorted, sometimes upside down, as if Watanabe has plunged into an illusion.

It should make him happy. But when the piano player starts taking requests, Watanabe finds himself singing a sad,

lonely song: "Fall in love, fair maiden . . . for there is no tomorrow . . . for today will never come again." It could be the love
song of Jack and Rose in *Titanic*. But what a sad, sad song.

* * *

As a worker at City Hall, Mr. Watanabe has spent 25 years in the
drudgery of paperwork, going through the motions and refusing to apply himself with any passion or care. "Now he has neither determination or initiative," the narrator informs us. "City
Hall and its senseless drudgery killed them both." A coworker
has nicknamed Watanabe "the Mummy."

Like many of his self-absorbed colleagues, Watanabe seems
to have no interest in helping people. It's just a job, a paycheck,
security. Similarly, the doctor who discovers Watanabe's stomach cancer dodges his patient's questions. It's possible he
wants to spare Watanabe the painful truth, but in this environment it seems just as likely that the doctor himself wants
to avoid discomfort and hardship. Denial seems to be epidem-
ic in this culture.

Perhaps that is part of the point. *Ikiru* was released in 1952,
and Kurosawa is portraying Japan in the misery of its World War
II defeat. People are throwing themselves into willful forgetful-
ness, crowded together and dancing to music of other nations as
if trying to forget their own. In their sober hours, they have lost
all resolve. New generations are turning their eyes to Western
culture and embracing new social trends. There is a dark cloud
of despair and regret hanging over the city. It is as though in
those frequent images of Mr. Watanabe standing hunched in
the darkest portion of the frame, his back turned to the camera,

we are seeing a picture of the shame of the whole nation.

* * *

Watanabe's son Mitzuo is no help to him. Like the old couple in Ozu's *Tokyo Story*, Watanabe can only watch and despair as Mitzuo and his wife cast off tradition, move on with their lives, and embrace a Western style of independence and materialism. To them, Watanabe represents an eventual inheritance, and that's all. They're waiting for him to die.

So they are startled when Watanabe strikes up a playful friendship with Odagiri, a young woman who has just resigned from the office. As he runs around the city with this impetuous spirit, Watanabe rediscovers laughter and the joy of companionship. Her radiance helps him see things clearly.

Noting her lack of spending money, he tries to return her kindness by buying her gifts and tokens of affection. But Odagiri's a rather naïve and innocent young woman, and when Watanabe becomes dependent on her for happiness, she realizes that she has let this go on too long. He'll have to learn that she is not the answer to his troubles—she is only pointing the way.

When Watanabe finally turns in the right direction, his epiphany is unforgettable and heralded by a chorus of "Happy Birthday." He is, in a sense, born again, and he returns to the office a changed man.

In his sermon entitled "Growing Up," Frederick Buechner writes, "Children that we are, even you and I, who have given up so little, know in our hearts not only that it is more blessed to give than to receive, but that it is also more fun—the kind of holy fun that wells up like tears in the eyes of saints, the kind of blessed fun in which we lose ourselves and at the same time begin to find ourselves, to grow up into the selves we were created to become."[2]

At last, Watanabe is learning what God *really* desires for us. He is following his heart, yes, but he is training his heart to follow the way of wisdom. Back at work, Mr. Watanabe takes up the cause of the angry housewives, determined to build a park that will serve the neighborhood. He wants to give the world something meaningful.

Serve the citizens? From the reaction of the bureaucrats around him, you'd think that he had announced he was off to join the circus. And after Watanabe has completed his mission, his achievements become local legends. Ashamed of their own hard-heartedness, Watanabe's colleagues strive to rob "the Mummy" of the glory he deserves. If we listen to their attempts to rationalize his behavior, we hear echoes of the ways people have tried to discredit and dismiss Christ over the centuries.

It is as though Mr. Watanabe's transformation makes him a fool in the eyes of the world—but a holy fool indeed. We remember the words spoken by the intoxicated novelist early in the film, words that become a sort of prophecy: "Behold the man. This man bears a cross called cancer. . . . If you were diagnosed with cancer, you'd die on the spot. But . . . that's the moment he started living. Right?"

Ikiru means "to live."

Notes

1. Terry Mattingly, "*Titanic*, Satanic?" Scripps Howard News Service, March 30, 1998.
2. Frederick Buechner, *Secrets in the Dark* (San Francisco: HarperSanFrancisco, 2006), p. 144.

PART FIVE

Summoned by Music and Light

CHAPTER
THIRTEEN

Pours Forth Speech

*Who are you whom I so faintly hear, who urge me ever on? What voice
is this that speaks within me, guides me toward the best?*

JOHN SMITH IN *THE NEW WORLD*

The Call of the Color Blue

The first thing that Julie unpacks in her new Paris apartment is
a mobile of blue glass shards, which she hangs in the middle of
a room illuminated by large windows so that the crystals shine
and the strands sway and clatter together.

Julie's spirits have brightened since her decision to move
into a new neighborhood. But as she walks slowly around the
blue menagerie, the lights mesmerize her and then draw emotion to her face. She may not even know why. But we have seen
these very stones hanging in "the blue room," a personal and
precious place in the house where she lived with her husband,
Patrice, a world-renowned composer, and her daughter, Anna,
until a car crash tore them from her life. Now, these stones suggest more than a memory—they are like strands of suspended
crystalline tears, pieces of sharp-edged grief that Julie has not
been able to express. Or perhaps they are the notes of a sad

melody that she cannot compose into a whole.

Earlier in Krzysztof Kieslowski's film *Three Colors: Blue*, we learned that Patrice's last composition—a grand symphony expressing hope for the unification of Europe—remains unfinished. When the news of his death reached television, rumors surfaced that Julie may have composed the music herself. We do not know if this is true. But it is clear that she has failed to compose anything to give shape to her anger and grief. She has determined to follow her impulses, to flee the familiar rooms and the unfinished symphony.

As Julie closed up the old house, just before her move, she found her housekeeper weeping in the pantry.

"Marie, why are you crying?" she asked.

"Because you will not," sobbed Marie, leaning into Julie's embrace. "I keep thinking of them. I remember everything."

Julie refused to cry and locked up all of her memories.

*   *   *

The color of those cold blue fragments begins to visit Julie at unexpected moments. A bright blue light, like the probing ray of an otherworldly presence in *Close Encounters*, shakes her back to full awareness. The flare is accompanied by full, bold orchestral notes that press on her like a summons.

This haunting may happen while she swims or in the middle of a conversation. It occurs one night while she sleeps on the stairway outside her door, having accidentally locked herself out of the secure new apartment.

Viewer interpretations of the light will vary. For me, it seems to be the spirit that inspired the composition—a call for the reunification of broken things. But if Julie answers that call, it will take her back to pick up and complete what has been left undone.

Julie is more intent on escape. She seals herself off from her neighbors and tries to prevent new relationships. The pain is too great. Commitment, responsibility, craft—these things have come to ruin. She will live freely, independently. Money is no issue, so she will live without a vocation.

As Julie basks in the sunlight, delirious with denial, we watch as an old, feeble woman hobbles past. *Things mean things,* I remind myself. Why this old woman? Why focus on her? Ah, yes. The old woman is alone with no one to help her. The dangers of Julie's isolation have not become real to her yet. But they will if she does not answer that call.

Blue is the first of the films in Krzysztof Kieslowski's *Three Colors* trilogy. Each movie—*Blue, White* and *Red*—represents one of the colors of the French flag, which symbolize, in turn, liberty, equality and fraternity. Of course, these three themes do not begin to summarize what the films convey—many other themes suggest themselves to us through the course of the stories—but these three might prove helpful as starting points for those who want to engage with and discuss the trilogy. They're offered like lenses that will reveal different truths. When we start considering a theme, we begin mapping the interconnectedness of details and events.

When Americans make films about liberty, they usually tell stories about the glory of independence and the need to break away from the expectations of others and follow a personal dream. Kieslowski's portrayal of one woman pursuing liberation gives us a strikingly different impression of individualism. The more Julie tries to break free, the more she imprisons herself, cutting herself off from her relationships and her calling. Unless she turns back, the music she loved will never be played at all.

Moving Pictures

In Kieslowski's *Blue*, every scene—in fact, almost every shot—unfolds like a poem.

We are challenged to stop asking what will happen next and begin considering what is happening now. What can we learn from the moment? The more I watch the film, the more I'm learning to consider the movement of light, the color of a room, the brief hint of tension in the lines of Julie's face.

In one shot, Kieslowski employs a camera the size of a filament to zoom in close and glide along a staff of musical notation. We hear the notes being played—a simple, melancholy melody on piano keys. The notes blur as they appear on the right side of the frame, come into sharp focus in the center, and then fade again as they slide off to the left. Suddenly, we reach the end of the notes, moving along stark, straight, horizontal lines. Were they the last strokes of Patrice's pen as he composed? Perhaps.

I think of a heart monitor, and a flat-lining heart, a life suddenly halted. Or perhaps it represents Julie's journey. We are looking at her steps along a path and then—out of the blue?—she has leapt off the page, which waits for her to return and follow the song to its conclusion.

When Julie visits a café, a man seated on the sidewalk outside performs a song on a recorder. The music drifts in through the window and Julie basks in the melody as if resting in the sun. It is an arresting motif, because it is so familiar. Julie knows it is impossible that it is from Patrice's compositions, which she destroyed. Yet it is so similar.

Julie holds a sugar cube above the surface of her espresso. An edge of that perfect, white cube touches the opaque surface and draws the coffee in, blackening, holding its shape as long as it can while it fills with darkness. In the same way, the music has brought Julie to the edge of the past, and she is welling up with emotion.

Kieslowski provides a long, extreme close-up during which we can see only the coffee cup, spoon and saucer on the café table where Julie sits listening. We watch as shadows slowly shift, but nothing else changes. Hours pass, and Julie sits there without touching anything. She is so caught up in thought that she has not refilled her cup. But she cannot have left, or the waiter would have cleared the table.

Kieslowski communicates so much with so little. If he were moving any faster, we would lose the detail and the fullness of his world.

* * *

Kieslowski leaves clues for us to consider—little windows into understanding the state of Julie's heart. When we take the time to think about them, we begin to participate in the film in a way that popular commercial cinema doesn't allow. There are long passages in *Blue* in which no one says anything and we must shift our attention to what we see in order to discern what is happening.

Julie never says a word about what the glass mobile means to her. But because we have spent so much time looking at it and so much time watching Julie look at it in a certain way, it becomes almost a character in the film.

When an exotic dancer who is Julie's neighbor, exhibiting no boundaries or sense of privacy, barges into her new apartment and walks up to touch the mobile, we tense up in alarm. All we need to see is Julie's face to know her sense of fear and violation.

A Song for Reunification

Thanks to Kieslowski's delicate development of moments and images, the time I have spent with Julie in those silences has made the film grow into something like a liturgy for me. As if running beads through my fingers, I move through a progression of meditations that help me process my own deep sense of grief. I am moved by the film, from one place to the next, each time coming to reconcile a little more with my own loss.

In the mid-'90s, I suffered a grievous betrayal and a loss that still aches. While friends and families surrounded me with prayer and help, the wounds were of a sort that no one's words could heal. The suddenness and the severity caused me to feel as if I had been rushed into surgery in a case of mistaken identity—that someone had carved out vital organs without anesthesia. Then I was left to tend to the wounds without any needle and thread to sew myself up again. It was just me and the silence of God.

Once I was able to move forward again, I became inclined to embrace escapism, just to distract my attention from the pain. Some of those pursuits were rewarding and healthy. A few were ill-advised and merely wasteful. I moved to a new place and tried to begin again. Like Julie, I avoided places that held painful reminders and steered clear of contexts that brought back memories. On my desk, stories were left half-written. Projects remained unfinished. I invested in activities and relationships that were easy, that made no demands, and that allowed me to go on running from my calling.

"Time," a friend told me. "Time will heal it all." But it's not true. Time doesn't heal things. Time can help you forget or preoccupy you with other things.

Blue became a way I could move through my loss by experiencing someone else's journey rather than facing my own pain directly. It coaxed me to give creative shape to the grief, just as Julie eventually responds to the call of the music. The film became a sort of personal Gethsemane for me, a place to go and rage, weep and then muster the strength to finish what had been left undone.

While I've never been visited by a blazing blue light, I did at last attend to a still, small voice that coaxed me back to those unfinished stories. I filled my stories with my questions in order to purge them from my head and heart. My own pursuit of storytelling ultimately showed me things about myself that I hadn't understood—my weaknesses and need.

In the same way, the words that filled the symphony for the reunification of Europe must have given Julie healing and hope. If we investigate the words of Patrice's symphony, sung in Greek by a choir over the closing montage of the film, we suddenly realize the true power of the song and understand why it has become so important for Julie to accept it and offer it to the world.

The lyrics are the text of 1 Corinthians 13:1—"If I speak in the tongues of men and of angels, but have not love, I am only a resounding gong or a clanging cymbal . . ."

What a Picture Is Worth

Images speak. Like music, they convey things that mere words cannot communicate. The power of the image is different from the power of the narrative. That's a secret great filmmakers know.

The power of narrative lies in the succession of events: This happens and then that happens. Most films we will see in our lifetime are forms of illustrated narrative—storytelling. Since they are designed to dazzle us with intensifying surprises over the course of two hours, we become focused on *what happens next.*

In previous chapters, I focused on characters and the values they embody, and choices and the consequences they bring. But film and the stage are unique in that they give us an experience of imagery in motion. Imagery speaks even when nothing is *happening,* offering us something more than provocation to anticipate *what's next.* Furthermore, cinema is distinct from theater. While the stage offers us particular moments only once, never to appear in quite the same way again, cinema gives us captured moments and allows us to study them more and more deeply with each look. We can revisit a specific moment, a specific span of time, searching for new possibilities.

Understanding the way that great art "speaks" is not just about interpreting the moral of a story. It takes patience and learning to do more than follow the narrative. A friend will watch a film that I have come to cherish, and he'll come to me with an apologetic frown, saying, "I'm sorry, but it was just too slow for me. There didn't seem to be much happening."

I know what he means. But lately I've been increasingly grateful for films in which not much happens. Weary of constantly taking in information from the news, e-mail, web pages, television, movies, the telephone and radio, I find myself longing for a vacation. And that longing has led me to seek movies that satisfy in a very different way from narrative. This art is not about what happens next. It's a style that gives me space to have my own thoughts while engaging the director's vision. I'm not simply being led along—I'm a willing participant. It gives me pictures and sounds to consider rather than developments to anticipate.

Increasingly, I find myself preferring to see a great film again instead of a new release. I find myself drawn to slow, contemplative films than fast action movies. I take so much pleasure in discovering all that things can mean that I'm not so thrilled by the buildup to another explosion or surprise. Yoda would be proud— I'm trying to "unlearn what I have learned." We can find new freedom when we stand still, when we stop running from one thought to the next, and give ourselves time instead to absorb each moment and explore it.

This isn't about movies, ultimately. This kind of moviegoing is an education in how to live.

Talking with director Darren Aronofsky, whose film *The Fountain* reminds us of the importance of savoring the moment,

I learned a little about his recent adventures. He told me about a visit to Tokyo, and it was interesting to note which moment, out of that whole exotic trip, stood out to him. "On the street, we bought a salted cracker from this guy who was frying them up and selling them to schoolkids," he said. "We watched, just amazed by how patiently he picked through them before he picked the right one to give you. That's so different from getting a hot dog in Manhattan, where they'll just slap one on the bun and hand it to you." When he said that, I thought of the difference between the filmmaking of artists and the moviemaking of most commercial entertainers.

Aronofsky shook his head, bewildered again as he thought back. "Watching that, we saw that we've become so detached from the reality of the moment. We've lost touch with it. We escape in so many ways, with TV and video games. But that kind of attention to the moment is amazing—to remember that within every moment there are infinite possibilities."

In Psalm 46:10, the Almighty exhorts us to "know that I am God." He also tells us how: "Be still . . ."

Music healed the rift between a mother camel and her child. The mystery of incarnation, in art as in nature, performs a quiet, intimate work.

* * *

Cinematographer Louis Schwartzberg, whose inspiring work is celebrated in the documentary *America's Heart and Soul*, is devoted to capturing the possibilities of particular moments. He's interested in stories—don't get me wrong—but his gift is in being at the right place at the right time for instants of revelation in color and light.

His discipline has resulted in a massive library of imagery that is used as stock photography for movies and advertising by people who know the power of unscripted beauty and want to bring it into their own work.

"I think quality is important," Schwartzberg told me during an interview for ChristianityTodayMovies.com. "Cinematography . . . it's not there just to be pretty. It makes a greater emotional impact in telling a story. Beauty is a way of having you fall in love with your subject matter. It's an emotional connection. It's not intellectual. Beauty makes you fall in love with nature so that hopefully you'll protect it. Beauty makes you fall in love with your baby so that you won't throw it out with the bathwater when it cries. I'm fascinated with beauty, and that's what I try to capture with my moviemaking."

Schwartzberg is also not about to give up the discipline of *film*-making. Digital cameras just don't do it for him. "I *love* shooting film," he told me. "I know the medium. It's like an old craft . . . like oil painting. I just know what film can do. Digital is getting better and better all the time, but there's something about it that feels too electronic to me. I just love the colors and palette of film. When I shoot film, I can actually feel the light etching into the emulsion. That to me is like an ancient craft . . . chasing the light."

Chasing the light. Yeah, that's about right. For me, living my whole life in busy cities, constantly moving from classes to desk jobs to meetings to shopping, it's a rare and rejuvenating privilege to sit quietly and give my eyes a rest from manmade busyness and let them drink in the grace of what God has made.

I strongly suspect that the success of Peter Jackson's *The Lord of the Rings* trilogy had as much to do with the awe-inspiring spectacle of New Zealand's mountains and forests as it did with the suspense and the manmade special effects. We knew we were going back for the sequels to learn *what happened next*. But is it possible that we might have been responding, oblivious, to another appetite . . . the desire to gaze on the kind of wild beauty that God designed as an environment for us all? Is that why *The Fellowship of the Ring* lifts my spirits—the way it makes the stuff of creation front and central, whereas we have pushed it into our peripheral vision, an occasional vacation destination?

It was this communicative power of nature that the beloved poet, theologian and Trappist monk Thomas Merton wrote about in his journals during his years of living and strolling around on the property of the Gethsemani monastery. Although I cannot see the place with my eyes, the beauty Merton observed reaches me through his journal entries.

At the end of a day of basking in its colors, he wrote a particularly beautiful description of the light, the field, and the woods, and concluded:

> I looked at all this in great tranquility, with my soul and spirit quiet. For me, landscape seems to be important for contemplation. Anyway, I have no scruples about loving it. Didn't Saint John of the Cross hide himself in a room up in a church tower, where there was one small window through which he could look out at the country?[1]

Later in the same journal, he recorded an afternoon of searching for an opportunity to sit down and study a book. But as he searched, natural wonders continued to distract him and minister to him as much or more than reading ever could. Eventually, he surrendered.

> I just listened to the clean water flowing and looked at the wreckage of the horsebarn on top of the bare knoll in front of me, and remained drugged with happiness and prayer.[2]

The more I spend time with the work of artists and filmmakers who are similarly patient and attentive to the visual poetry of faces, light, nature and revelatory details, the less I'm satisfied with noisy, frantic entertainment that shows no care for aesthetics. When they invite me to look deeply at something beautiful rather than fleetingly at many forgettable sights, the process becomes healing and rejuvenating. Just as that blue light and that persistent anthem summon Julie to return to the hard road of love, art's capacity to draw us into contemplation has led me through dark and uncertain times.

Since then, it has led me into unexpected blessings, and I'm left fumbling for words that will convey the pleasure I take in "chasing the light."

Transported to a New World

As Terrence Malick's film *The New World* begins, birds and crickets are rejoicing. We move slowly over the surface of the water, which reflects the sky.

Malick asks us to look at this water for so long that a certain suspense arises. At first, I was anxious to see what's next. But I've come to suspect that the moment is not just an incidental, arbitrary picture used to build suspense. The moment is all about how *this* water reflects *this* sky. I am supposed to *be here* for this.

What comes to mind is the Scripture about the beginning of time: "And the Spirit of God was hovering over the waters" (Gen. 1:2). I am taken back to creation. To Eden.

I am also thinking about light and reflection. Earth is mirroring back the glory of the heavens, but it does so darkly, and the reflection is not distinct.

Our gaze is then turned directly into the light, a span of bright sky caught between the open arms of a young woman looking upward. She offers a simple introductory prayer: "Come, spirit. Help us sing the story of our land. You are our mother, we your field of corn. We rise from out of the soul of you."

The mystery above has raised a soul up from the earth, like a green and growing thing. Reaching brown arms skyward, the woman cups light in her hands and pulls it toward her eyes. It is a purposeful physical gesture, a ritual. She's saying something important. She wants to catch that light, that spirit, and draw it into herself.

*   *   *

Fish swim past the lens. We're underwater, looking upward. Through the wavering veil, this smiling Native American princess reaches out and runs her hand though the water as if she's inviting us up, through time and memory, into her world.

The music—the strings and horns of Wagner's "Vorspiel" from *Das Rheingold*—swells and courses like a stream that becomes a rushing river. It perfectly enhances the way that the imagery continues to draw us forward, forward, always forward into something new. As these images and sounds accumulate, the momentum becomes exhilarating. It only stops when we find ourselves drawn into a manmade enclosure, where the things of nature disappear and we are trapped inside the crude machinations of human fear and ego.

But before we encounter anything like hell, we will meet other travelers to this Eden. We meet Captain John Smith, a man who inadvertently repeats the gestures of the princess. He does not yet know her. He is chained in the darkness of a ship's holding cell. We first notice his eyes, bright and burning in the shadows. He too is drawn to the only piece of sky available—the shaft of light through the barred window in the ceiling. He lifts his hands to it, trying to catch rain to cool his thirst.

We watch through the eyes of the agitated natives as ships full of British explorers approach the coast of what will become known as the Virginia territory. The natives are drawn to this bizarre sight, scrambling along, concealing themselves in the trees.

They do not know that, in the minds of the arriving Europeans, it is the year 1607. It is as though they can hardly focus their eyes on the frightening foreign craft. They peer out suspiciously through the branches, alarmed by what they are seeing. But the child princess steps forward into the open in wonder and curiosity, without fear.

* * *

Surrounded by spears, swords and guns, Captain Newport brings his men ashore. They busy themselves exploring, testing and tasting the water, excitedly scooping up oysters and declaring that they will live like kings.

Behind Newport's narrow gaze is a mind calculating the next steps in his country's occupation of this land. His face seems hewn from stone, hardened from travel and the company of difficult men. He moves as if assuming ownership of any ground where he plants his feet. The natives annoy him. They are an inconvenient detail. "We must be careful not to offend the naturals," he says. "We may be obliged to trade with them."

Moments before a noose is draped around Smith's head, Newport suddenly pardons him. Perhaps he realizes he needs all the help he can get. "You come to these shores in chains," he warns Smith. "You are under a cloud."

In a Malick film, words like these cannot be as incidental as they seem. Sure enough, even after his bonds are broken, Smith moves about the land like a man seeking to escape the chains of his past, his culture and his own lust for discovery and achievement.

*   *   *

Malick's cameras follow Smith as he puts distance between himself and the other men. While they chop down trees and erect fort walls, Smith wanders through long grass, marveling, as if drawn by the light of this place. When he takes a boat up the river in search of the king's camp, we hear his own personal prayer: "Who are you whom I so faintly hear, who urge me ever on? What voice is this that speaks within me, guides me toward the best?"

Brusque and gruff, Newport is full of talk about God giving the British this "promised land," this "Eden." But Smith seems to actually believe it, the way he takes each step cautiously, as if expecting the Almighty Himself to appear in the trees. With the glory captured by Emanuel Lubezki's cinematography, we might expect the same thing.

While Smith doesn't see the Almighty—not directly—he does stumble upon a wonder that will haunt him for the rest of his life. As the call grows sharper, his attention seizes on the shape of a curious girl who is peering at him through the grass like an inquisitive deer.

* * *

Their courtship is the most beautiful half hour of film I have ever seen.

History gives the 12-year-old girl many names, but we know her as Pocahontas, which means "playful one." And their flirtatious dance is rather playful.

It's as though we're seeing Adam and Eve discover each other for the first time. As they cautiously sift each other's words, the princess strives to learn his language. She learns quickly, as if born to occupy the space between the cultures. Intensely curious, she practices his words. "Sky. Sun. Water. Wind. Eyes. Lips. Ears." Each new discovery is a joyous revelation that sets her dancing.

Malick frames shots in such unlikely ways that it is as if we have never seen a man and a woman touch each other before. When she slowly removes a feather from her hair and places it in his hands, we half expect a choir to burst into chorus. And when she leans slowly against him, we know that she has placed all trust in him, this one she says is "like a god" to her.

But Smith is not a god. And they are not Adam and Eve. Each in turn idealizes the other's culture. Smith calls the Native Americans "gentle, loving, faithful, lacking all guile and envy. They have no jealousy. No sense of possession." Looking at Smith, Pocahontas thinks, "You have no evil in you. I belong to you." This sets the stage for devastating disappointments and betrayals.

In one memorable sequence, dark clouds move over the land. A line of birds unfurls like a whip. Lightning breaks through the darkness and thunder rolls. Pocahontas, standing in the water and smiling in awe, suddenly appears vulnerable and naïve, stepping into charged and dangerous territory.

* * *

In the Jamestown camp, things are spiraling downward. The men and the children are starving, yet they spend their days digging into the earth in search of gold, the only wealth they understand. Their territory has become a colorless world stripped of natural life. A gang of boys, half-mad, greets Smith on his return to the settlement from his time among the Powhatans and tell him of sickness and desperation: "They're eating all the dead."

Damnation is like this, Smith thinks to himself as the cultures turn against one another with arrows and spears. He offers up his own desperate prayer: "Lord, turn not away thy face. . . . I have not hearkened to your voice."

But it is not war that tears Smith away at last from his true love. It is ambition. Newport puts his hand on Smith's shoulder and offers him a chance to travel farther and discover yet another world. "I remember when you had ambition," Newport says to him. "Shall you not press on?"

*   *   *

"There's something I know when I'm with you that I forget when I'm away."

Those are Pocahontas' words to Smith, and her mistake is in believing that he is the source of the light, that knowledge she so desires. It is through him she has seen the light. But he is not the light.

Saint John of the Cross wrote that man is like a window through which God is shining. If the window is clean and undefiled, it allows us to see past it, to the light. We hardly notice it at all. And yet, if a man gives evidence of any kind of arrogance or ego and self-interest, then that window becomes noticeable. It is not fulfilling its purpose. It is not merely a vessel for the light.

Malick is constantly drawing our attention to windows, shafts of sunshine, and the way the trees catch and throw the light.

But as moviegoers, we have been conditioned to give glory to what reflects and takes credit for the light. We love rogues like Captain Smith, the adventurer, the fearless and independent man.

Those who recognize that coursing Wagner music that returns again and again may suspect why Malick has chosen it. As Manohla Dargis observed in her *New York Times* film review, this Wagnerian prologue from the Ring cycle represents the forswearing of love for gold and power. Smith, for all of his gentleness and potential as Pocahontas' true love, has made his choice. Malick is clear-eyed enough to see that there is no turning back.

*   *   *

It was with utter astonishment that I watched Terrence Malick introduce yet another suitor for Pocahontas more than halfway through the film. This man was not so arresting, not so fierce and magnetic. This man was almost transparent in his meekness.

We're introduced to a widowed farmer named John Rolfe, who resembles John Smith, but with one fundamental difference. It's in the eyes.

In a typical big screen epic, the rival for the heroine's heart is a man confined by tradition, seeking marriage and oozing evil from every pore. Rolfe has all the makings of a big screen villain—he's traditional, he grows tobacco, and what is more, he's a Christian. His gaze, unlike Smith's, is quiet, gentle and inquisitive. He's drawn to this broken princess out of a shared sense of suffering.

"Are you kind?" she asks him, unsure whether she can ever trust any man to be honest with her again. Rolfe's response is a gaze of such grace that it's likely some filmmaker will invite Christian Bale to play the next big-screen Jesus.

When Smith returns at the end of the film, Pocahontas faces a terrible choice. Will she return to the man who seemed like a god, the one she worshiped as the source of the light? Or will she remain with Rolfe, who is "like a tree" to her, someone who grows toward the light with such sincerity that she finds comfort in his shade?

*   *   *

Malick has crafted a landmark of American mythology that contradicts so much else in our cultural lexicon. He has given us a story that sets aside the pursuit of happiness for something greater—the apprehension of joy.

Some critics have already drawn parallels between his Pocahontas story and recent headlines regarding foreign occupations, homeland security and "culture wars." But Malick's movie transcends convenient correlations. He is not so concerned with which culture is right or wrong. He's watching the ways in which individuals in either camp behave as children of God.

Malick returns frequently to images of trees that tower and sway with heads disappearing into the heavens. In one easily overlooked moment, Pocahontas gazes at a tree that, despite a broken branch, continues to grow toward the light. In this, Malick reminds us that regardless of which society gains supremacy or what is lost along the way, what matters most is how we respond to the summons of that heavenly light—whether we encounter it in nature or in art.

It's remarkable, really. Even as he depicts a woman who apprehends the mysterious call of the Divine through the language of nature, so Malick himself, through the beauty of his work, enables us to sense that summons ourselves.

As Merton wrote in *No Man Is an Island*:

> In an aesthetic experience, in the creation or the contemplation of a work of art, the psychological conscience is able to attain some of its highest and most perfect fulfillments. Art enables us to find ourselves

and lose ourselves at the same time. The mind that responds to the intellectual and spiritual values that lie hidden in a poem, a painting, or a piece of music, discovers a spiritual vitality that lifts it above itself, takes it out of itself, and makes it present to itself on a level of being that it did not know it could ever achieve.[3]

* * *

I can think of few filmmakers who transport me to a new level of being with the power of Terrence Malick. More than any film I've seen since *Three Colors: Blue* and *Wings of Desire*, Malick's *The New World* makes me want to seize the people I love and bring them into a theater to enjoy it on the largest screen possible.

That is because Malick, like Kieslowski, communicates through images more than plot. The dialogue in *The New World* can be frustrating, even exasperating, for we are listening to only fragments of the characters' conversations and thoughts. If their words are considered without taking into account how they relate to the visual communication, they can sound like so much processed cheese. Most directors rely on their script to do the talking. For Malick, words are just seasoning. He lets his pictures speak, and he gets out of the way.

In a 1943 letter to Sister Penelope, C. S. Lewis wrote, "'Creation' as applied to human authorship seems to me to be an entirely misleading term. We rearrange elements He has provided. And that is surely why our works never mean to others quite what we intended; because we are recombining elements made by Him and already containing His meanings.

Because of those divine meanings in our materials it is impossible that we should ever know the whole meaning of our works and the meaning we never intended may be the best and truest one."[4]

Acting on my recommendation, a friend caught a screening of *The New World* and returned raving about its dazzling imagery. Yet he confessed that as he watched Smith and Pocahontas meander through the woods, he thought, *Why can't they walk faster?*

I remember a time when I would have agreed. But now, at this point in the journey, sometimes I wish that the characters would slow down. Or step out of the frame altogether so that I can just watch the light.

Notes
1. Thomas Merton, *The Sign of Jonas* (New York: Harcourt Brace Jovanovich, Inc., 1953) cited in *Through the Year with Thomas Merton* (New York: Image Books, 1985), pp. 105-106.
2. Thomas Merton, *The Sign of Jonas* (New York: Harcourt Brace Jovanovich, Inc., 1953), p. 225.
3. Thomas Merton, *No Man Is an Island* (New York: Dell Publishing Company, 1955), p. 55.
4. Walter Hooper, ed., *C. S. Lewis Collected Letters, Vol. 2: Books, Broadcasts and War 1931-1949* (New York: Harper Collins, 2004), p. 554.

Chasing the Light

Wherever you turn your eyes the world can shine like transfiguration.
You don't have to bring a thing to it except a little willingness to see.
Only, who could have the courage to see it?

MARILYNNE ROBINSON IN THE NOVEL *GILEAD*

When we open our eyes and dream
We open our eyes . . .

"HOW TO DREAM," A SONG BY SAM PHILLIPS

"Flickerings" of the Future[1]

On July 4, 2003, I realized that something had changed.

I was walking through a maze of campsites scattered like the world's largest circus during the twentieth anniversary of the Cornerstone Festival, a week-long alternative Christian music extravaganza run by Jesus People U.S.A. Nearly 20,000 campers had gathered in the middle of a 20-acre patch of farmland near Macomb, Illinois, four hours west of Chicago. Everywhere I went, my eardrums were pummeled by waves of throbbing bass as bands of all musical colors clamored for attention from the various exhibition tents.

But there was more than music going on at Cornerstone that summer.

An unremarkable storage shed stands a fair distance from the concert stages. For most of the year, it houses equipment. But on that day, the shed caught direct sunlight in the near 100-degree heat while several hundred people inside sweated silently in the dark, shoulder to shoulder.

The storage shed had become a makeshift cinema. Over the doors hung a hand-painted sign that read "Flickerings Film Festival." It was only noon, but already the people had spent hours straining to listen while the roaring industrial-strength fans circulated heavy humid air. The movies began at 9:30 A.M. and continued until 9:00 P.M.

This was not a screening of *The Passion of the Christ* or *The Chronicles of Narnia: The Lion, the Witch and the Wardrobe*. Nor was it a marathon of the *Left Behind* movies or another franchise popular among churchgoers, such as *The Lord of the Rings*. This morning, it was a series of amateur short subjects. The people in the makeshift theater had just finished viewing a feature-length documentary on gun control, during which others eager to join them were turned away at the door. Someone had scrawled "sold out" on a piece of cardboard with a Sharpie. Soon they'd take in an obscure foreign film, followed by a documentary about Jacques Derrida.

An intellectual's film festival drawing capacity crowds in the middle of Illinois farmland? And the attendees are Christians? What is going on here?

* * *

The first time I saw Mike Hertenstein, I thought he looked like a youth-camp counselor. He drove up in a golf cart and invited me on a quick tour of the Cornerstone Festival. In his baseball cap, dusty red T-shirt and shorts, he didn't look like an arts-awareness activist. But his work mixes the responsibilities of an art critic, a youth minister and a prophet in the wilderness. His wilderness is the Church. His vision is a revival of profound artistic sensibilities within it.

As he putters along in his cart, no one can see the print on the back of his T-shirt: "So many subtitles, so little time."

Mike is one of many agents responsible for setting in motion this continental shift in churchgoers' perceptions of popular culture and art. But his approach is unique. He wants to expose moviegoers to the provocative and over-looked work of filmmakers who explore spiritual themes. He wants to draw Christian artists out of their old enclaves to break new ground.

For Flickerings 2003, Hertenstein called for amateur film-makers to submit short films following a list of strict limita-tions. It's his version of the "Vows of Chastity" enforced by filmmakers who participated in the Dogme 95 project, an avant-garde filmmaking movement started by a group of Danish filmmakers including Lars von Trier (*Dogville*, *The Five Obstructions*). Dogme 95 encouraged filmmakers to adhere to a strict code of minimalist filmmaking, and his famous "Thou Shalt Nots" forbade genre movies, postproduction work, cam-eras other than hand-held video cameras, sound added beyond what takes place within the scene, superficial action (murder, gunplay, car chases), and more.

Filmmakers who accepted Von Trier's Dogme 95 challenge introduced influential and revelatory films that proved just how much of what we see in mainstream cinema is unnecessary and how a more efficient mode of filmmaking could captivate audiences. This series of arresting, unconventional films included critically acclaimed titles such as *Breaking the Waves*, *The King Is Alive* and *The Celebration*.

Hertenstein had adapted Von Trier's dogma, customizing it for religious artists, detailing different restrictions: Refrain from the use of popular religious symbols, including the cross. No church scenes. No conclusions that involve a conversion to Christianity. No Scripture verses. No music with lyrics. No End Times scenarios. Show; don't tell.

By these rules, Flickerings' founder coaxed Christian artists away from the simplistic, didactic, sentimental and condescending qualities often found in contemporary Christian art and entertainment, nudging them toward the language of metaphor. This unsettled some artists. They worried that viewers wouldn't "get their message." It's true—some didn't get their message, but some did. And some got more than the filmmakers had ever meant to convey.

Even as Hertenstein challenged artists on their own work, he provided attendees with a feast of overlooked international cinema. What better way to draw Christians into healthy and relevant discussions than to show them provocative works of art?

It happened again and again during the course of the week: *Code Unknown* stimulated conversation and some epiphanies. *Not of This World* introduced viewers to an amusing, emotional Italian parable about a nun and a Laundromat owner. *The King*

Is Alive took us on an excruciating journey of moral, civil, marital and intellectual disintegration. *Hell House*, a troubling but objective documentary on heavy-handed evangelical tactics, provoked debate over the methods with which zealous Christians share the gospel. Hertenstein followed this with even more ambitious programs in 2004 and 2005. In 2006, he hosted a festival of films by the Italian director Roberto Rossellini, reintroducing Christian viewers to the spiritually and politically challenging works like *The Flowers of St. Francis,* a treasure almost forgotten by American moviegoers.

* * *

Yes, something has definitely changed. In the heat of the Flickerings Film Festival, people are going to extremes to discover a new language for spiritual matters. Tired of pat answers and mere preachiness, more and more believers are turning to art to experience truths that cannot be reduced to a paraphrase.

God promises that we will be changed when we see Him. This pursuit of what film critic André Bazin calls "holy moments" becomes an exercise of transformative recognition of God in the everyday world. You could call it "practice," the art of becoming ready for the day we see Him in His fullness. Such discipline carries over into encounters in the humdrum of daily existence, in walks at the park, in unexpected moments of eye contact between friends and strangers.

Wise men studied the skies and then set out after a star, which led them to the Christ child. Those with eyes to see will be drawn to follow beauty and truth, and they will encounter God.

In the multiplex. On DVD. In post-viewing discussions on-line, at home and, increasingly, at the local church. This summer, they will go searching again in a hot storage shed on a patch of farmland near Macomb. Inquisitive moviegoers will be out there chasing the light.

* * *

For the big studios, the future of film is in digital effects, franchises, comic book adaptations and big-budget remakes with expensive celebrities. Too often they give us pornography masquerading as art—indulgent in sex, but also in violence, political agendas and religious sermonizing—appeasing whatever appetite consumers bring.

For those who hunger for art, the future of film belongs to a generation of creative artists who have discovered that they can afford what it takes to make a good movie without the big budgets, celebrities and special effects. These amateurs have priorities other than earning big studio paychecks, achieving magazine-cover fame and winning popularity contests like the Oscars. Some will focus on realizing their unique artistic visions. Once they develop a method of distribution—we can see the beginnings in the emergence of YouTube and other online video services—these new visionaries will show us how the studio system has stifled rich and diverse expressions from around the world. Many of the great films of the next era will be discovered at independent film festivals and in the blogs of watchful cinephiles rather than at major studio press junkets.

The works that stand the test of time will be those that capture our imaginations and speak to our deepest spiritual longings. They will reveal the truths that cannot be told. This will occur not through argument but through visual poetry—images worth a hundred thousand words or, better, worth a long and reverent silence.

Ministers of Light

There is so much more I wish I could share with you, so many marvels I have seen along the way. Given time, I would start with Ingmar Bergman's *Winter Light*, Wong Kar-Wai's *In the Mood for Love* and Errol Morris's *Fast, Cheap and Out of Control*. I'd write about the Coen brothers' *Barton Fink* and *Fargo*, Wes Anderson's *The Life Aquatic with Steve Zissou*, and Robert Bresson's *Au Hasard Balthazar*.

I'd explore the challenging contributions of contemporary artists such as Hou Hsiao-Hsien, Mike Leigh, David Lynch, Guillermo Del Toro, Jim Sheridan, Sofia Coppola, Peter Weir, Jim Jarmusch, Aki Kaurismäki, Thomas Vinterberg, Tom Tykwer, Richard Linklater and Denys Arcand.

Iranian filmmakers Abbas Kiarostami, Jafar Panahi and Majid Majidi have recently offered penetrating journeys into spiritual conflicts tormenting the present-day Middle East. Mira Nair's *Monsoon Wedding* is an ebulliently colorful, deeply moving comedy set in India that explores issues of marital fidelity, abuse and healing. Documentarians Errol Morris (*The Fog of War*) and Steve James (*Hoop Dreams*) are elevating their genre to the level of high art. *Stevie*, James's personal testimony about serving as a Big Brother to a troubled boy, has become for me a soul-searching, transforming work of nonfiction film that I revisit frequently and share with friends.

In interviews, many of today's most provocative directors confess their admiration for the same list of predecessors: Robert Bresson, Akira Kurosawa, Yasujiro Ozu and Carl Theodor Dreyer. The works of two more-recent directors—Krzysztof Kieslowski and Andrei Tarkovsky—are also mentioned with reverence. It is worth noting that these past masters are all known for works of an intensely spiritual, religious and, in some cases, Christian nature.

Tarkovsky's semi-autobiographical work, *The Mirror,* is a rush, a plunge into dream and memory, in which scenes morph from one chapter of his life to the next. Sometimes the camera will turn a full circle, and by the time it comes all the way around, we find that the room has changed entirely and we are in another time.

Marvels arrive with such drama and flourish that they could not have been humanly orchestrated. Watching *The Mirror,* I saw a woman sit on a fence and stare across a vast field toward a dark wood. All was still and peaceful. Then, without warning, a gale force wind rounded the corner, rushed toward the camera, set the field to thrashing and made me want to rise and run for shelter. It thrills me just to think about it, remembering how unexpectedly that invisible force bore down on the audience. I think of it whenever I look out across a field and often even when I am indoors and at peace. The spirit can move so suddenly and turn my world around.

That is how art has worked in my life. There have been so many moments at the movies that have become a part of my history, giving me images that function as vocabulary, enhancing what I experience when I am away from the screen.

Flickerings of the Past

In *A River Runs Through It*, the two Maclean boys kneel beside their father on the bank of a river. Like the good Presbyterian minister he is, the father says to them, "Long ago, rain fell on mud and became rock. . . . But even before that, beneath the rocks are the words of God. Listen."

And so I try. When I look up at the screen and see sunlight, God is speaking. It doesn't matter if it's a sunrise over New York City in a comic book movie. It might be the sunlight over vivid trees in Majid Majidi's *The Color of Paradise*, a spectacle made much more poignant by the fact that a blind boy is climbing one of the trees. A filmmaker might make a terrible movie, but one good image within it can stay with me, mysterious, burning. And that can enrich my appreciation of moments I experience after leaving the theater.

* * *

During that sacred, middle hour of the day, when I can leave my desk and my assignments behind, I walk to The Grinder, an espresso stand a few blocks from Seattle Pacific University. There, I sit in a blue canvas recliner, enjoy the sunshine, and visit with the ever-joyful barista and owner, Kristen Wilhite. Life is just a little brighter at Kristen's coffee stand. I've been drinking double-tall Americanos there for more than a decade.

Just as Kristin's company improves the taste of the coffee, so too a scene from *Wings of Desire* enriches every cup she pours. On that cold day when Damiel becomes a human being, he hurries off to buy a cup of coffee. He has watched people savor coffee for so many ages, and now he gets to try it for himself. He takes it into his hands the way the faithful take a cup of communion wine. The heat through the cup, the steam, the blackness, the flavor—his eyes widen in amazement.

In that moment, coffee became sacramental to me. I savor it all the more because the movie made me aware of the privilege.

But I sometimes get a laugh out of ordering, because I remember Steve Martin ordering "a half, double, decaffeinated, half-caf with a twist of lemon" in *L.A. Story*. At a diner, I imagine drinking straight from the coffee pot as nonchalantly as Bill Murray in Jim Jarmusch's *Coffee and Cigarettes*. Sometimes, on special occasions, I pour espresso over a single scoop of vanilla ice cream, just as Julie does in *Three Colors: Blue*.

At the Mar T Café in North Bend, Washington, I order cherry pie, because Special Agent Dale Cooper relished cherry pie at that very restaurant in the *Twin Peaks* series, refusing to let the grim and grisly details of the murder case interfere with his apprehension of glory. I also remember how cherries were savory enough to foil an attempted suicide in Abbas Kiarostami's *A Taste of Cherry*.

Whenever I go out to breakfast with longtime friends like Ben, Danny, Todd and Wayne, our conversation is rife with references to movies. Looking at the menu, I order chorizo and eggs, because the dish inspired a passion in Charles Grodin during Martin Brest's comedy *Midnight Run*. Nothing has influenced our sarcastic jabs more than watching Grodin test Robert De Niro's patience in that movie. It brings humor to the mundane. All I need to say is "Today's your lucky day," or "Why are you so unpopular with the Chicago police department?" and we'll end up reciting whole scenes together.

From our days of playing in a college band called The Garbage Chute Flyboys—a name inspired by something Princess Leia shouted in *Star Wars*—to the updates we send each other via e-mail every week, so many of the things that bind us are strengthened and enhanced by the art we have experienced together.

*   *   *

In the summer of 1991, I worked with fellow Seattle Pacific University students at a camp on Whidbey Island in Puget Sound. The property was bordered to the north and the south by thick woods, which were teeming with life: mosquitoes, deer, bald eagles, red foxes and rabbits. We were immersed in the grandeur, and we became close friends.

In the evening, I would stand at the edge of the sapphire waves, reflect on the day and listen. The tide waters whispered, washing in and out of my thoughts, taking what was forgettable and leaving behind what was important. I felt like *Star Wars'* Luke Skywalker, the farm boy, staring off at the two suns of Tatooine and dreaming of a life of adventure. I could almost hear the strains of John Williams' music in my mind. But instead of dreaming about going to war, I felt a strong creative impulse. I wanted to respond to what I had seen. Perhaps this is what the psalmist felt after a day of tending sheep on the hills—an urgent desire to answer glory with new songs.

On Wednesday nights, my friends and I would faithfully gather and hike up into the dark northern woods, following flashlight beams, to congregate underground in a cold military bunker. Gathering around a single candle, we passed around a flashlight and read poetry, fiction, plays and essays, including many original works. We listened to echoes of William Shakespeare, A.A. Milne, E. E. Cummings, John Milton, Emily Dickinson and tales of the great, green, greasy Limpopo river.

The gathering was, of course, inspired by *Dead Poets Society*. To make it our own, we called it the Thomas Parker Society, for Lieutenant Thomas Parker, the bunker's namesake. The film had made a lasting impression on us. Life should be lived with passion, and great art should be savored in good company.

The friendships formed in that circle continue today. So does the Thomas Parker Society, which just celebrated its fifteenth anniversary.

* * *

When Anne and I drive eastward from Seattle to Montana or wind our way along the road from Kingston to Port Townsend, we often pull over to watch horses move across a field. I have not been horseback riding, a lack that makes my wife shake her head in dismay, for she loves the nature of horses as much or more than the nature of chocolate.

But horses fill me with awe. They are so massive, muscular and graceful. I might never have grown to appreciate them if my parents hadn't taken me to see Carroll Ballard's adaptation of *The Black Stallion*. I'll never forget those tense, holy moments when young Alec, marooned on a desert island, slowly approached that magnificent black stallion, offering a handful of wet green seaweed in hopes of making a friend.

If a gust of wind casts leaves up into the air, I watch them fly, because I have been taught to notice and celebrate the playfulness of wind in *American Beauty*. Yet I also think of those cyclones of yellow leaves in Zhang Yimou's *Hero*, which spin around the two dueling swordswomen.

Car crashes in *Punch-Drunk Love* and *Crash* have made me a little more watchful on the road. And thanks to *The Station Agent*, I try to be extra careful with hot beverages while driving.

Sometimes, when the morning sun breaks over the hills ahead of us, I hear those rising strains of a song and half expect Julie Andrews to come dancing and spinning over the mountaintop singing, "The hills are alive!" Or I remember a plucky banjo melody and hear Kermit the Frog and Fozzie Bear singing along in pursuit of their dreams during *The Muppet Movie*.

And if we drive by night, we turn off of the freeway to wander along back roads, looking for the darkest possible place where we can get out and stare up at the stars. This reminds me of the scene in which the Muppets, stranded in the middle of nowhere, gather around a campfire, despairing for their failing dreams. Kermit, whose journey began with a solo bicycle ride from the swamp to the city, wonders if he might have been crazy to pursue that calling in the first place. But the Great Gonzo, that crazy daredevil, spends that dark hour staring up at the glittering constellations. The heavens inspire a powerful longing inside of this scraggly, flightless bird, just as they do for those magnificent flocks of geese in *Winged Migration*. And yet, Gonzo reminds me of an even higher calling when he sings:

> *Sun rises, night falls, sometimes the sky calls.*
> *Is that a song there, and do I belong there?*
> *I've never been there, but I know the way.*
> *I'm going to go back there someday.*

Even when my parents first took me to see *The Muppet Movie* (I was only nine at the time) that song tugged at my heart. I have always been haunted by that sense that I have forgotten my homeland. Like Stands With a Fist in *Dances with Wolves*, struggling to remember her native tongue, I'm taking my first feeble steps in the right direction with a premonition that it will all come back to me and the darkness will lift. The stars flicker like faint hints and reminders.

In the morning, after Anne and I have set up our camp, I stroll into the woods to look for trees worth climbing, not only because it takes me back to those apple-boughs of my childhood backyard but also because an animated Bilbo Baggins climbed an animated tree in the middle of Mirkwood forest in the Rankin/Bass production of *The Hobbit*. When Bilbo stuck his head up above the wood, he saw that the treetops were a vast stage for dancing, fluttering butterflies, and he said, "There are moments which can change a person for all time. I suddenly wondered if I would ever see my snug hobbit hole again. I wondered if I actually wanted to."

*   *   *

Near Flathead Lake in Montana, I watched Anne walk ahead of me on the trail, carrying her journal and her pen through the profusion of summer colors. I followed, in no hurry, catching glimpses of a story that would grow to engulf my imagination. I remember Olivier bringing Julie back to her calling in *Three Colors: Blue,* just as Anne coaxes me back to stillness and to writing. I think of John Rolfe in *The New World*, enchanted by the quiet and mysterious princess. He was a man acquainted with grief and loss, but the quiet mystery of Pocahontas drew him to risk his heart again.

When I think back to those first days Anne and I traveled and wandered together, I recall images of Paris and cautious flirtation in *Before Sunrise*. And even though the film had not arrived yet, the memories take on the vivid color and romantic energy of *Moulin Rouge*. People don't believe me when I explain that it was Anne's idea, not mine, to have our friend Todd play the closing anthem of *Star Wars* on the piano for our wedding recessional.

When Anne writes poetry, scattering words across the page and then sculpting them with scrupulous tenderness, I'm reminded of watching the documentary *Rivers and Tides: Andy Goldsworthy Working in Time*, mesmerized as Goldsworthy places stones, grass blades, leaves or branches just so, until he has crafted a fragile sculpture that breathes with inspiration. When she reads the lines she has composed, I see Goldsworthy casting dust out into wind, and I watch the words carried along in artful spirals.

As I watch her work in the garden, she gently touches the silvery green leaves of a ladies' mantle. She shows me how the fine bristles on the leaves cause rain water to bead and slide away. She pulls the plant softly free of the soil, cupping its muddy roots and transplants it to a new home. I am as awestruck as the angel Damiel watching Marion on the trapeze. He stood back in amazement, as if he could watch for hours.

Back home, I think of Bilbo's treetop epiphany again when I am lying in bed, unable to sleep, weighed down and racked with worry from the crises of the day. My fears can manifest themselves like the Red Knight in *The Fisher King*, and I realize how weak my faith has become. I want to push my way up through the darkness to catch a glimpse of hope.

A car passes outside, sending a sharp spot of light jittering across the dark wall of the bedroom, and I think of those mysterious lights that flicker in *The Double Life of Veronique* and *Three Colors: Blue*, reminding me to be vigilant for signs of God even in the darkness. Perhaps even now, in my trouble, God is moving. Perhaps the beacons have been lit, as they were in *The Return of the King*, and help is on its way. Perhaps a sign of hope is being smuggled through the chaos, the way Theo and Kee carry an unlikely infant through a battle zone in Alfonzo Cuaron's *Children of Men*.

On Saturday mornings, when I don't have to rush off to the office, it's Norm Gunderson of *Fargo* who inspires me to sit up, put on my slippers and robe and shuffle off to the kitchen to fry some eggs and bacon for Anne, just the way he does for Marge.

Later in the kitchen, as Anne stirs up a pot of gumbo, I mince garlic cloves, chop carrots and slice yellow peppers. When she's ready for them, she reminds me of Buttercup in *The Princess Bride*, and I hand her the bowl, saying, "As you wish."

* * *

For years, a hunched old man in a wheelchair attended our Sunday morning church services. Sometimes he was disoriented, unable to recognize people. No matter how many times I introduced myself, he always called me Steve. His life was full of difficulty, but he attended every worship service he could. When our pastor invited people in the congregation to pray, he often spoke a prayer in his broken, rasping voice.

Once, as the ushers passed loaves of communion bread down the pews, each congregant breaking off a piece, I watched this dear, devoted believer take the bread from the usher, raise it to his face and then—I almost shouted in surprise—he used it as a towel to mop his sweating brow. Then he handed it back to the usher and thanked him.

It was funny, yes, but later I thought of Christopher from *Babette's Feast*—a man who lost some of his wits along the way, but who was so like a child drawn to rumors of glory, accepting each new wonder with reverence.

I miss that dear churchgoer now that he's gone.

When I think of the road ahead, I wonder if I will have the passion to continue answering the call if my circumstances are overcome by storms. Where will I be, and how will I respond if I see my death coming?

I cringe, thinking of the old man in *Magnolia* whose death is a miserable plunge into regret and confessions that come too late to make a difference. I feel a surge of inspiration watching as that heroic young woman of *Sophie Scholl: The Final Days* finds strength in Christ to resist the Nazis all the way to a glorious sacrifice, just as a heroic child follows the call of mystery in *Pan's Labyrinth* and risks her life to save an infant from the hands of a devil. I think of that last, soft, forgiving smile of Denzel Washington in *Malcolm X*. In *Watership Down*, the Black Rabbit of Inle drifts down from the sky, calling Hazel's name, and Hazel quietly and willingly lies down and surrenders, knowing that the story is far from over. It's a scene of such mysterious peace.

A lot will depend on how attentive I am to the light.

*   *   *

So the journey continues for me. Each film is a new world. Some of them are dead ends and disappointments. In others, I see the light in a new way, calling me in a new direction. These revelations help me to think more clearly about my future. They also help me understand my past. Like Pocahontas with her beloved, beauty moves me to say, "There is something I remember when I'm with you that I forget when I'm away."

Looking back now, I see that in one way or another, I was chasing the light from the time that it first caught my attention. That guiding beacon, that call, might make a fool of me yet—inspiring me through an undeserving scoundrel with symphonies in his head. A man trained to be a missionary who would rather go running to feel God's pleasure. A statesman of conviction with an allegiance to God over country. A small and humble hobbit willing to carry a burden into enemy territory. A Native American princess who keeps reaching into the light, no matter what it costs her. A frog on a bicycle, pursuing a dream of making people happy. A weary, wounded camel mysteriously healed by a song.

I suspect that when we have forgotten ourselves, open to the coursing light, we may reflect it as well. Darkly. But that may be enough.

Note

1. Portions of this section were originally published as an essay, "Through a Screen Darkly," in *Image* journal, Number 42, Spring/Summer 2004.

Additional Resources

Visit LookingCloser.org/Darkly for more exclusive content, including:

- Two bonus chapters of *Through a Screen Darkly*

- A chapter-by-chapter guide to further commentary, film reviews and interviews with filmmakers and actors related to films referenced in this book

- A collection of questions to help film discussion groups explore the movies they watch together

- A list of books for further reading on the intersection of faith and art (periodically updated)

- Recommended film review resources (periodically updated)

Recommended Titles for Film Discussion Groups

Note from Jeffrey Overstreet

Are you ready to discover some thought-provoking films? The following list includes movies I recommend for groups of discerning adults to view and discuss together. However, before you begin, please note these important disclaimers:

1. This is not intended as a comprehensive list of great films. Rather, this is a list of films I have selected from those that have been particularly significant for me in my personal moviegoing journey thus far. I have also found that most of them will serve as challenging and provocative fodder for discussion among discerning viewers.

2. As I mentioned above, I've compiled this list with discerning adult viewers in mind. Some films contain elements that could be alarming, distressing or even offensive to some viewers. *Read about the films ahead of time.* Pay attention to what the film is rated, and why. Make sure that those in your discussion group do not go into the film unprepared. You'll find reviews of these films online at places such as ChristianityTodayMovies.com, RottenTomatoes.com, Metacritic.com and, of course, at LookingCloser.org.

These resources will help you determine which selections are appropriate for your viewing group. If you can't find sufficient information about a particular title, don't hesitate to send me an e-mail. (My address is posted at LookingCloser.org.)

Films for General Adult Discussion Groups

Alien; dir. Ridley Scott
Almost Famous; dir. Cameron Crowe
Amadeus; dir. Milos Forman
American Splendor; dir. Shari Springer Berman and Robert Pulcini
The Apostle; dir. Robert Duvall
Babette's Feast; dir. Gabriel Axel
Being There; dir. Hal Ashby
Big Night; dir. Campbell Scott and Stanley Tucci
Born into Brothels; dir. Zana Briski
Capote; dir. Bennett Miller
Chariots of Fire; dir. Hugh Hudson
Citizen Kane; dir. Orson Welles
The Color of Paradise; dir. Majid Majidi
Crash; dir. Paul Haggis
Dead Man Walking; dir. Tim Robbins
Dead Poets Society; dir. Peter Weir
The Decalogue (a series of 10 short films); dir. Krzysztof Kieslowski
Do the Right Thing; dir. Spike Lee
Dr. Strangelove; dir. Stanley Kubrick
Empire of the Sun; dir. Steven Spielberg
The Exorcism of Emily Rose; dir. Scott Derrickson
Fargo; dir. Joel and Ethan Coen
Fast, Cheap and Out of Control; dir. Errol Morris
Fearless; dir. Peter Weir

Final Solution, dir. Cristobal Krusen
Finding Neverland; dir. Marc Forster
The Fisher King; dir. Terry Gilliam
The Fog of War; dir. Errol Morris
The Fountain; dir. Darren Aronofsky
Gattaca; dir. Andrew Niccol
Ghost World; dir. Terry Zwigoff
The Gleaners and I; dir. Agnes Varda
Gosford Park; dir. Paul Thomas Anderson
The Gospel of John; dir. Philip Saville
Grave of the Fireflies; dir. Isao Takahata
Harold and Maude; dir. Hal Ashby
Henry V; dir. Kenneth Branagh
Hero; dir. Zhang Yimou
Hoop Dreams; dir. Steve James
Hotel Rwanda; dir. Terry George
House of Sand and Fog; dir. Vadim Perelman
In America; dir. Jim Sheridan
In the Bedroom; dir. Todd Field
The Insider; dir. Michael Mann
Insomnia; dir. Christopher Nolan
Italian for Beginners; dir. Lone Scherfig
Jean de Florette; dir. Claude Berri
The Last Days of Disco; dir. Whit Stillman
Last Orders; dir. Fred Shepisi
Limbo; dir. John Sayles
Lone Star; dir. John Sayles

Lord of the Flies; dir. Peter Brook
Malcolm X; dir. Spike Lee
Man Facing Southeast; dir. Eliseo
  Subiela
A Man for All Seasons; dir. Fred
  Zinnemann
The Man Without a Past; dir. Aki
  Kaurismäki
Manon of the Spring; dir. Claude Berri
Mansfield Park; dir. Patricia Rozema
*Master and Commander: The Far Side of
  the World*; dir. Peter Weir
Metropolitan; dir. Whit Stillman
Million Dollar Baby; dir. Clint
  Eastwood
Millions; dir. Danny Boyle
The Mission, dir. Roland Joffé
Modern Times; dir. Charlie Chaplin
The Mosquito Coast; dir. Peter Weir
The New World; dir. Terrence Malick
Nine Lives; dir. Rodrigo Garcia
No Direction Home: Bob Dylan; dir.
  Martin Scorsese
Nobody's Fool; dir. Robert Benton
O Brother, Where Art Thou? dir. Joel
  and Ethan Coen
Pan's Labyrinth; dir. Guillermo Del
  Toro
Personal Velocity; dir. Rebecca Miller
Picnic at Hanging Rock; dir. Peter Weir
Pieces of April; dir. Peter Hedges
The Player; dir. Robert Altman
Ponette; dir. Jacques Doillon
Promises; dir. Carlos Bolado, B.Z.
  Goldberg, Justine Shapiro
The Queen; dir. Stephen Frears
Quiz Show; dir. Robert Redford
The Remains of the Day; dir. James
  Ivory
*Rivers and Tides: Andy Goldsworthy
  Working with Time*; dir. Thomas
  Riedelsheimer
The Road Home; dir. Zhang Yimou

A Room with a View; dir. James Ivory
The Royal Tenenbaums; dir. Wes
  Anderson
Rushmore; dir. Wes Anderson
Saved! dir. Brian Dannelly
The Searchers; dir. John Ford
Searching for Bobby Fischer; dir. Steve
  Zallian
The Secret of Roan Inish; dir. John
  Sayles
Sense and Sensibility; dir. Ang Lee
Shadowlands; dir. Richard
  Attenborough
Shall We Dance? dir. Masayuki Suo
Shattered Glass; dir. Billy Ray
The Shawshank Redemption; dir. Frank
  Darabont
Signs; dir. M. Night Shyamalan
Sophie Scholl: The Final Days; dir. Marc
  Rothemund
The Station Agent; dir. Thomas
  McCarthy
The Straight Story; dir. David Lynch
Super Size Me; dir. Morgan Spurlock
Tender Mercies; dir. Bruce Beresford
The Thin Blue Line; dir. Errol Morris
*Thirteen Conversations About One
  Thing*; dir. Jill Sprecher
Three Kings; dir. David O. Russell
To Kill a Mockingbird; dir. Robert
  Mulligan
The Truman Show; dir. Peter Weir
Twelve Angry Men; dir. Sydney Lumet
Unbreakable; dir. M. Night
  Shyamalan
Unforgiven; dir. Clint Eastwood
The *Up* Series; dir. Michael Apted
  (*28 Up, 35 Up, 42 Up*)
The Virgin Suicides; dir. Sofia Coppola
Watership Down; dir. Martin Rosen
Whale Rider; dir. Niki Caro
What's Eating Gilbert Grape? dir. Lasse
  Hallström

When Harry Met Sally; dir. Rob
Reiner
The Widow of St. Pierre; dir. Patrice
Leconte

Wit; dir. Mike Nichols
Witness; dir. Peter Weir
Zelig; dir. Woody Allen

For Ambitious Discussion Groups

2001: A Space Odyssey; dir. Stanley
Kubrick
The 400 Blows; dir. François Truffaut
Andrei Rublev; dir. Andrei Tarkovsky
Apocalypse Now; dir. Francis Ford
Coppola
Au Hasard Balthazar; dir. Robert
Bresson
Babel; dir. Alejandro González
Iñárritu
The Ballad of Jack and Rose; dir.
Rebecca Miller
Barton Fink; dir. Joel and Ethan
Coen
Before Sunrise, and *Before Sunset*; dir.
Richard Linklater
The Big Kahuna; dir. John Swanbeck
Blade Runner; dir. Ridley Scott
Brazil; dir. Terry Gilliam
Brokeback Mountain; dir. Ang Lee
Caché; dir. Michael Haneke
Café Lumiere; dir. Hou Hsiao-hsien
The Celebration; dir. Thomas
Vinterberg
Children of Men; dir. Alfonzo Cuaron
Cinema Paradiso; dir. Giuseppe
Tornatore
The Circle; dir. Jafar Panahi
Claire's Knee; dir. Eric Rohmer
Code Unknown; dir. Michael Haneke
Crimes and Misdemeanors; dir. Woody
Allen
Days of Heaven; dir. Terrence Malick
Diary of a Country Priest, dir. Robert
Bresson

Dirty Pretty Things; dir. Stephen
Frears
Distant; dir. Nuri Bilge Ceylan
Dogville; dir. Lars Von Trier
Donnie Darko; dir. Richard Kelley
Down by Law; dir. Jim Jarmusch
L'Enfant; dir. Luc and Jean-Pierre
Dardenne
Eternal Sunshine of the Spotless Mind;
dir. Michel Gondry
The Five Obstructions; dir. Lars Von
Trier
The Flowers of Shanghai; dir. Hou
Hsiao-hsien
Full Metal Jacket; dir. Stanley Kubrick
George Washington; dir. David
Gordon Green
Grizzly Man; dir. Werner Herzog
Hannah and Her Sisters; dir. Woody
Allen
Husbands and Wives; dir. Woody Allen
The Ice Storm; dir. Ang Lee
Ikiru; dir. Akira Kurosawa
In the Mood for Love; dir. Wong Kar-Wai
Jesus of Montreal; dir. Denys Arcand
Junebug; dir. Phil Morrison
Lantana; dir. Ray Lawrence
The Life Aquatic with Steve Zissou; dir.
Wes Anderson
The Life of Brian; dir. Terry Jones
Lost in Translation; dir. Sophia
Coppola
Love and Death; dir. Woody Allen
Magnolia; dir. Paul Thomas
Anderson

A Man Escaped; dir. Robert Bresson
Mean Creek; dir. Jacob Aaron Estes
The Mirror; dir. Andrei Tarkovsky
Natural Born Killers; dir. Oliver Stone
Ordet; dir. Carl Dreyer
Paris, Texas; dir. Wim Wenders
The Passion of Joan of Arc; dir. Carl Theodor Dreyer
The Passion of the Christ; dir. Mel Gibson
The Pianist; dir. Roman Polanski
Punch-Drunk Love; dir. Paul Thomas Anderson
Ran; dir. Akira Kurosawa
Rashomon; dir. Akira Kurosawa
The Return; dir. Andrei Zvyagintsev
Ride with the Devil; dir. Ang Lee
Rosencrantz and Guildenstern Are Dead; dir. Tom Stoppard
Rosetta; dir. Luc and Jean-Pierre Dardenne
Safe; dir. Todd Haynes
A Scanner Darkly; dir. Richard Linklater
Secrets and Lies; dir. Mike Leigh
The Seventh Seal, dir. Ingmar Bergman

The Son; dir. Luc and Jean-Pierre Dardenne
The Sweet Hereafter; dir. Atom Egoyan
Solaris; dir. Andrei Tarkovsky
Stevie; dir. Steve James
A Taste of Cherry; dir. Abbas Kiarostami
The Thin Red Line; dir. Terrence Malick
Thirteen; dir. Catherine Hardwicke
Three Colors: Blue; dir. Krzysztof Kieslowski
Three Colors: Red; dir. Krzysztof Kieslowski
Three Colors: White; dir. Krzysztof Kieslowski
Three Times; dir. Hou Hsiao-hsien
Tokyo Story; dir. Yasujiro Ozu
Waking Life; dir. Richard Linklater
The Wind Will Carry Us; dir. Abbas Kiarostami
Wings of Desire; dir. Wim Wenders
Winter Light; dir. Ingmar Bergman
The World; dir. ZhangKe Jia
Yi-Yi (A One and a Two); dir. Edward Yang

Visit LookingCloser.org/Darkly for a guide to post-viewing discussions, including a list of helpful questions for group leaders.

Also, visit the site for further film recommendation lists, organized by theme, including a special list for children. These lists will be expanded and revised periodically.

A Word from the Author About Post-viewing Discussions

I've enjoyed and supervised many film screenings and led quite a few post-viewing discussions. Some have been greatly rewarding. But a few frustrating experiences have taught me to employ a few basic guidelines for discussion. I would highly recommend these ideas for groups.

- After a screening, give viewers at least 10 minutes to stand up, stretch, eat some dessert, ponder in silence and even walk around a bit before launching into discussion of a film. Some viewers prefer to let a film "settle" for a while before they discuss it. Some even prefer to wait a day or two. Art works mysteriously, and by rushing to analyze and criticize we can interfere with its quieter, more subtle effects.

- When discussion starts, begin by asking viewers to volunteer thoughts on what impressed them about the film or what resonated with them. Try to dissuade others from reacting or responding to these comments right away. Cultivate a feeling of safety in the group so that people will feel comfortable participating without fear of being laughed at or rejected.

- Hold off harsh criticisms of the film until later in the discussion. If viewers dive hastily into complaints, a group can quickly narrow its perspective and lose track of the larger picture or intimidate inexperienced viewers.

• As the discussion proceeds, don't impose too many pre-determined questions on the discussion. Let the conversation wander. See where it goes. Even the group leader may be surprised at the direction a film discussion can take and the revelations that are shared by different viewers.

• If it's difficult to get discussion started, read a review of the film aloud, preferably a review by a film critic who has a strong—even controversial—opinion about the film. That'll get 'em talking.

• Come prepared with information about the film—the year it was made, a list of the director's other films, the cast and their character names. This will be useful if viewers have questions.

• If any individuals begin to dominate the discussion, interrupt by saying, "Let's hear from some others who might not be so bold or who might not be comfortable pushing their way into the fray." Or, if a conversation needs extra structure, viewers can always take turns, proceeding in a circle to prevent the conversation from becoming imbalanced.

• Be careful to observe the nature of other viewers' responses. The conversation should stay focused *on the work* and on sharing a mix of interpretations, not on criticizing the opinions of others. Disagreement is acceptable as long as there is respect and courtesy. Everyone comes to a film with different experiences and perspectives.

· Encourage the group to consider the film again at a later date, when they might make new discoveries and even change their opinions. Rarely can one come away declaring a final word on a work having only just encountered it. Some of my favorite films, such as *Three Colors: Blue* and *Ordet*, are features that did not impress me much during my first viewing. I needed to look closer.

For a list of recommended post-viewing discussions, visit LookingCloser.org/Darkly.

More Relevant Resources from Regal

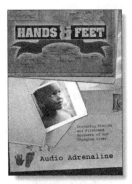
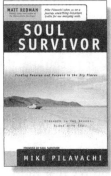